GUSTA\

PROFILES IN POWER

General Editor: Keith Robbins

GUSTAVUS ADOLPHUS

Michael Roberts

Second Edition

LONGMAN
London and New York

Addison Wesley Longman Limited
Edinburgh Gate,
Harlow, Essex CM20 2JE, England
and Associated Companies throughout the world.

*Published in the United States of America
by Addison Wesley Longman, New York*

First published as *Gustavus Adolphus and*
the *Rise of Sweden*, by English Universities Press, 1973
Second Edition published by Longman Group, 1992
Second impression 1998

British Library Cataloguing in Publication Data
A catalogue record for this book is
available from the British Library

ISBN 0582 09001 6 CSD
ISBN 0582 09000 8 PPR

Library of Congress Cataloging in Publication Data
Roberts, Michael, 1908-
Gustavus Adolphus / Michael Roberts. – 2nd ed.
p.   cm. – (Profiles in power)
Originally published: Gustavus Adolphus and rise of Sweden. London:
English Universities Press, 1973.
Includes bibliographical references and index.
ISBN 0-582-09001-6 – ISBN 0-582-09000-8 (pbk.)
1. Gustaf II Adolf, King of Sweden, 1594-1632.   2. Sweden–
–History – Gustavus II Adolphus, 1611–1632– I. Title.   II. Series:
Profiles in power (London, England)
DL706.R76   1992
948.5'02'092–dc20   91–45108
[B]   CIP

Set in 11/12 Linotron Baskerville

Transferred to digital print on demand 2001

Printed and bound in Great Britain by Antony Rowe Ltd, Eastbourne

CONTENTS

. . . .

LIST OF MAPS

Chapter 1

BACKGROUND

If in the year 1660 the ordinary man in the street had been asked to enumerate the great powers of Europe, he would almost certainly have replied that there were four great monarchs overtopping all the rest: the Emperor, the kings of France and Spain, and the king of Sweden. A century earlier, in 1560, no one would have dreamed of including Sweden in the list. Though Gustavus Vasa (who died in that year) had a well-deserved reputation for political craft and financial greed, the country over which he ruled lay too far out on the periphery of European politics to be much more than a possible makeweight in the perennial struggle between Habsburg and Valois, and was indeed very much less a part of Europe than (for instance) Poland. Yet it was just in this year, 1560, that the first foundations were laid for Sweden's later greatness; and in 1660 that greatness reached its apogee. In the second quarter of the seventeenth century Sweden burst upon the European firmament like some new star, big with portents: a political analogue to that *nova* in Cassiopeia which had so disturbed the watchers of the sky in 1572; flaring for a brief space with unnatural brightness, and thereafter declining into insignificance; something unforeseeable, and to contemporary observers scarcely capable of rational explanation. When Gustavus Adolphus began his reign, in 1611, no man could have imagined this imminent incandescence. But twenty-one years later, when Gustavus met his death at Lützen, the situation was very different. When he fell, it seemed that Europe had lost a master. In the last months of his life it had not been extravagant to think of him as a possible candidate for the Imperial throne. In the years

1

that followed, men debated whether his chancellor, Axel Oxenstierna, might not be made Elector of Mainz. In 1648 Queen Christina joined Louis XIV as co-guarantor of the great peace settlement of Westphalia, which laid a basis for international relations which was to endure until the French Revolution. By 1660, Sweden had attained her natural geographical limits, had built up an empire which made her the dominant state in the Baltic, and was besides a German power, represented in the Imperial Diet (as France never was) in virtue of her membership of no less than three of the Circles of the Empire.

A fragile and precarious greatness. Twenty years after 1660, Europe had come to see that the youthful giant was plainly somewhat weak at the knees; twenty more, and Sweden's neighbours were gathering for the kill; a further twenty, and she had sunk irrevocably to the position of a state of the second order. After 1721 her overseas possessions shrank to no more than a shred of Pomerania; which remained as a memento of empire, a kind of Calais, preserved as a keepsake after all the rest was gone.

Yet if the Swedish empire proved a transient phenomenon, it did not vanish without leaving strong traces behind it; if Swedish military might proved insecurely based, it had been real enough in the 1630s and 1640s. The creator of that military power, the architect of that empire, was Gustavus Adolphus. The ascendancy of Spain in the sixteenth century, the economic predominance of the Dutch in the seventeenth, are not to be explained in terms of personalities: the greatness of Sweden, on the other hand, does seem to be directly related to the character and ability of her rulers. The military genius of Gustavus Adolphus, the olympian statesmanship of Axel Oxenstierna, the restless energy of Charles X, between them erected a great political edifice; the blinkered obstinacy of Charles XII finally destroyed it. In this very limited sense, and for a very limited period, Geijer's old dictum that 'the history of Sweden is the history of her kings' holds good. But it is a dictum which implies a view of history unacceptably narrow; and tells us nothing of the means which made their achievements possible, nothing of the Swedish people upon whom their policies bore so heavily, nothing of the political constants which affected their calculations and their actions.

All these conquering monarchs were the prisoners of circumstance, constrained and limited by political and social situations which they had inherited, and which were largely outside their control; and they had to take things as they found them. The imperial adventures of the seventeenth century were in the main their reaction to these internal and external pressures; in so far as the empire was planned at all, it was planned as a response to Sweden's geopolitical situation, or as a desperate attempt to outface the economic facts of life.

In the sixteenth and seventeenth centuries Sweden was confronted, whether she liked it or not, with the possibility of having to wage war simultaneously on two fronts; and her foreign policy was necessarily conditioned by that fact. Denmark and Norway threatened her from south and west; Muscovy loomed darkly over the eastern horizon. The danger from Denmark took its rise in the confused history of the fifteenth century, for much of which Sweden had been merged with Norway and Denmark in a united Scandinavian kingdom whose centre of gravity lay in Copenhagen. The Union had had a chequered history, and from the 1440s onward Sweden more often than not had pursued a virtually independent existence under its own regents. But it was only in 1523 that Gustavus I, the founder of the Vasa dynasty, finally broke loose from the Union and established his country as a fully independent sovereign state.

It was a state of vast dimensions, stretching northwards from the Småland border to the Arctic, until it petered out on the tundras in a no man's land which was still the preserve of the nomadic Lapps; while on the other side of the Gulf of Bothnia it included the associated territory of Finland, which had been conquered and colonized by Swedish expeditions in the thirteenth century, and was to remain an integral part of the Swedish realm until it was lost to Russia in 1809. But, big as the country was, in the eyes of Swedish statesmen it was not big enough for safety. To east and west, actual or potential enemies impended over its shaggy frontiers and menaced its security. When independence came in 1523, the Danes were able to retain control of the provinces of Halland, Skåne, and Blekinge, which formed the natural southern limits of the Swedish half of the peninsula, and were on economic as well as political grounds highly desirable possessions. This situ-

3

ation meant that the kings of Denmark straddled the narrows of the Sound, one foot planted in Elsinore, the other in Hälsingborg; and from this point of vantage they exercised a patrimonial control of all the shipping that passed between. The Sound, they contended, was a stream flowing through Danish territory, rather than an international waterway; and they applied this theory by taking toll of merchantmen entering and leaving the Baltic. With the proceeds they built a formidable navy. They were thus in a position to cut off Stockholm from all maritime contact with western Europe, if they chose to do so. Nor was this all. Strung out eastwards across the Baltic from Copenhagen, the Danish-held islands of Bornholm, Gotland, and Ösel provided bases from which the Danish navy could keep Swedish trade within the Baltic under surveillance, and if need be could threaten Sweden's communications with the Hanseatic ports of Germany and Livonia. The west, again, the Norwegian kingdom (still linked to Denmark by a personal union) retained possession of the province of Bohuslän; while half-way up the Scandinavian peninsula the Norwegian provinces of Jämtland and Härjedalen thrust far to the eastward across the mountains that divide Scandinavia from north to south.

Jämtland and Härjedalen, it is true, were more of a piece of geographical inconsequence than a serious anxiety: in every Swedish-Danish war they fell more or less into Sweden's hands. But Bohuslän was another matter, for its southern frontier came so close to the northern limits of Halland that the two were separated only by a narrow (and highly vulnerable) strip of Swedish territory. Through that strip ran the Göta river, and at its mouth successive Swedish sovereigns established successive fortresses – first Nya Lödöse, then Älvsborg, finally Gothenburg – in an effort to prevent these pincers from closing. As yet, it is true, not much Swedish trade went this way, for land-communications between Älvsborg and central Sweden were very difficult; but, bad as they were, they provided Sweden's only direct line of access to the North Sea and the markets that lay beyond it. If Denmark should decide to close the Sound, they offered the only means of obtaining those supplies of Bay salt without which the country could not long survive.

It was a state of affairs which the kings of Sweden must sooner or later seek to alter, if ever the land were to thrive;

4

and in itself it made good relations with Denmark difficult. But the difficulty became an impossibility in the face of Danish aspirations to restore the shattered fabric of the Scandinavian Union and once more to subject the Swedes to rule from Copenhagen. From 1523 to 1611 Sweden's constant suspicion of Denmark was based on fear: fear of a Danish attempt at reconquest. There were, indeed, periods when common political interests, reinforcing an obstinately persistent sense of the underlying unity of the North, produced a relaxation of tension and a grudging co-operation; but the roots of enmity lay too deep to be easily plucked up.

The threat from the east was older than that from the west. The conquest of Finland had long ago involved Swedes and Russians in rivalry for the control of the eastern march-lands of Karelia. In 1323 the Treaty of Nöteborg had attempted to define spheres of influence in this region. It had left the Russians a large slice of eastern Finland, and drawn a frontier which would have given them access to the northern end of the Gulf of Bothnia. But the line of the boundary thus established was always in dispute, and the pressure of Swedish colonization soon pushed far beyond it. The weakness of Russia in the period of the 'Tatar yoke' had ensured that the process should meet with little opposition, and by the close of the Middle Ages the limits of Finland were much as we know them today. The consolidation of the Muscovite realm in the later fifteenth century, however, had reopened the question. The reign of Ivan III saw the beginning of Russia's attempt to break out to the Baltic, and a revival of Russian attacks upon Swedish positions in Finland. By the 1540s the threat to Finland's eastern frontier had clearly developed; so clearly, that even the wary and parsimonious Gustavus Vasa was contemplating a preventive war, in order to scotch the danger while Ivan IV was still a minor. In the 1550s frontier incidents did indeed lead to a three years' war. It settled nothing; but it left the Swedes with a lively sense of the danger to be apprehended from Moscow's expansive policies: henceforward Muscovy, no less than Denmark, was a likely enemy. For the next two centuries it would be one of Sweden's major concerns to ensure that the two did not join forces against her.

In the 1560s the collapse of the old crusading Order of the

5

Livonian Knights initiated a crisis which lasted for more than thirty years. The vacuum of power which was the result of that collapse presented Ivan IV with a chance to effect a lodgement on the Baltic coast. In 1559 his armies captured Narva, and for the first time the merchants of western Europe were able to trade directly with the Russians without being mulcted by greedy Hanseatic middlemen. But it was not only Muscovy that was interested in the acquistion of Livonia. The disappearance of the Livonian Knights presented to other states opportunities too tempting to be ignored: to Poland, for instance, which was obviously concerned in keeping the Russians out; to Denmark, which had old claims to influence in this region. With Poland, Sweden had as yet no quarrel; but she had no wish to see Muscovy established as a Baltic power. Still less could she afford to allow this area to pass under the control of Denmark: a Danish occupation of Reval would threaten Finland; it would mean the forging of one more link in the chain of Danish encirclement. Even Gustavus Vasa, had he lived, would probably have been unable to sit still and allow events to take their course; and Eric XIV, who succeeded him in 1560, had certainly no intention of doing so. When the town of Reval, equally alarmed by the prospect of subjection to Russia, Denmark, or Poland, offered in desperation to put itself under the protection of the king of Sweden, the offer was at once accepted. A Swedish expeditionary force was sent to Estonia. Reval became a Swedish town; and remained so until 1721.

It was a fateful decision. For it meant, among other things, that the first stone of the Swedish empire had been laid. And the thing had been done (it is worth remembering) for reasons which were essentially defensive. No doubt Eric XIV, like his father, was anxious to obtain a share in the tolls and dues which could be levied on the Russia trade by sovereigns in possession of suitable end-ports; but each would have preferred to establish a staple in Finland. Economic considerations certainly played a part in the creation of the Swedish empire, and as it expanded they increased in importance, if only because the cost of defending it grew increasingly heavy. But to begin with such considerations were subordinate: the problem was at bottom political; a problem of security, a problem perhaps of survival.

But the antithesis between political and economic factors

in the history of the Swedish empire is an unreal and false antithesis. From beginning to end they were twin aspects of the same question. Security implied the command of the resources to pay for it; and those resources could be obtained only by war. It may well be doubted whether in 1560 Eric XIV had any more idea of founding an empire in Livonia than Gustavus Adolphus had of founding an empire in Germany in 1630. Each found himself enmeshed in a catena of circumstances and dilemmas; each felt himself led by strict political logic to steps whose consequences no one could foresee. The acquisition of Reval might seem a limited objective: the event proved that it was the setting in motion of a train of events which carried men along whether they would or no. The defence of Reval could hardly be ensured unless a possible enemy were denied control of the adjacent territory from which an attack upon it could be mounted. Once acquired, that territory in its turn prescribed fresh objectives for a defensive strategy. Military logic transformed a limited commitment into an open-ended programme of logical aggression. Eric XIV took over Reval: within a decade it had become a question not of Reval only but of Estonia. From 1570 to 1595 Sweden fought a desultory war with Russia to retain that province. Not until 1581, when Pontus de la Gardie crowned his victories with the triumphant capture of Narva, did the struggle begin to turn in Sweden's favour; not until 1595 was she able, at the Peace of Teusina, to extort relatively satisfactory terms from her adversary. At Teusina the Tsar recognized Sweden's right to Estonia, and agreed to a redrawing of the Finnish frontier on lines which gave legal sanction to the extension of Swedish colonization since 1323.

Thus by 1595 the danger of Danish encirclement had been averted, the Russian drive to the sea had been halted, and Sweden had acquired her first overseas province. But in the course of doing so she had also acquired a new potential enemy. The Poles had forced Russia to acknowledge their right to Livonia in 1583; and Livonia, in their view, (and historically they were quite right) included Estonia. After 1583, therefore, Polish interests clashed with the interests of Sweden. One possible way of settling the controversy lay through a dynastic union; and it was in the hope of gaining Estonia at the price of collaboration against Russia that the

Polish magnates in 1587 elected Sigismund, the heir to the Swedish throne, as their king. It soon became apparent that they had miscalculated: Sigismund's Swedish subjects, it appeared, were not prepared to allow him to cede Estonia. Thus the Poles felt themselves to have been cheated, and henceforward only awaited a favourable opportunity to assert their claims. That opportunity came in 1600, when Sigismund (for purely domestic reasons) was deposed by his Swedish subjects, and the crown usurped by his uncle, King Charles IX. It was this Charles IX who was the father of Gustavus Adolphus. The ensuing quarrel between the usurper and the deposed, the dynastic split within the Vasa family, was in some ways an accident extraneous to Swedish political traditions. But one element in it was the fact that Sigismund's obligations as elected Polish king conflicted with his duty as a hereditary Swedish monarch. And one reason why they clashed was the rivalry of Sweden and Poland for the control of Estonia. Thus Eric XIV's venture had added a new dimension to foreign policy: the hostility of Poland. It had entailed commitments and created vested interests which were not easily to be jettisoned. It had already involved Sweden in a quarter of a century of war, and it was to prove a fruitful breeding-ground of wars in the future. The threat from Russia had indeed been warded off for the present; and the anarchy which engulfed that country in the years after 1605 made any recurrence of that danger unlikely in the immediate future. But the latent threat from Denmark remained: indeed, the new king of Denmark, Christian IV, was perhaps more interested in the possibility of restoring the old Scandinavian Union than any of his predecessors since 1523. As the seventeenth century opened, Sweden found herself in a perilous world.

It must be the part of a prudent statesman to see to it that if war proved to be unavoidable, at least it should be a war against no more than one enemy at a time. But Charles IX was not a prudent statesman. He had driven Sigismund from Sweden by methods which were violent and unconstitutional, and in doing so he had imported into Swedish foreign policy a confessional element which had never hitherto been of much importance. Since the reign of Gustavus Vasa, Sweden had been a Lutheran country; but Sigismund, the son of John III by a Polish princess, had been brought up a Roman Catholic:

8

this was one reason why he had been an acceptable candidate for the Polish crown. His endeavour to obtain a measure of toleration for Roman Catholics in Sweden was met with a compact and successful resistance by the Swedish Estates, and especially by the clergy; and it was not difficult for Charles to beat the Protestant drum and represent what was really a struggle for power as essentially a religious issue. The deposition of Sigismund, and the accession of Charles, was made to assume the aspect of a victory of militant Protestantism over the aggressions of the Counter-Reformation. There was an element of truth in this; for Sigismund was a pupil of the Jesuits, a zealous son of the Church, and in him the Papacy saw the instrument appointed by God for the recovery of Scandinavia to Rome. Protestant Europe, all the same, listened with pointed scepticism to Charles's attempts to represent his cause as one aspect of the general religious struggle, and the more responsible Lutheran princes disapproved of what had happened. Yet though Charles's appeals to Protestant solidarity for the moment fell remarkably flat, he had struck a note which was to reverberate strongly in the next reign. Charles himself might not be a very credible candidate for the part of Protestant Hero; but with Gustavus the case would be altered. The dynastic quarrel, the Swedish – Polish rivalry for control of Estonia, had already been given confessional overtones.

Yet in 1600 a war with Poland was not inevitable. The Polish magnates had little sympathy for Sigismund's natural desire to recover his hereditary kingdom; they were more interested in thwarting his attempts to strengthen the monarchy than in campaigns in Estonia; and the victory of the Counter-Reformation in Poland was still far from complete. If Charles had been content to stand on the defensive in Estonia, Sigismund might well have found it impossible to raise an adequate army from his unruly subjects. But Charles did not stand on the defensive: he invaded Livonia. By doing so he rallied to Sigismund's cause the mass of the Polish nobility, who could not afford to see Sweden controlling the great trade-artery of the Düna down which the produce of their *latifundia* flowed to the grain-markets of Amsterdam.

Thus Charles initiated a Swedish-Polish war which was to last, with truces of longer or shorter duration, for some sixty years: it was among the most troublesome political

9

heirlooms which he bequeathed to his successor. The war went ill for Sweden: at Kirkholm in 1605 Charles sustained the most crushing defeat ever to be inflicted on a Swedish army, and was lucky to escape with his life. It would have gone still worse, had not Sigismund's efforts been crippled by domestic insurrection, and his attention distracted to a political objective even more tempting than the conquest of Estonia. This was nothing less than the incorporation of the Muscovite realm into Poland. A Polish-backed Pretender seized the Russian throne on the death of Boris Godunov in 1605. Though his career came to a violent end within a year, it initiated a period of anarchy and civil war which reduced Russia to impotence and presented obvious opportunities for foreign intervention. Sigismund could not resist the temptation to use them. He would have liked to obtain the throne of the Tsars for himself, or, failing that, for his son, Ladislas; and he did in fact manage to find sufficient partisans in Russia to secure Ladislas's election. A Polish garrison established itself in Moscow; a Polish army besieged Smoleńsk.

In the face of this new development the war in Livonia became a secondary issue, and the campaigns there declined into desultory operations, unmemorable even to the military historian. For however the fighting might go in Estonia, Charles IX could not afford to see a Polish Tsar in Moscow. Hitherto, the waters of the Baltic had safeguarded him against any attempt at invasion from Poland; for Sigismund had no fleet. But now the back door to Stockholm, by way of Finland, would lie open to Sigismund's assault: Sweden would have lost her ditch. Polish intervention in Russia had already forced Charles to meddle in Muscovite politics: by the Treaty of Viborg (1609), Vasily Shuisky, the boyars' Tsar, had purchased Swedish assistance against the Poles by the promise of territorial concessions. But at Klushino, in 1610, he and his Swedish auxiliaries sustained a disastrous defeat, and that defeat was shortly followed by his deposition. Ladislas, it seemed, would now have a clear field. In this crisis, the Swedish commander in Russia, Jakob de la Gardie, came to an agreement with those elements which were not prepared to accept a Catholic Pole as their ruler, and secured from them an offer of the crown to one of the sons of Charles IX – preferably the younger son, Charles Philip. Charles IX died before reaching a decision on this offer, but in the meantime de la Gardie set about establishing a Swedish protectorate in north-western Russia as a base from which Charles Philip might one day assert his authority over the whole country. It was an open question whether his candidature had much chance of success; but it seemed obvious to de la Gardie that Sweden must use the prevailing chaos to strengthen her bastions on that side. She must have Kexholm, and the Karelian isthmus, and Ingria; and if it were possible she must retain the great trading city of Novgorod, which de la Gardie had already seized by a *coup de main*.

By 1611, then, the war against Poland was mainly being fought on Russian soil; and by that transference had begun to make sense in terms of the historic traditions of Swedish foreign policy. But if the venture were to be successful it was vital that there should be no complications in the west. Neither the army nor the navy was in any condition to take on another enemy, and Charles IX's evangelical diplomacy brought no hope of aid from outside. Sweden stood alone, without an ally, and with no very cordial friend. In this situation common sense dictated that every effort should be made to maintain good relations with Denmark. It ought not to have been impossible. Christian IV, it is true, was young, ambitious, and more than ready to see Sweden's difficulties as Denmark's opportunity; but his council was resolutely pacific, fearing that a successful war might enable the monarchy to strengthen its constitutional position against the aristocracy: only flagrant Swedish provocation would avail to stop its dragging its feet.

That provocation Charles IX rashly proceeded to offer. His navy blockaded Riga, interrupting Danish trade to that port; his privateers preyed indiscriminately upon shipping within the Baltic. At the same time, he was pursuing an aggressive policy in an area which had latterly been acquiring a new international importance: the Scandinavian Arctic. The trouble began as a dispute over the right to tax the nomadic Lapps; and it became acute when Charles IX began to buttress his claims by a systematic policy of colonization of this inhospitable region. This obscure controversy had wider implications than might at first sight appear. In the last resort it was one aspect of that geopolitical predicament which lay at the root of Swedish foreign policy. On the one hand it represented an attempt by Sweden to find a way round the

11

barrier of the Sound by a thrust to an ice-free port in the neighbourhood of the present Narvik; on the other, it cloaked an ambition to provide Sweden with a base for an attack on the Kola Peninsula, and the eventual conquest of Archangel.

In 1553 Willoughby and Chancellor had opened the White Sea route to Russia; in 1584 the new town of Archangel had been founded as a port for the English trade which began to take that way. For those who were prepared to face the stormy northward passage, the White Sea route offered the advantage of evading the Danish Sound dues, and not unnaturally the kings of Denmark looked upon it with disfavour: the desire to exercise a discouraging surveillance of the trade was one reason why Denmark was so anxious to make good her claims to the Arctic coastline. In Sweden the question wore a different aspect. Since the time of Gustavus Vasa it had been an object of Swedish policy to persuade traders to Russia to deal with the Muscovite through Swedish-controlled ports: at first through Helsingfors or Viborg, then (after 1560) through Reval, and lastly (after 1581) through Narva. But success had been only moderate: the tolls tended to be too high; the Swedes lacked entrepreneurs with sufficient capital to provide the long credit needed for discharging the functions of a middleman, and so were forced to rely on foreigners; and there were too many alternative ports available in the Baltic. If Charles IX's attack on Livonia had been successful, if Riga had passed into Swedish hands, the case might have been altered. But Archangel offered fresh possibilities, and no competitors in sight.

Thus, from the Danish point of view, Sweden's ambitions in Livonia, and Charles IX's forward policy in the Arctic, appeared to be (as in fact they were) complementary halves of a consistent plan which aimed at bringing more and more of the Russia trade under Swedish control. For decades the kings of Denmark had asserted a claim to a kind of tutelage over Baltic waters, but now, for the first time since the decay of Hanseatic power, the ascendancy of Denmark was beginning to be challenged: the Swedish blockade of Riga, Swedish intervention in Russia, Swedish designs in the Arctic, added up to a challenge which not even the reluctant Danish council could ignore. In April 1611 Christian IV's herald delivered Denmark's declaration of war. Seven months later Charles IX was dead.

So Gustavus Adolphus succeeded his father at a moment when the traditional policies of his country, and the dynastic controversy with Poland, had produced a situation which was both dangerous and new. The problem of the west had become merged with the problem of the east; security (and perhaps even independence) had been jeopardized by the attempt to strengthen those financial resources without which security must always be precarious.

Gustavus Adolphus was thus in many ways the prisoner of circumstances. His policies, at least to begin with, were the legacies of the past; always they were limited by the logic of history and the unalterable facts of geography. If this was true in the field of international relations, it was no less true in regard to domestic affairs. He had to work within the framework of the existing social structure and in the light of constitutional traditions; and his foreign policy was bounded (if indeed it was not largely determined) by the natural resources of the country over which he ruled.

Those resources gave little promise of providing the wherewithal for the acquisition of an empire. In comparison with France, or England, or Spain, Sweden seemed but a poor country; and a poor country she was in fact to remain throughout her entire imperial career, and for long afterwards. As late as the first half of the nineteenth century, C.J.L. Almquist saw in 'Swedish poverty' a main influence in the shaping of the Swedish national character. By a curious paradox it was not the least of the factors which led to the emergence of his country as one of the great powers of Europe, for poverty at home could most easily be compensated by rich pickings abroad. A poor country, then. Poor first of all in manpower, which the mercantilists considered the basic prerequisite for national strength: in 1611 the population of Sweden-Finland probably did not exceed 1,300,000; and, since the realm was so extensive, it was thinly scattered. A great part of the land was lake and forest; a wilderness of wood and water, very difficult to traverse except in winter; a land where man was still dwarfed by nature. Except for Stockholm, which was perhaps as big as Norwich, there was no town of any significance when measured by the standards of continental Europe. There were no great urban concentrations of population. Hence there was no wealthy middle class

13

to be mulcted by royal tax-gatherers or persuaded to unwilling loans in times of financial need; no great accumulations of merchant capital in native hands, and very few native entrepreneurs to finance industrial development or exploit the mineral resources of the soil. There were virtually no professional classes either, apart from the clergy, for as yet there was no centralization of justice other than that which was provided by the king in person, and until Sweden was equipped with a Supreme Court there would be no regular profession of the law. It was no wonder that, of the four Estates comprising the Swedish Diet, that of the Burghers was at this time by far the least important.

It was not to commerce and industry, however, that kings of Sweden mainly looked for their revenues. They did no doubt draw an income in cash from import and export duties; but essentially they depended upon revenues in kind, and these they converted into specie as necessity might require or opportunity offer. Iron and copper, fish and pelts, butter and tar, hides and grain, constituted the greatest part of the crown's resources; and all converged upon the royal warehouses, to be disposed of when the market was favourable, or when foreign creditors were to be paid. The bulk of this income in commodities was applied directly to the remuneration of the crown's servants, who were then left to make the best bargain they could from the sale of the miscellaneous articles and comestibles which were assigned to them by way of payment. Gustavus Vasa in his day had grown rich on the plunder of the Church, and by vigilant administration and business acumen had amassed a great hoard of coined money in the royal vaults at Stockholm and Gripsholm; but the half-century of war which followed had more than dissipated these resources. The lands of the crown, and the private estates of the Vasa family, were still of great extent – far greater than those of any of the nobility – but the cost of war had long since outstripped these hereditary revenues. Nevertheless, the monarchy relied on the land for the running of the state: rents in kind from the royal manors, taxes in kind from freehold peasants, taxes at half-rates from peasants on noble estates. For Sweden was overwhelmingly a peasant country. In all but the worst years she was self-sufficient except in the vital article of salt, though the fiscal demands of the king's government ensured that there was little margin of safety against a bad season. Most peasants had at some time in their lives to fall back upon bread-substitutes made of bark or bones, lichens, or dried fish-roes.

This austerity of living was not confined to the peasantry. It appeared, with modifications, at all social levels, when set in comparison with conditions in the richer countries of Europe. It showed itself in the miserable living conditions of many of the clergy, in the hardships of the academic life, in the unimpressive dimensions of churches and cathedrals, in the aspect of the capital, where goats were found grazing on the turf-roofed wooden houses, and in the modest domestic circumstances of most of the provincial nobility. Even the high aristocracy had scarcely as yet caught the idea of comfort: they spent their revenues on buying more land or richer clothing, but they lived in icy castles or unpretentious wooden granges, and scarcely any of them dreamed of maintaining an establishment in Stockholm. A select few had acquired a sufficient command of polite accomplishments to make a presentable show upon a foreign embassy, but it was only at court, under monarchs such as Eric XIV and John III, both of whom had aesthetic and cultural interests, that the spirit of Renaissance Europe made any impression upon the harsh and ungracious aspect of a society which was half-isolated, culturally retarded, and still in all essentials mediaeval. Royal patronage provided the only encouragement for the fine arts; royal interest in building produced a 'Vasa Style' of architecture which owed something to both Italian and Polish influences. A troupe of venturesome Elizabethan players did indeed visit Sweden in the 1590s, but they played to audiences to whom drama as a form of literature was a novelty, and toured a country which had so far failed to produce a poet writing in his own language. That language had perhaps suffered less change than English in the previous two or three centuries, but as yet it had developed neither richness nor flexibility. For political polemic, doomsday sermons, and royal eloquence it was a splendid vehicle: vivid, rude and pungent; but it was hardly adapted to the expression of complex ideas, and those who spoke it would have been hard put to it to produce a sonnet. Not that they made the attempt. They stuck to syllabic verse; and terrible verse it could be, as Charles IX's doggerel autobiography sufficiently testifies.

This economic and cultural backwardness did not provide a promising base for greatness. The stony soils of the moraine-lands, the all-pervading wood and water, rendered the country incapable of supporting the burden of taxation which a rich land such as France could endure, for here a grudging nature was unable to repair the abuses of man: the risk that farms might become derelict and revert to the waste was always a check upon fiscal exorbitancies. The exiguous population felt severely the loss of manpower entailed by war, famine and pestilence. There were limits to what any Swedish king could expect from his country, and only in Charles XII's *Götterdämmerung* were those limits really exceeded.

In another way, too, the social structure seemed ill-adapted to the needs of a great power. The absence of a strong middle class meant that the government, and the central government in particular, suffered from a shortage of competent trained administrators. Before the Reformation the Church had supplied some of the personnel required, but thereafter no churchman had occupied ministerial office. Judicial functions were discharged by the nobility (or their deputies), and on the whole they discharged them well, for they had for centuries been the hereditary custodians of the law. But despite the nobility's increasingly clamant demand for a monopoly of the major offices of government, they were only just beginning to be the class of statesmen, bureaucrats, and administrators which they were to become later in the century. Charles IX tried to compel them to serve the state, but the strained relations between monarchy and nobility which characterized his reign were not conducive to willing service. Meantime, the lack of any class of professional lawyers deprived the government service of the opportunities for recruitment which were normal in the states of western Europe; and the sorry condition of the University of Uppsala made it an unpromising forcing-house for potential civil servants. It was no wonder that the apparatus of government was scanty, primitive and undifferentiated. Charles IX ruled personally with the assistance of his bailiffs and of a handful of upstart secretaries who had received their training in foreign universities and shed their scruples in the process. Such a central administration, so antique in its form and so *ad hoc* in its methods, was quite unfitted to the carrying on of a great European war, and still less to ruling an empire.

Yet Sweden, though in so many respects she seemed to be unripe for the destiny which was soon to overtake her, had advantages and sources of inner strength which were denied to some of the greater states of Europe. For instance, when compared with France, or Spain, or the Netherlands, it was a unified country. It had, no doubt, been formed by the growing together of various provinces. But despite differences of dialect, strong provincial loyalties and institutions, and a local government which rested heavily on provincial magnates, the king's authority was not qualified by provincial privileges: the last manifestations of provincial independence had been definitively crushed by Gustavus Vasa. The towns were too weak, and too dependent on the crown, for municipal liberties to present obstacles to national policies. Trade moved unimpeded over the whole country: there were no internal customs barriers to create artificial and local famines. Since Sweden had never been a feudal country, there was no trouble about feudal immunities or offices; and though the over-mighty subject had presented problems during the turbulent fifteenth century, Gustavus Vasa's heavy hand had disposed of that danger for ever. When after 1632 (as again after 1660) the high nobility took charge of the state during the minority of the sovereign, they inherited the monarchical tradition of unity. Though great magnates such as Per Brahe or Magnus Gabriel de la Gardie might keep a princely state in their counties of Visingsö or Läckö, they never sought to use them as power bases from which to bring pressure to bear upon the crown: a Henry of Navarre, a Biron, a Bouillon, had no place in Swedish society, and a Condé was inconceivable.

The unity of the state was matched by the unity of the Church. The imagined threat of recatholicization in the time of Sigismund had called forth a definition of the country's theological position; and an apprehension of danger from Calvinism under Charles IX had only made that definition the sharper. Sweden was a solidly Lutheran country, more fully united in religion, less troubled by heresies and sectarian divagations, than any state in Europe except Spain. In an age of religious strife this was no insignificant advantage. Moreover, the clergy were well placed to ensure that it was an advantage that should not be lost, for they formed one of the four Estates of the Diet. On matters of religion their views would ordinarily prevail, if only because the crown relied upon them to act as unpaid civil servants and expected them to preach the nonsense out of men's heads.

Against such nonsense as remained when their sermons were over the king had a further resource. It was provided by the presence in the Diet of the Estate of Peasants. As there had never been any feudalism in Sweden, so also there had been no villeinage. The peasant in Sweden was a free man and had always been so. When, during the fifteenth century, representative institutions began to crystallize, it seemed natural that the peasants should form a part of them. Nowhere else in Europe had the commonalty so direct a voice in the affairs of state; nowhere else could the sovereign meet the accredited representatives of the masses face to face and persuade them to compliance with unpopular policies by appeals to their duty to God and to their country.

Thus Sweden was not quite as unapt for a career of greatness as might at first sight appear. Though still poor, she had great resources of copper and iron which were soon to make her richer. Though the king's revenues might still be paid in butter or tar, they were at least thereby rendered less vulnerable to erosion by the price revolution. Though surrounded by foes, she was strategically upon the inner lines; and in her forest barriers, and the intricate labyrinth of skerries that fringed her coasts, she had defences provided by nature against invasion. Sweden was not without assets. And not the least important among them was Gustavus Adolphus himself.

Chapter 2

THE ACCESSION CRISIS AND ITS CONSEQUENCES

Gustavus Adolphus was born on 9 December 1594, the eldest son of Charles IX's second marriage with Christina of Holstein. He is said to have been a child of unusual promise. If so, native genius was improved by a careful education, which his father took pains to supervise. Although it was not until 1604 that the resolution of the Diet of Norrköping finally confirmed Charles's usurpation and recognized Gustavus as his heir, it is clear that for some time before this his education had been designed to fit him for the responsibilities of kingship. As his principal tutor Charles selected Johan Schroderus, better known by his noble name of Skytte. The choice proved to be excellent, for Skytte was not only a man of comprehensive learning, but also a pedagogue who succeeded in implanting in his pupil that capacity for concentrated application, that strong intellectual curiosity, that wide-ranging expertise, and that sense of duty, which in the end made him the greatest ruler of his age. Gustavus Adolphus liked and respected Skytte, and in many ways his approach to political and religious questions reflects Skytte's influence.

The training to which he was subjected added up to a formidable educational programme. He was thoroughly grounded in the Latin classics (for Latin was still the language of diplomacy), and in later life could throw out a casual reference to Seneca to enforce an argument; and he was well drilled in Ciceronian rhetoric, for Skytte (like Charles IX) knew what a powerful political asset the gift of words might be to a king. He knew some Greek too, and he had an enviable command of modern languages: from his childhood, German was as familiar to him as Swedish, and he is said by the end of his life to have been more or less acquainted with eight other languages, including English and (a proper distinction) Scots. He was given instruction in the elements of law, and as king showed an informed interest in the cases which came before him for revision. He learned history, too, and liked it; and later he was to try his hand at writing a history of his own times. He was passionately interested in all those fantasies about Sweden's heroic Gothic past which did duty for a history of Swedish antiquity; and undoubtedly he saw himself as the last of a long line of (mostly imaginary) warrior-kings who in the great days had sallied out from the North to conquer Europe and topple the empire of the Caesars. Sweden might appear insignificant now, but is was a comforting reflection that she had once led the world, in the arts of peace and war alike.

Finally, there were the essentials, the training no king could do without in that age of religious wars. The first of these was theology; and here the influence of Skytte, and the example of Charles IX, combined to produce in Gustavus Adolphus a type of Protestantism less doctrinally rigid than was usual in Sweden at that time. Of course he was a sound Lutheran; but he was less eager than some of his episcopate to pronounce damnation upon Calvinists: this was to be useful when the time came to look for friends in Germany. As he grew older the limits of his charity expanded; at the close of his life he seems to have been prepared to entertain the idea of toleration even for Roman Catholics.

The second essential was a knowledge of the military art. He approached it on the theoretical level through the study of mathematics, optics and mechanics, and was in later life emphatic upon the necessity of these disciplines to a good commander. It was Skytte, too, who taught him the history of the art of war, from Caesar, Vegetius, Aelian and Frontinus down to the new Dutch style of fortification as expounded by Simon Stevin, and the tactical innovations of Maurice of Orange. But Skytte was without military experience, and in order to supplement his theoretical instruction Gustavus had to rely on what he could pick up from a two-months' intensive course from Jakob de la Gardie, on leave from the Swedish armies in Livonia. All this provided no more than a foundation on which to build, and only experience could prove whether he was capable of building on it. The reign would be half over before he really made his mark as a commander: like many another great soldier, Gustavus was essentially self-taught.

Thus equipped, and still a few weeks short of his seventeenth birthday, he confronted a situation which might have daunted an experienced leader and a more mature statesman. Charles IX's war with Denmark was proving disastrous: the Swedish armies had been incapable of meeting the Danes in battle; the Swedish navy had shown itself incompetent to keep the seas; the Danes had taken Kalmar, Sweden's bastion on the east coast. In Russia was a force which was desperately needed at home, but which could not be withdrawn without leaving the field there open to the Poles. And before anything could be done on either front, Gustavus had to face, and somehow to surmount, a major constitutional crisis.

The crisis was a direct consequence of Charles IX's usurpation. In the first place, Charles's accession had not only excluded Sigismund and his descendants from the throne, it had also quietly pushed aside the next person in order of succession – Charles's nephew, Duke John of Östergötland, the son of John III by his second marriage. In 1604 John had renounced his claims in favour of Gustavus; but the Diet which confirmed this arrangement had laid it down that if Charles should die while his son was still a minor, the government was to remain in the hands of a regency until he reached the age of eighteen, and was not to be wholly entrusted to him until he was twenty-four. But in November 1611 he was not yet seventeen. Secondly, the rule of Charles IX had provoked widespread discontent in large sections of the nation. The deposition of Sigismund had brought political ruin to those members of the Council who had felt bound by their oaths of office to stand by him. At Linköping, in 1600, four of their leaders had been judicially murdered, at Charles's instigation, by an extraordinary tribunal drawn from the Estates. Their deaths were not only a blow to the high aristocracy: they entailed also the wreck (for the moment) of a constitutional cause. For the Council had been champions of a long-standing tradition of aristocratic constitutionalism which aimed at imposing checks and limitations on the crown, and which stood for the rule of law and resistance to arbitrary power.

21

Charles, on the other hand, represented a tradition of personal kingship inherited from Gustavus Vasa; and by capitalizing on the anti-aristocratic feelings of the lower Estates he was able to run the country as a sort of parliamentary despotism. If, as happened from time to time, there appeared some sign of restiveness among his subjects assembled at the Diet, he blackmailed them into co-operation by threats of abdication – threats which were effective because it seemed that only he stood between them and Sigismund's restoration; and that would entail handing over Sweden to Rome. A new submissive Council replaced the old constitutionalists, and government passed into the hands of a group of imported Livonian nobles and able but ill-reputed secretaries of mean extraction. The high aristocracy was in disarray, split in two by the events of 1600: there was scarcely a great family which did not have close relatives in exile at Sigismund's court. Inevitably there were plots and intrigues which compromised those who remained at home; and to these Charles reacted by savage measures of retaliation in which forms of law were set aside, and men were convicted on hearsay evidence or unsubstantiated delations. To most of the high nobility it seemed that their king was a tyrant who governed by terror. No doubt it is true that Charles and his secretaries acknowledged an obligation to rule within the law, and that they even (on paper) subscribed to the ideal of a 'mixed monarchy'; but what mattered in the eyes of the nobility was not Charles's theories but his practice.

By 1611, then, the nobility was profoundly alienated, and saw in the accession of a minor the opportunity to limit the monarchy and restore the rule of law. But it was not only the nobility that was discontented. Throughout his reign Charles had waged a guerrilla warfare with his episcopate, who attacked his latitudinarian theology, resented his meddling in ecclesiastical appointments, and suspected him of being a crypto-Calvinist. The lower Estates were wearied by his repeated summonings of the Diet and his threats of abdication. The Council vainly remonstrated against the rashness of his foreign policy; the commonalty grumbled at the burdens which that policy entailed. The country which Gustavus inherited was sullen, resentful and deeply divided. But on one point at least almost everybody was agreed: the existing regime must not be suffered to continue: 'God in Heaven', wrote a contemporary pamphleteer, 'preserve us from such another bloody and oppressive reign as this has been.'

At the Diet which met at Nyköping in December 1611 the discontented took their chance to hold monarchy to ransom. Gustavus was informed that the Estates would be prepared to ignore the resolution of 1604, and accept him immediately as king with full powers, 'seeing that God . . . has made up in understanding what is lacking in years'; but only if in return he accepted a Charter which should safeguard them against the abuses of the previous decade. It was a bleak ultimatum, and Gustavus had no choice but to accept it.

The result was the Charter of 1 January 1612. It reads like a sort of Grand Remonstrance: a devastating indictment of prevailing malpractices and illegalities.[1] It bound the monarchy, in terms more explicit than any Swedish monarch had submitted to since 1523, or would submit to again before 1719, to rule in terms of the constitution. Henceforward the consent of the Council would be required for the making of new law, for all major acts of foreign policy, and for the summoning of the Diet. No new taxes were to be imposed, no new troops were to be levied, without the Council's knowledge and the consent 'of those concerned' – a phrase which might imply the consent of the Diet, but which also left the way open for separate bargains between the crown and individual Estates, or for negotiations on a provincial basis. The liberties of the Church were secured against royal encroachments. And the nobility was firmly established in the seats of power by a clause which laid down that membership of the Council, and all the most important civil and military offices, were to be reserved to noblemen of Swedish birth: there was to be no recurrence of the abhorred 'rule of secretaries'.

Though these terms represented a softening of the demands originally put forward, they were sufficiently stringent. Whether he liked it or not, Gustavus had no option but to swallow them. If the country were to be extricated from the desperate position in which it found itself, the prime requisite was a restoration of confidence between crown and people, the relaxation of the tensions which had been generated in the preceding reign, the reconciliation of those elements in society which Charles had alienated: in short, a process of 'healing and settling'. For without the collaboration of the nobility a youth of seventeen could scarcely hope to carry on the government. The acceptance of the Charter made all these things possible.

The constitutional crisis was uncommonly sharp while it lasted, but it was necessarily short, and it left no aftermath of bitterness behind it. Nevertheless, the historic struggle between royal authority and aristocratic constitutionalism, though it might for the moment be pretermitted, had not vanished overnight: it remained latent, and would recur once Gustavus was dead. But the reconciliation of 1612 was real, and it lasted for the whole of the reign. The symbol of that reconciliation, and its most important immediate result, was the appointment as chancellor of the man who had had the main hand in drafting – and extorting – the Charter: Axel Oxenstierna.

So began that remarkable collaboration which was to endure for the rest of Gustavus's life: a partnership of Sweden's greatest king with her greatest statesman. It was a partnership of equals, in which each contributed qualities which the other lacked. Their temperaments were very diff- erent: Gustavus dynamic, impetuous, 'ever *allegro* and *courage*'; Oxenstierna imperturbable, tireless, unhurrying; the one sup- plying inspiration, the other ripe wisdom and many-sided administrative ability. As Oxenstierna himself once remarked, it needed his phlegm to temper the king's choler. Though Oxenstierna was the embodiment of the tradition of aristo- cratic constitutionalism, and Gustavus inherited a good por- tion of his father's dynamic view of kingship, their association of over twenty years was unbroken by a single open clash. At first, indeed, there are signs that the king was concerned to make it clear that he would take decisions independently of his chancellor; but in later years he consulted him about everything – including strategy – and lamented when separa- tion made it impossible to obtain his advice in good time. What was it, then, that bound them together? It was agree- ment on two basic matters: foreign policy and administrative reform. They might – and occasionally did – differ on the best means to secure the objectives which were common to both, but such differences of opinion never disturbed their relation- ship, which was throughout one of complete frankness, trust, and in the end, affection. Oxenstierna saw it in terms of loyal service to a master whom he admired and respected; Gustavus came to see it almost as a necessity of life. At a dark moment in December 1630, he addressed a moving letter to his chancellor:

> And so I urge and entreat you, for Christ's sake, not to lose heart if the issue be otherwise than we would have it. I know that I may rely upon you to take care of my memory, and to look after the welfare of my family as you would that God should look after you and yours – and as I myself will look after them, if God permit me to live so long that you should need my help in that way. . . . If anything should happen to me, my family will become objects of compassion; for they are women, the mother a person of no judgment, the daughter still a young girl; likely to make a mess of things if they are given their head; in danger, if others gain an ascendancy over them. Natural affection forces these lines from my pen in order to prepare you – as an instrument sent to me from God to light me through many a dark place – for what may happen: it is, in all the world, the care that lies heaviest upon me. Yet this too, as also my life and soul and everything that God has given me, I commend into His keeping; hoping always the best in this world, and after this life peace, and joy, and felicity. And the same I wish for you when your hour shall come.
>
> I remain, for as long as long as I live, ever your gracious and affectionate
>
> Gustav Adolf.

But if Oxenstierna throughout the reign held an uncontested primacy among the king's servants, he was not the only minister to enjoy the king's confidence. Gustavus had a justified respect for the abilities, and a warm appreciation of the personal attachment, of his old tutor, Johan Skytte, whom he insisted on admitting to the Council in 1617, in the face of the obvious repugnance of Oxenstierna and his aristocratic friends. It may be that the king was not unwilling to create a kind of counterpoise to the aristocratic monopoly of high office. He had a strong filial piety; and his own sketch of the troubled history of the 1590s shows how completely he identified himself with Charles's rancorous attitude to his political opponents. In 1612 he was by no means disposed to make a clean sweep of all the men who had served his father. Skytte stood, then, in many ways, for the attitudes and traditions of the reign of Charles IX. Relations between Skytte and Oxenstierna were never easy. As long as the king

25

lived their dislike was cloaked in a decent courtesy; but after his death incompatibility passed into scarcely disguised hostility, and produced a deep division in Swedish politics which was to last for more than a generation.

For the moment, however, these discords were muted, or were resolved into the national unison which Gustavus contrived to evoke. Certainly he could not in his early years afford to quarrel with the ancient families, if only because the main danger to his throne seemed to come from aristocratic exiles committed to Sigismund's restoration and in dangerous contact with their cousins and brothers at home. So the Charter was followed immediately by the grant of fresh privileges to the nobility; and those privileges were extended in 1622. But before the reign was many years old, the tact and persistence of Oxenstierna (who had relatives of his own in exile), and the trust which the king's personality inspired in former adversaries, had succeeded in reconciling an appreciable number of those whom his father had persecuted and proscribed. A steady trickle of exiles returned home, and those who remained abroad were less able to rely on sympathy for their cause: it was a striking sign of the success of his policy that no less than four of the sons of the men whom Charles had brought to the block at Linköping had by 1632 been admitted as members of the Council.

Though Gustavus succeeded in healing the wounds which Charles had inflicted, and though in time the nobility rallied strongly round the throne, his attitude to them differed less from his father's than might appear. He gave them privileges, certainly; he dangled before their eyes the prospect of extensive land grants in conquered Ingria; he offered a career open to talents: 500 commissions should be reserved to them, he assured them in 1625, if only they would agree to contribute to financing a standing army. But he exacted service in return, as Charles had also tried to do: unlike his father he was able to get it. Charles had made extensive assignments of farms and revenues to the nobility in the expectation that they would furnish him with cavalry. They took the assignments; but they were slack about the *quid pro quo*. From the beginning of the reign Gustavus made it clear that he was not prepared to tolerate this state of affairs,[2] and within the first five or six years almost all of these assignments were resumed by the crown: it was the first *reduktion*, and it was not to be the last. The king needed cavalry which could be relied upon to materialize when required; he needed the alienated revenues; and as early as 1612 the Peasantry had demanded their resumption, as an alternative to increased taxation. By the end of the reign he had so schooled the aristocracy that it became for the first time a nobility of service, and thus capable of running the country in his absence, or in the event of a minority. But state service also carried with it the idea of status according to rank in the service, as against the older concept of status as determined by birth. Since Gustavus was prepared to take able men wherever he could find them, the emergence of a new hierarchy of rank-by-service would produce, in the two generations after his death, social strains and conflicts which were scarcely foreseen in 1632.

Moreover, the privileges which Gustavus granted the nobility in exchange for their support proved less substantial in fact than they appeared on paper. True, they obtained an enlargement of their fundamental privilege of exemption from taxation; but for the last decade of the reign this became an increasingly illusory concession, and remained so for the rest of the seventeenth century. As one extraordinary war-tax followed another, the nobility found it impossible to preserve their immunity. The king argued them into acquiescence by appeals to their patriotism; and by 1632 the concessions of 1612 and 1622 had in fact been largely eroded. Even Oxenstierna's domestics could not obtain exemption from inclusion in the 'files' from which the army was recruited. Taxation at half-rates for the nobility's peasantry tended to turn into taxation at full rates, and the total exemption of labourers on noble manors was jeopardized. The nobility themselves paid some of the new personal taxes; and if they preferred to call them 'contributions', the name did not disguise the reality. Charles IX may have been at odds with the old nobility, Gustavus may have contrived to maintain good relations with them, but at bottom there was not much difference in this matter between father and son: Per Brahe, head of the oldest noble family in Sweden, and lord of the great county of Visingsö, later remarked that Gustavus was 'a potentate whose humour it was to stick his fingers into other men's privileges in order to abridge them, that his power might be greater thereby'.

Thus the victory of the nobility in 1612 did not, in the

event, pave the way to an aristocratic oligarchy – at least, for
so long as Gustavus lived. Nor were its constitutional consequences what might have been expected. There was, indeed,
a resolute effort by the king to restore the rule of law; the
royal bailiffs who oppressed the subjects were brought to
book; the regime of spies and delations came to an end;
judicial procedure was regularized; and there was an end to
political trials by extraordinary tribunals. At the coronation
in 1617 Gustavus explicitly accepted the principle that king
and subjects were bound to each other by reciprocal oaths.
The curriculum of the University of Uppsala in the 1620s,
which reflected the influence both of Skytte and Oxenstierna,
prescribed as its textbook in politics not Bodin but Althusius,
the theorist of mixed monarchy. But if the Charter represents
the idea of a balanced polity, Gustavus took care that it
should be a balance tipped in his favour. In the draft of a
speech made to the Stockholm Diet of 1617 he defined the
king's authority as paternal, and spoke of his subjects as good
children occasionally in need of correction: not for nothing
had Charles IX commissioned the translation into Swedish,
by Skytte's brother, of James I's *Regium donum*.

The force of the king's personality, and the dangers which
confronted the country, soon induced his subjects to accept
an interpetation of the Charter which certainly did not accord
with the spirit in which it was drafted. In high matters of
state (if he happened not to be away on campaign) he did
often seek the opinion of his Council; but it does not seem
that he ever in practice felt bound to obtain their *consent*, as
the Charter required. When he turned to them it was sometimes for advice, more often simply for comment, rather than
for authorization. In the great debates on whether or not to
intervene in Germany, and if so whether offensively or
defensively, he set out the arguments against the course on
which he had in fact already determined; expounded them
fairly, eloquently, and at length. On less crucial occasions the
provisions of the Charter were simply ignored: he might
inform the Diet, or a section of it, on matters of foreign policy
after they had been decided; but the peace of Stolbova, the
alliance with Denmark in 1628, the truce of Altmark, were
concluded without even the simulacrum of consent. Still more
obviously was this the case after the landing in Germany: the
Pomeranian and Brandenburg treaties, the Contingent Con-

federation with Hesse, the treaty of Bärwalde, were his personal work, though he took care to seek Oxenstierna's advice, and sometimes (but not always) took it. Until Oxenstierna was summonded from Elbing to join him at Mainz – a period of sixteen months – Gustavus was his own, his sole, foreign minister; and he missed his chancellor sorely. 'As to your coming here, God knows how necessary it would be for us, both for your counsel and for conducting negotiations, since we have to direct our affairs here virtually alone . . . we can't manage it single-handed, and there is no one but you with the authority to deal with these things.'

In regard to the burdens of taxation, and to conscription-levies, he mostly found it prudent to observe the Charter's requirement that the assent of the Diet be obtained. But as those burdens increased during the 1620s there were clear signs that he was prepared to dispense with that requirement in an emergency; and to some extent he carried the Council with him in this. In 1627, for instance, the Council flatly declared that conscription-levies were entirely a prerogative matter, needing no assent; and (what is even more remarkable) in 1636 Axel Oxenstierna reiterated that assertion. By 1627, indeed, it is possible to detect an authoritarian tone in the king's pronouncements which he had previously been careful to avoid. In that year he had sharp exchanges with the Council about the continuation of the Stock-and-Land Tax. When the Council submitted their formal Resolution in reply to the royal Proposition, Gustavus rejected it, drew a Resolution himself, and demanded that they sign it. Their reply was to leave it unsigned for a fortnight, 'to the king's indignation'; and when the Resolution of the Diet affirmed that of the Council, his response was simply to draw up that Resolution also to conform to his own views. The Diet, in an attempt to excuse their obstinacy, informed him that their eventual capitulation proceeded 'from their affection and good inclination'; the king replied tartly that he was not concerned with their affection: what they did was a mere matter of duty. A year later the point was rammed home with all possible clarity: 'It is not a question of whether I have the right to make impositions without advice, nor of what your privileges may permit; what we have to look to is the temper of the commonalty and the necessity of the times; and it is not a question of what they are *bound* to pay, but of what they *can*

29

pay.' The king must have his money and his men, despite the audible groans of his lieges; and though he could on occasion be moved to compassion, and allow mitigations in particular cases, the country's welfare must normally override private rights. The Stock Tax was doubled in 1624, and reimposed in 1626, without the consent of the Diet. The Three Marks Aid – a poll tax on all males over the age of twelve (paupers and nobles included) was never granted by the Estates. In 1631 the Mill Tax was summarily ordered to be paid in silver, which made it many times more burdensome than before: this too was in fact arbitrary and unconstitutional taxation. The provision in the Charter that no additional burdens were to be imposed, nor new taxed levied, without the consent 'of those concerned' in fact left Gustavus free to decide for himself who was 'concerned', and this by no means always meant the Diet: it might be a 'Trade Meeting' of various towns; or a separate meeting for Finland; or an agreement with the nobility on a matter which concerned them alone; or the king might send 'commissioners' round the country (as in 1630) to persuade the 'commonalty', if the Diet should prove recalcitrant. The provision of the *Riksdagsordning* of 1617[3] that in case of discrepant answers from the various Estates the king might take 'that which seems best to him' was on at least one occasion used to force through his preferred solution. It is true that he did not follow his father's tactics of using the Diet as a political weapon against the aristocracy; but his preference for verbal rather than written forms for the transaction of business reflects his well-grounded confidence in his ability to talk them into doing what he wanted.

After his death events would make it apparent that the situation in his lifetime had been exceptional. The ideals and policies of the men who had imposed the Charter once more came to the surface of politics; the more certainly, since the political nation very soon came to feel that the objectives for which the war was being fought were no longer what they had been. Within a year of Lützen members of the Council would be saying that it was time to end the German commitment, and therefore to reject that abdication of constitutional principles to which (on the whole) they had been a party while he was still there to animate them with his spirit. And so it fell to Axel Oxenstierna, the man who above all had been responsible for the Charter, to reaffirm many of its provisions in the Form of Government of 1634,[4] and to replace the quasi-autocratic arrangements of the last years of the reign by what was destined to be its alternative: the rule of an aristocratic oligarchy.

Thus, against all probability, Gustavus emerged from the crisis of his accession with regal authority essentially unimpaired; and monarchy remained personal, after 1611 as before it. But with a difference. In the first place, the attempt which Charles had made to exercise direct supervision over all branches of government was abandoned: the business of state was now too heavy for such methods, which even in Charles's time had been outmoded. There had to be delegation, and Gustavus recognized this. In the second place, there was a difference of personality, of tone and manner. Charles IX had ruled against the grain of the nation; Gustavus ruled with it. His popularity, his personal prestige, enabled him to enlist the institutions of government – the Council, the Diet, the provincial administration, the Church – behind the policies he considered necessary; and consultation produced an appearance of collaboration which was not wholly illusory, since in fact it reflected something like a national consensus. Without such a consensus, the sacrifices which his policies demanded would scarcely have been tolerable to his people.

. . .

NOTES

1. English translation in M. Roberts, *Sweden as a Great Power 1611–1697* (London, 1968), pp. 7–10.
2. English translation of his stringent Proclamation of 26 November 1612 in ibid., pp. 94–5.
3. English translation in ibid., pp. 11–12.
4. English translation in ibid., pp. 18–28.

Chapter 3

RECOVERY (1612–20)

By January 1612, then, the constitutional crisis was over; the Charter had been signed, and Gustavus was free to devote all his attention to the pressing problems of war and foreign policy. Here, as in the domestic field, his line of action was more or less prescribed for him by the circumstances in which he found himself. Somehow or other he must extricate his country from the Danish war; he must take measures in Russia which would ensure that that country did not fall under Polish control; and he must parry his cousin Sigismund's attempts to reverse the verdict of 1600 and recover the Swedish throne for the elder Vasa line.

For the moment, the mere struggle for survival must engage all his attention. But on the assumption that that struggle would be successful, it must also be his concern to see that Sweden's perilous isolation was broken, and to enlist friends or allies for assistance if the threat from Denmark should recur, or Sigismund persist in his designs. The most likely places to find them would probably be in Germany or the Netherlands, and success might well entail reciprocal obligations which would draw Swedish foreign policy into wider engagements on the Continent. It is with these things that the period from 1612 to 1620 is concerned: with the deliverance of the country from the dangers which beset her, and with the beginning of the process which in the second decade of the reign was to involve Sweden directly in the great controversies of Europe. By 1620 the heritage of Charles IX would have been liquidated, at least as regards Denmark and Russia; Sweden's diplomatic isolation would have been broken; the worst of the domestic problems would have been overcome;

and a start would have been made with a great programme of internal reform and reconstruction. But to reach even these relatively modest goals took seven or eight years of arduous endeavour.

The first priority was the war with Denmark, for this was a threat to Sweden's existence as an independent state. It had gone badly under Charles IX, and it did not go much better under Gustavus. The native Swedish levies were not fit to engage the professional troops of Christian IV; the Swedish fortresses were incapable of resisting the siege tactics of continental warfare. Sweden's best defence consisted in the difficulty of conquering a densely forested and poorly provisioned country, in the ambushes which traditional Swedish tactics prepared for an invader, and in Christian's inability to find the money to pay his mercenary armies. It was a war of border forays, reciprocal harryings and devastations, with grim atrocities on both sides; and it left a long memory of bitterness behind it among the Swedish peasantry. Gustavus showed some awareness of the strategic advantages of operating on the interior lines; but Christian's plans for an advance on Stockholm through Östergötland never gave much promise of being able to surmount the geographical and logistical difficulties. Battles were few, though skirmishes abounded: Gustavus nearly perished in an affair near Vittsjö, when his horse went through the ice of a frozen stream; Christian was caught returning from a foray, and was lucky to escape with his life at Kölleryd. The Danes' command of the sea enabled their fleet to assist in the capture of Öland, to make harassing landings in the rear of the Swedish armies, and at last, in the closing stages of the war, to threaten Stockholm's outer defences from the skerries. Much more important, it enabled them to take Sweden's two key strongholds. Kalmar had fallen in the last months of Charles's life, and the vain effort to recapture it has given to the struggle its name of the War of Kalmar; but the capitulation of Älvsborg, in May 1612, was the most important single event of the war, and decisively affected the terms of peace. Its fall meant that the Swedish west-coast fleet, which had taken refuge in the harbour, had to be scuttled at its moorings; and it meant also that the mercenary troops which Gustavus had been raising in western Europe could no longer land at a Swedish port, and were driven to attempt to reach Stockholm by way of

Norway. But despite these disasters, despite the inefficiency of the Swedish administration, the exhaustion of the Swedish treasury, and the inadequacies of Swedish tactics, it was plain by the end of 1612 that Christian IV lacked the resources to exploit success. He might indeed win the war, but he could not really hope to reconquer Sweden. And when his brother-in-law, King James I, offered his mediation, Christian was glad enough to accept it. He was, after all, in a strong bargaining position.

This was reflected in the terms of the Peace of Knäred, which was concluded on 21 January 1613. It registered the abandonment of those provocative policies of Charles IX which had been the immediate cause of war. Sweden promised that her ships would levy toll on merchantmen trading to Riga only if the port were actually blockaded and besieged; Denmark was permitted to quarter the Three Crowns (the arms of Sweden) in her coat of arms; and Sweden relinquished all pretensions to the Arctic coastline and all claims to tax the coastline Lapps. In other respects there was to be a reciprocal restitution of conquests; but with one vital reservation. The treaty provided for the payment by Sweden of a war indemnity of one million *riksdaler*; and until it was paid, Denmark was to retain in her hand Älvsborg, the Göta estuary, and seven adjacent hundreds, as a pledge for its payment. There can be little doubt that Christian calculated that the exhaustion of Sweden would make a punctual payment of this huge sum impossible, and that Älvsborg and the seven hundreds would go to Denmark by default. If that happened, he would have a stranglehold which would enable him at a later opportunity to throttle Sweden's independence. He had barred Charles's attempted break-out through the Arctic; he had Sweden's solitary North Sea port in his hands; and it seemed of minor importance that the treaty should have confirmed Sweden's exemption from the Sound Tolls, for now it would be easier than ever to isolate her by shutting the Sound: the Peace of Knäred might well give him what he had been unable to win by war.

The ransom for Älvsborg fell with crushing severity upon a country which seemed already at the end of its tether. From all over the southern provinces came the same story of devastated villages and abandoned farms. The king could not pay his tailor so small a sum as thirty *daler*; he could not provide his courier to Finland with money to buy provisions on the journey. The hand-to-mouth expedients of the treasury would have broken down without loans from Jakob de la Gardie and the Queen Mother. On top of all this came Älvsborg's ransom; to be paid in four equal yearly instalments beginning in January 1616, and to be paid, moreover, in *riksdaler*, which were not the ordinary circulating medium in Sweden.[1] But, whatever the cost, the ransom had somehow to be collected; and in 1613 the Diet agreed to a special tax for four years to pay for it. It was of unprecedented severity: every adult Swede, with the solitary exception of the Queen Mother (who was left to make such contribution as she thought proper) was to pay upon a scale proportioned to his or her means: the king himself, and Duke John of Östergöt- land, promised 32 per cent of the revenues from their estates; and the yield of the tax was to be safeguarded by being paid into a special fund. But the ordinary necessities of government were so great that Gustavus was forced to raid the fund and apply some of it to other uses; the tax had to be levied for six years instead of four; and in the end nearly double the original amount was raised. The difficulty of obtaining *riksdaler* was met mainly by the sale of copper on the international market; even so, Älvsborg would have been lost without Dutch assistance: a Dutch loan of 150,000 *rdr* was secured to meet the second instalment; and only the arrival of a consignment of copper at Amsterdam in the nick of time prevented a default on the third. When in January 1619 Älvsborg was finally recovered, on the payment of the fourth instalment, Sweden found herself in debt to the Dutch to the tune of a quarter of a million. The whole affair was a vivid revelation of the country's financial weakness.

Yet though the burden at times seemed insupportable, and though the effort provoked more than one popular disturb- ance, the sacrifices had perhaps been worth while. Denmark got her million; but she lost Sweden. With the recovery of Älvsborg, Christian had missed his best chance. It would be another five years yet before it became apparent that the balance in the Baltic was shifting in Sweden's favour, and for many a day the old fear of Denmark, and memories of the War of Kalmar, would be a major element in Swedish foreign policy. But when, in 1619, Christian met Gustavus at Halmstad, it was a clear sign that, for the present at least, he

35

had laid aside all thoughts of reviving the Scandinavian Union.

Meanwhile Gustavus had been hacking his way through the labyrinthine confusions of Russia. At the moment of his accession the prospects looked not unpromising: the Polish garrison in Moscow was closely besieged in the Kremlin, and an embassy from Novgorod was in Stockholm soliciting his approval of Charles Philip's acceptance of the Russian throne. The 'Second National Rising' declared for Charles Philip in 1612; and on 25 October the Poles in Moscow capitulated. Two hundred Russian cities were said to have accepted the Swedish prince as their Tsar; the candidature of Ladislas had become a political impossibility, and no other rival seemed in prospect. In January 1613 the Russian delegates met to elect a Tsar; on 7 February they agreed in principle to offer Charles Philip the throne. But now, when all seemed plain sailing, the game was thrown away. Perhaps it had never been played with much conviction: there was a general reluctance to commit the young prince to the hazards of Russian politics; there was the difficulty about religion. The resolution to send Charles Philip to Russia was delayed; when at last he arrived at Viborg on his way there it was too late. The Cossacks were irreconcilably opposed to any foreign Tsar, whether Swede or Pole; and on 21 February, under threat of force, they compelled the abandonment of Charles Philip and the election of Michael Romanov. The policy of Jakob de la Gardie had been ruined by procrastination.

Perhaps it was just as well; but it did pose the question of what policy was to take its place. One possibility was to withdraw Swedish forces from Russia altogether; but this would give Sigismund a dangerously free hand. He had not by any means abandoned his ambition to make his son Tsar; but now he pursued it, not by recruiting a party in Russia (which had become impossible), but by force of arms. For the next six years Polish forces would be engaged in exhausting hostilities on Russian soil. It was always possible that they might be successful; and to guard against that event Sweden must labour to erect the strongest possible barrier on that side. The only practical policy therefore seemed to be to extort from the new Tsar the maximum territorial concessions while he was still weak; if possible by diplomacy, if not, by war. Diplomacy was indeed tried: at a conference at Viborg in

1613 Gustavus put forward a schedule of what he wanted. His demands did not err on the side of moderation. He asked, in effect, for the cession of the provinces of Kexholm and Ingria, and, in addition, for the towns of Gdov, Pskov and Archangel; or (as a last resort) for a million *riksdaler* – which would have come in handy for paying Älvsborg's ransom. His policy had thus two aims: on the one hand to establish a broad belt of Swedish territory as a protection for Finland, with perhaps a buffer-state for Charles Philip centred on Novgorod; on the other hand, the control of some of the main trade-routes to Russia. Archangel would offset the defeat by Denmark in the Arctic; Pskov, Gdov and Novgorod would put Sweden in a position to direct the trade that passed through them to Swedish-controlled ports.

It was a policy which nicely balanced the need for security against the means for supplying that need. The only thing wrong with it, in 1614, was that it had no chance of being accepted by the Russians. The Viborg talks broke down on the exorbitance of the Swedish demands. Nothing now remained but to try to enforce at least some of them by war. Thus Sweden found herself, as Poland also did, committed to still deeper involvement in the Russian imbroglio.

For Sweden, as for Poland, it proved uphill work. The Russians could usually be beaten in a battle between approximately equal forces; but the climate was murderous, communications difficult. The country was devastated, so that armies starved, and in the wake of starvation came plague. Nevertheless, when Gustavus went over in June 1614, he found the Ingrian fortresses firmly in Swedish hands, and he was accordingly able to direct his main efforts against Gdov and Pskov. Gdov was taken in 1614; but the Swedes could make little impression on Pskov, which in 1615 and 1616 resisted all attempts to take it: at no stage of his career was Gustavus much of a hand at sieges. Yet perhaps in the end Pskov was saved as much by diplomacy as by the tenacity of its defenders. The Swedish Council was pressing Gustavus to make peace with the Tsar before Sigismund disentangled himself from his Russian adventure, and to seek the good offices of the Dutch and the English, both of whom had a strong interest in ending a war which interfered with their trade. Under their joint mediation, talks began at Diderina in 1615; and Sir John Merrick, the English mediator (whose membership of the Muscovy Company inclined him to favour Russia), negotiated with some skill to stave off a final assault upon Pskov.

The Swedish demands remained high: both Gustavus and Oxenstierna stood out for stringent terms. They did so not only in order to obtain a barrier against Poland, but also in order to cut Russia's claws while she was still disabled. The prospect of controlling the Russia trade, tempting as it was, was not an objective for which they were prepared to fight indefinitely; hence they were ready to drop their claims to Archangel and the White Sea ports. What moved them was the old fear of Russia's power, and of the threat which that power might one day present to her neighbours. The Russian, in Oxenstierna's opinion, was 'a false and at the same time a mighty neighbour; in whom, by reason of the guile and treachery which he has (as it were) drunk in with his mother's milk, no faith is to be reposed'. The Swedish negotiators fought obstinately to push back that power. And with some help from the Dutch mediators they did in fact do remarkably well. By the terms of the Peace of Stolbova (27 February 1617) Sweden renounced Charles Philip's pretensions to the Russian throne and relinquished her demand for Novgorod and Pskov; but she acquired the whole of the provinces of Kexholm and Ingria, with their strong fortresses of Kexholm, Nöteborg, Jama, Ivangorod and Koporé. These gains meant that Estonia and Finland were now firmly buttressed to the eastward; indeed, they were linked by a kind of land-bridge, for the Gulf of Finland was now entirely encircled by Swedish territory: a man might ride from Stockholm to Reval without quitting Swedish soil. The Karelian isthmus, the mouth of the Neva, the site of the future city of St Petersburg, were now all in Swedish hands. Russia was cut off from access to the Baltic, and for almost three-quarters of a century she was pushed back towards Asia. It was a result of far-reaching significance for the history of Europe. Gustavus was keenly conscious of its importance for Sweden, not merely as a satisfactory settlement of a war too long drawn out, but as a safeguard for future generations: in his triumphant speech to the Diet of Örebro in 1617 he spelt out to his hearers the strategic implications.[2] Rivers and lakes, they were told, would now provide such a barrier as the Muscovite would not find it easy to overleap; the Tsar would not be able to launch a single ship on the Baltic; vaguely defined economic opportunities would now be open for exploitation. Ingria, it was true, was now desolate from the ravages of war, but it was nevertheless a rich country needing only cultivation: 'You of the Nobility, why do you tread on each others' toes here at home, and wrangle and quarrel for a handful of wretched farms? Go you over to this land and found great estates there, as much as you list. . . . I will give you privileges, immunities and all favour.' It was the first time that a Swedish sovereign had dangled such a bait before his subjects. But it is note-worthy that the inducement was offered *after* the acquisition of Ingria, and not as a reason for acquiring it: neither this war, nor those that followed it in Sweden's Age of Greatness, were made in order to satisfy the appetites of a 'feudally-acquisitive nobility', or to 'shut the mouths of complaining peasants, and other troublesome commoners' – though some historians have thought so.[3] Some noble settlements in Ingria did in fact occur (Skytte, for one, was granted a barony there); but in this reign the new province was perhaps best known in Sweden as the probable destination of those who obstinately refused to pay their taxes, or were convicted of poaching the king's game, or of cutting down his oak trees. Yet it was a major success; and it was his first. He lost no time in making use of the advantage thus gained. The immediate consequence of the Peace of Stolbova was the renewal of the war in Livonia.

At the moment of Gustavus's accession both Poland and Sweden had been too preoccupied with other problems to have resources to spare for a direct confrontation. The war in Livonia had accordingly languished; and a series of armi-stices, extending from the beginning of 1611 to the autumn of 1616, put the quarrel temporarily into cold storage. Anything better than an armistice or a truce was out of the question, for Sigismund would never renounce his right to the Swedish throne. Nothing really was changed; the war went on, but it was fought now with the weapons of propaganda, conspiracy and plot. On these terms Sigismund had a considerable advantage. A small but formidable group of Swedish exiles pursued a relentless vendetta against the usurping dynasty in Stockholm, and remained unappeased by the milder temper of the new sovereign and the emollient efforts of Oxenstierna. Their propaganda was designed to enlist the sympathy of

Europe, but also to seduce the discontented in Sweden. It was reinforced in the latter aspect by the Jesuit seminary at Braunsberg, which offered a better education than could be had at Uppsala, and was designed by the Papacy to do for Sweden what Douai had done for Elizabethan England. In the troubled early years of the reign, when burdens were heavy and the rule of law as yet imperfectly restored, the exiles believed that conditions were propitious for sedition. The Swedish government was nervous, for Polish agents were known to be at large in the country; one of them even contrived to get himself appointed secretary to the Estate of Peasants. In 1616 it became clear that this was no longer merely a dynastic quarrel. For in that year there was founded, by the Austrian Count von Althann, a peculiar kind of crusading order, among whose objects was the recovery of Sweden for Rome. Sigismund had married a Habsburg (indeed, two); and in 1613 he concluded an alliance with the Emperor Matthias. Two years later, Matthias did his best to get Sigismund off the hook in Russia by offering his mediation, and in 1616 Sigismund reciprocated by helping the Emperor to reduce his rebellious subjects in Silesia. Poland was now recognizably the most easterly outpost of the Habsburg system; and the foundation of the Althann Order made it plain that the Protestant occupant of the Swedish throne might be threatened not only by a dynastic rival, but by the whole might of the Counter-Reformation.

The response of Gustavus to this new situation came in 1617. It took the form of both military and legislative action. The duchy of Courland had been disturbed by a quarrel between the dukes and their nobility, as a result of which Duke William had been forced to seek refuge in Sweden. In 1616 a member of the Courland nobility, Wolmar von Farensbach, took the opportunity to approach Gustavus with a tempting offer: to betray the fort of Dünamünde into Swedish hands. Dünamünde guarded the mouth of the Düna, which was a vital trade-artery for Lithuania and Livonia; its possession would put an expeditionary force within striking distance of Riga. The latest truce with Poland had just run out; Sigismund was still grappling with the Russians; the Peace of Stolbova gave Gustavus a free hand. In 1617, therefore, the invitation was accepted, and an expeditionary force sent over. Farensbach did his part, and contrived the seizure of Dünamünde: the dragging war with Poland suddenly moved from cold to hot. But the Swedish commander, Nils Stiernsköld, made no effort to exploit the initial surprise: no incursion into Courland, no attempt upon Riga. A somewhat peripheral and casual operation enabled him to take Pernau, but with that his military imagination seems to have been exhausted. By early 1618 the campaign was petering out; before the end of the year the Truce of Tolsburg, to last until November 1620, brought it to an inglorious end.

Action on the domestic front was a good deal more trenchant. At the Diet of Örebro, in February 1617, Gustavus obtained the assent of the Estates to legislation designed to provide security against Polish treason and plot. This meant legislation also against Roman Catholics. The Statute of Örebro was a penal statute of the Elizabethan type, prescribing the penalties of treason for contact with Sigismund, drastic punishments for correspondence with the exiles, outlawry for those who went to Catholic universities, and loss of civil rights for any who might lapse to Catholicism. Its object was purely political. It was not in intention a piece of religious persecution, and its operation was limited to the duration of the war against Poland. The Statute of Örebro was panic legislation, for the internal threat, though real, was not serious; the number of Catholics in Sweden was negligible. After 1617 there was nothing that could reasonably be called a plot. Not until after 1626 would Sweden be in real danger from the forces of the Counter-Reformation.

Nevertheless, the identification of Sigismund's cause with that of Roman Catholicism had an immediate and long-lasting effect upon Swedish foreign policy, which henceforward took on a more specifically confessional aspect. On the one hand, Gustavus was led to seek friends and allies among the Protestant states; on the other, the comparative indifference of most evangelical princes to Charles IX's appeals to Protestant solidarity began to give way to the idea that it might be desirable to draw Sweden into the camp of the Protestant activists in Germany.

In 1613 Gustavus had scored an important diplomatic success by concluding an alliance with the Dutch. It was not an alliance based primarily on religious considerations: it sprang rather from the United Provinces' fear of a Danish domination of the Baltic, which the Peace of Knäred seemed

41

to have brought nearer. The Dutch resented Christian IV's high-handed treatment of their shipping during the War of Kalmar; it was obviously in their interest to try to restore an equilibrium in the Baltic by bolstering up Sweden. Lübeck, and some other Hanse towns, had similar feelings. Thus the Peace of Knäred, disastrous as it was, produced its own antidote. In 1613 the Dutch had concluded with Lübeck a treaty which had a point against Denmark; now they reinforced it with a defensive alliance with Sweden.

Just as fear of Denmark had driven the United Provinces over to Sweden's side, so too had Christian IV's restless ambition won friends for Gustavus in Protestant Germany. For Christian meddled in the affairs of the Lower Saxon Circle; he intrigued to obtain secularized north-German bishoprics for his sons; he offended the Hanseatic towns by his commercial policies and his foundation of Glückstadt. As between Sweden and Poland he was indifferent: he had no wish to see Gustavus's struggle with Sigismund supported by other Protestant states; but obviously he would himself be in danger if there were a Catholic crusade against Scandinavia. In the Protestant cause as such he took little interest, unless it should happen to coincide with his own; and to the leaders of the activist party in Germany he was somewhat suspect. Prominent among those leaders were Maurice of Hesse-Cassel and Frederick V of the Palatinate; and both were connected by family ties with the Vasas. Gustavus's mother was Maurice's cousin; Charles IX's first wife was Frederick's aunt. Maurice and Frederick had been among the few German princes to champion the cause of Charles IX. It was not surprising, therefore, that as the situation in Germany gradually slid towards the catastrophe of the Thirty Years War they should have begun to speculate on the possibility of enlisting Sweden on their side. An embassy from Maurice arrived in Stockholm in 1613; another from Frederick a year later. There was some idea of inviting Sweden to join the Protestant Union. In 1615 the ties between them were drawn closer by the marriage of Gustavus's half-sister Catherine to John Casimir of Pfalz-Zweibrücken-Kleeburg, who henceforward became a kind of unofficial observer and publicity agent for Sweden in Germany.

If the great religious war which men were expecting should break out, Gustavus had no intention for the present of allowing himself to be dragged into it. From the beginning he made his position clear. If it came to a fight between the Protestant Union and the Catholic League, he would do what he could to help. But he would do it in Poland, not in Germany. His struggle with Sigismund, in his view, exempted him from further obligations. It was one aspect of that vaster struggle which was impending; and his campaigns in Livonia were to be considered as a diversion, for they would effectively prevent Sigismund's coming to the Emperor's aid. The German Protestants received this line of argument with tactfully sympathetic noises; but it did not convince them. Whether convincing or not, however, the argument supplied the basis for the policy which Gustavus was to pursue for almost a decade. When the long-awaited explosion came with the Defenestration of Prague in 1618, he gave Frederick V eight guns and a quantity of good advice; but he was not favourably impressed by the reports which reached him from Bohemia.

An opportunity for collecting first-hand impressions of the state of German Protestantism came in the summer of 1620, some months before the débâcle of the White Mountain put an end to Frederick's Bohemian adventure. It was provided by Gustavus's search for a wife. His formidable mother having prevented him from marrying for love, he had made up his mind to marry for political advantage; and for some time he had been thinking that his best choice might be Maria Eleonora of Brandenburg. The Elector, George William, was a Calvinist; but Maria Eleonora was Lutheran, and, next to Saxony, Brandenburg ranked as the most important Lutheran state in Germany. George William, however, was appalled at the prospect of a Swedish marriage, for it seemed to him that it must jeopardize his chances of realizing a long-held Hohenzollern ambition. The cadet branch of his house, which since 1525 had ruled the duchy of East Prussia, became extinct in 1618, and in the normal course of events the duchy would pass to the main line of the Hohenzollerns. But East Prussia was a Polish fief, with the king of Poland as its suzerain; and George William had no title to the duchy until his suzerain granted him investiture. In these circumstances it would be a gratuitous provocation to allow his sister to marry Gustavus; not the less so since among the suitors for her hand was Sigismund's son, Ladislas. However, there was a party at

Berlin which favoured the Swedish match; and it was with their encouragement that in 1620 Gustavus undertook that romantic incognito journey to Berlin – 'for all the world like a comedy' – which so curiously anticipated the expedition of Charles and Buckingham to Madrid in search of the Infanta.

With this difference, however: Charles was led by the nose and came back empty-handed; Gustavus, thanks to the assistance of the strong-minded Electress-Dowager, accomplished his mission successfully. Not, however, without a good deal of difficulty; and it was with the idea of applying a little blackmail that he quitted Berlin for some weeks and made a round of other Protestant courts, with the professed intention of inspecting a few matrimonial alternatives. The expedient worked; but it was useful also in other ways. His tour of Germany enabled Gustavus to make a personal assessment of the Protestant leaders and their policies; and the experience left a permanent mark on him. He returned to Berlin with a strong impression of the feebleness, cross-purposes, selfishness, and military incompetence which vitiated the efforts of the Protestant party. That impression was never eradicated; indeed, all his later experience reinforced it. From the very beginning of his relationship with those who were one day to be his clients, his attitude to them was tinged with a trace of contempt which he did not always trouble to conceal, and which they certainly found difficult to bear.

The marriage was celebrated on 25 November 1620. It was not a success, domestically or politically. Maria Eleonora was a hysterical woman who pursued her admirably faithful husband with neurotic devotion during his lifetime, and luxuriated in orgies of grief after his death. She gave him no male heir; she gave him no moral or intellectual support. She was incapable of supplying his place in his absence; and he had the sense to exclude her from the regency. Politically, the marriage paid very meagre dividends. For Sigismund, it was an unpalatable diplomatic defeat; but it did not make George William less anxious not to offend his Polish suzerain, nor could it put any backbone into that invertebrate Hohenzollern. Nevertheless, it was a landmark of a sort. The Peace of Stolbova, the *détente* with Denmark, the Truce of Tolsburg, rounded off the period during which Gustavus's actions were determined by the situation which he had inherited. The Brandenburg marriage, and the closer contacts with the

German princes, mark the transition to a new period: they are the beginnings of that complex intertwining of the problems of Poland and of Germany which was to be characteristic of the second decade of the reign. Sweden was on the threshold of its emergence upon the great stage of Europe.

. . .

NOTES

1. The *riksdaler* (the Swedish equivalent of the German *Reichsthaler*) was a money of account: the silver *daler* of four marks was the domestic unit. Until 1628 the *riksdaler* was worth about 6.5 *marks*, or roughly 1.5 *daler*: thereafter it appreciated against the *daler*, and by 1632 was worth 14 *marks*. Sums expressed in *daler* have henceforward been converted for comparison, into *riksdaler* (*rdr*) at the rate of exchange of the relevant year.
2. English translation in Roberts, *Sweden as a Great Power 1611–1697*, pp. 134–6.
3. See, for example, Axel Strindberg, *Bondenöd och Stormakts-dröm.* (Stockholm 1937).

Chapter 4

POLAND AND THE PROTESTANT CAUSE (1620–28)

Gustavus Adolphus's place in the history of Europe rests essentially upon the effects of his intervention in the Thirty Years War: the rise of Sweden to the position of a great power was the direct result of that intervention. Yet in 1618, or 1620, Sweden's involvement in the tragedy of Germany was neither obvious nor even likely. The eviction of Frederick V from Bohemia, and subsequently from his hereditary electorate, and the collapse of Protestant resistance which followed, were not events with which Sweden was directly concerned. England, the Netherlands, the German Lutheran states, or even Christian IV's Denmark, might all seem more appropriately cast for the part of Protestant Paladin, for the interests of all were touched more nearly. To Sweden the danger from Poland was still the first consideration.

The old controversy about whether Gustavus was animated by religious or political motives has long since ceased to trouble historians. In the world of the early seventh century the two could scarcely be dissociated. Politics were to a large degree influenced by religion; the cause of religion was sustained by political weapons. Gustavus Adolphus was neither a single-minded Protestant Hero, nor a ruthless *Realpolitiker*: he was both. His Protestantism was based on education and founded in conviction; his piety was genuine; his sense of confessional solidarity was strong. Of course he was troubled by the threats to the religious and political independence of his fellow Protestants in Germany. But he was also concerned, as king of Sweden, to obtain the maximum advantage for his country. The outbreak of the Thirty Years War confronted him with the necessity of making judgments which should balance the interests of Protestantism against the interests of Sweden. He had to decide upon his priorities. In 1621 it was clear to him that the first priority must be Poland. By 1628 he had revised his opinion: under the pressure of events the first priority had become Germany.

It was not a matter of a simple choice between alternatives. The problem was a triangular problem; and the third element in it was Denmark. Denmark, like Sweden, was a Lutheran monarchy, and in Christian IV the German Protestants now saw a possible saviour. As a prince of the Lower Saxon Circle, as an enterprising collector of secularized bishoprics, he was as much threatened as they were by the resurgence of Imperial power and the flowing of the Catholic tide. If Gustavus could have been sure of Christian's goodwill, he might well have elected to devote all his attention to Poland and leave to Denmark the task of organizing German resistance. But he could not be sure, either now or later. In these circumstances, the prospect of the formation of a Protestant alliance under Danish leadership, or the establishment of something like a Danish protectorate of north Germany, was viewed in Stockholm from a political rather than a confessional angle. Sweden could not welcome any development which tended to enhance the power and influence of her Scandinavian neighbour. In Germany, as in the Baltic, the two countries were rivals. Only imminent and unmistakable danger would avail to force them to stifle their mutual distrust and unite for self-defence.

The interaction of the Polish, German and Danish problems appeared very clearly in the years 1620 and 1621. Before the battle of the White Hill Gustavus had not been unduly concerned about events in Bohemia. He had responded to Palatine appeals for aid merely by offering to renew the war in Livonia. He hoped that the German Protestant princes might form a defensive league of their own: the Protestant Union was plainly on its last legs (it expired in May 1621), and something had to be found to replace it. He therefore indicated that if such a league could be formed he would be willing to act *as its Director*. The proposal has its interest as being the first manifestation of a policy which would come to fruition in the last few months of his life. But whatever chances of acceptance it may have had were disposed of by the action of Christian IV. Christian was not prepared to see Gustavus as the self-constituted patron of German Protestantism, for he aspired to that position himself. His immediate reaction was to outbid him. In 1621 a congress of states of the Lower Saxon Circle met at Segeberg under Danish auspices; and at that congress Christian succeeded in creating a league of his own. It was designed on broader lines than Gustavus's modest proposals, for it was to include England and the Netherlands. In the event it remained no more than an ineffectual political fantasy, but from Christian's point of view this did not matter. What mattered was that his initiative gained him the alliance of James I and the United Provinces; that his authority in the Lower Saxon Circle was strengthened by the acquisition of the bishoprics of Bremen and Verden for his son Frederick; and that Sweden had been pushed firmly into the background. Gustavus was thus outmanoeuvred. He accepted the situation, and drew the appropriate conclusions. He turned his back upon Germany, not without prophetic warnings to the Protestant princes that sooner or later they would have to organize to defend themselves, and proceeded to devote his attention to Poland.

In 1618, at the time of the Truce of Tolsburg, Gustavus had been quite ready to keep the Polish war in abeyance. In return for a ten-years' truce he was prepared to allow Sigismund to go on calling himself King of Sweden, if only he would promise to stop his plots and propaganda. He was even willing to hand back Pernau (at that time his only foothold in Livonia) as the price of a real peace. But Sigismund had no intention of making a bargain of this sort. In 1620, however, the situation underwent an important change. Poland got herself involved in a war with the Turks, and in October the Polish armies sustained the appalling disaster of Cecora. The opportunity was obvious, and Gustavus did not hesitate to seize it. In July 1621 he landed with an army at the mouth of the Düna; two months later he had captured Riga.

Even the friends of Sweden were slightly shocked at this stabbing of Christendom in the back, but both friends and enemies recognized the importance of what had happened. The capture of Riga was something which concerned the whole of Europe; for Riga was one of the great cities of the Baltic, the outport for the rich corn-lands of Lithuania and

Livonia. By its acquisition Swedish ambitions to grow rich on the trade to Russia for the first time gained some plausibility. It was a success which marked a perceptible shift in the balance of forces within the Baltic: 'God forbid', Christian IV had said, 'that he should get it into his power.' It marked, too, a significant extension of Sweden's overseas dominions, a step forward towards a Swedish empire. For the terms of capitulation seemed to indicate that Riga was intended to be a permanent Swedish possession: her burghers were to send representatives to the Swedish Diet, her litigants were to appeal to the Supreme Court in Stockholm. As it turned out, Riga was to remain a part of the Swedish realm for exactly a century.

The essential object in taking Riga was to deny Sigismund a port from which he might launch a legitimist invasion, to constrain him to be reasonable by inflicting economic damage upon his subjects, and to lay hold of an asset which would be a valuable bargaining-counter when peace negotiations should begin. A firm peace was what Gustavus wanted: when Riga passed into his hands he expressly guaranteed to the burghers the right to return to the allegiance of the king of Poland if a peace should be concluded within three years. In 1622, in the course of negotiations for a truce, he made it plain that he was ready to retrocede Riga and all his conquests in Livonia in return for a peace, or perhaps for a truce of sixty years. A year later, in 1623, he was still prepared for the retrocession of Riga if he could get a settlement with Sigismund that would give him security. Thus for strictly political reasons he would have handed back what was to become the greatest city in the Swedish empire, and would have renounced all the obvious fiscal and commercial advantages which its possession would bring him. In the face of these facts it is difficult to maintain, as many Swedish historians in recent years have been inclined to do, that the motive-force behind Swedish foreign policy was a consistently pursued determination to obtain control of the trade with Russia. If Livonia eventually became a Swedish province it was not because Gustavus was animated by a spirit of political or economic imperialism. In October 1622 he accepted a truce which left Riga and Pernau in his possession; and thereafter the Livonian front relapsed into a state of suspended animation for more than two years.

In 1623 Sweden found herself once more moving to a crisis in her relations with Denmark. The immediate cause of tension arose from two provisions of the Peace of Knäred in 1613. One of them renewed the exemption of Swedish ships and goods from the Sound Tolls; the other provided for reciprocal free trade between the two countries. The Danes complained that each had latterly been interpreted by the Swedes in a manner inconsistent with the spirit of the treaty and prejudicial to Denmark's interests. Sweden was claiming exemption for ships from Riga and Pernau, and she had imposed a sales tax on certain commodities which the Swedes were exporting to Denmark.

In August 1622 Christian IV had sent an ultimatum demanding the removal of the sales tax within six months; in January 1623 he denounced the free-trade clause of the Peace of Knäred. The Swedish government played for time, but by November it felt sufficiently reassured about the situation in Poland to take a stiffer line. Both Gustavus and Oxenstierna toyed with the idea of using the lull in Livonia to launch a quick preventive war against Denmark, but in the end they decided to make a final effort to settle the dispute by negotiation. In May 1624 the parties met at Sjöaryd. There followed a month of tough negotiation and acute tension; but at last, on 29 June 1624, they reached agreement. Christian IV, for all his bluster, was short of men and money; his navy was only partly manned; and he accepted the terms on which Oxenstierna had insisted all along.

The agreement at Sjöaryd in June 1624 marks a turning-point in the relations between the two Scandinavian countries. On Christian's side it was tantamount to a capitulation: the sales tax was retained, the principle of free trade reaffirmed, and exemption from the Sound Tolls was to apply to any Swedish-owned ships and cargoes, irrespective of their port of origin. The result reflected the success of Gustavus's military reforms, and the revival of Swedish naval power.[1] It meant that the verdict of 1613 was set aside. Christian's challenge had been squarely met; and he had shrunk from a confrontation. The blow to his pride was severe. Henceforward he could no longer pretend to the sole *dominium maris Balthici*, but must be content to share it with his neighbour. The events of 1624 involved the final liquidation of his hope of reviving the Scandinavian Union. They registered the plain fact that in military and naval strength Sweden was now at least his equal; and they foreshadowed the day when Denmark's traditional primacy in the Baltic would slip from her grasp into Swedish hands.

The defeat of Denmark at Sjöaryd also had implications for Germany. In 1621 Christian IV had succeeded in his object of presenting himself as a patron of distressed Protestants more credible (and more accessible) than Gustavus. After 1624 the choice between them looked more open; certainly the need for some external support for the evangelical cause had become more urgent. The year 1622 had seen the collapse of Palatine resistance at Wimpffen and Höchst; Heidelberg fell in September, Mannheim in October, and Tilly's crowning victory at Stadtlohn followed in July 1623. Four months later the Emperor transferred Frederick's electorate to Maximilian of Bavaria as a reward for services rendered. Only prompt intervention, it seemed, could prevent the establishment of Imperial control, and the re-establishment of Roman Catholicism, in the three Circles of north Germany.

These disasters posed a particularly difficult problem for Sweden. To stand by and allow the Protestant princes to be overwhelmed was repugnant on grounds of religion and dangerous on grounds of policy. Yet the prospect of averting this calamity by the establishment of a virtual Danish protectorate in north Germany was only a little less objectionable. It seemed out of the question for Sweden to send aid as long as no peace was to be had from Sigismund. Gustavus continued to believe that the best solution would be for the Protestant princes to save themselves by their own efforts, but he had few illusions about the chance of that happening. One way out of the dilemma occurred to him: to transfer the seat of war from Düna to the Vistula. By fighting Sigismund in Prussia rather than in Livonia he might provide an effective diversion. The German Protestant princes clamoured for direct intervention, oblivious of the fact that peace in Poland was not to be had. They disliked the prospect of a Swedish attack upon Prussia: already they were inclined to suspect Gustavus of a deliberate plan to bring all the ports of the Baltic under Swedish control, and to turn the Sea into a Swedish lake. The suspicion provoked Gustavus's indignation: 'If I draw a pail of water from the Baltic', he wrote, 'am I supposed to be desirous of drinking up the whole sea?'

The day would come when force of circumstances would drive him to actions which lent some colour to the charge; but it had not arrived in 1623.

By 1624 the situation in Germany had become so grave that even sovereigns as pacific as James I and George William of Brandenburg were moved to take action. In that year both made approaches to Gustavus to persuade him to join in the formation of a general league of Protestant states and to collaborate in a common military effort against the Imperialists. To the English, Gustavus made it clear that he would not join the proposed league unless the Dutch were members of it; he insisted that there must be an Anglo-Dutch fleet of at least forty-eight sail in the Baltic, to protect his coasts and his communications; and the allies must see to it that a port of disembarkation in Prussia was put firmly in his hands. From Brandenburg he demanded even solider security, since George William's plan would involve him in operations in western Germany: the allies must therefore provide an army of 32,000 men, and pay them in advance; they must place in his hands two first-class harbours, one in the North Sea and one in the Baltic; the neutrality of Danzig must be guaranteed; Bethlen Gabor, the Prince of Transylvania (an old enemy of the Habsburgs) must be invited to join the alliance; and, most important, Gustavus must have the *Direktorium* – the supreme military and political control – of the allied forces.

These were conditions with which neither England nor Brandenburg was in a position to comply. They could not find the money or the men; they could not satisfy the political demands; they could not give naval protection. Above all, they could not accept Gustavus's stipulation about the *Direktorium* without grievously offending Christian IV. Gustavus had for a moment forced them to face reality; and they had not relished the confrontation. They therefore fell back upon the only possible alternative: an approach to Christian IV.

They met with an encouraging reception. After the humiliation of Sjöaryd Christian was eager to seize the chance to reassert himself. He was by nature rash and sanguine; and he was ready to close his eyes to the inconstancy of Brandenburg policies, the uncertainty of the English parliament's granting supplies, and the formidable nature of the military opposition he would have to encounter in Germany. In February 1625 he concluded an agreement with James I. He promised to lead an army into Germany, on condition that England provide 7,000 men to his 5,000; and he was prepared to settle for an annual subsidy of £180,000 as against the £400,000 which would have been required by Gustavus. Both parties were pleased: James I was getting a campaign in Germany at cut-price rates; Christian had trumped Gustavus's ace.

It was agreed that a congress should meet at The Hague in November 1625 for the purpose of constituting the proposed Protestant league. Only then did Christian begin to appreciate the true nature of the prospect before him. In September England had concluded with the Dutch the Treaty of Southampton, and that treaty bound the allies to make war, not in Germany, but against Spain. The fiasco of Buckingham's expedition to Cadiz had ended the hope of replenishing England's finances with the treasure of the Indies; parliament was no longer interested in providing money for the Palatine cause, and Charles I was in no condition to furnish it without parliamentary grant. Only a miserable rump of Protestant powers put in an appearance at the Hague Congress: Sweden and Bethlen Gabor held aloof; John George of Saxony was sharply disapproving; George William of Brandenburg, terrified by the advance of the Imperialist armies, hastily abandoned the movement he had helped to initiate. The great Protestant league proved still-born; and Christian was left to plunge to disaster with no better support than a pocketful of empty promises. Gustavus might well congratulate himself upon having evaded the pitfall into which Christian had stumbled.

For the moment, however, Germany appeared to be taken care of, and no immediate crisis seemed to threaten from that side. Christian IV might be expected to hold up the Imperialist armies for a campaign or two. Gustavus was free to turn once more to Poland, where the latest truce had just expired. The breathing-space might well be the last chance of bringing the Polish war to a conclusion, undistracted by anxiety for Germany. He must therefore force Sigismund to make a peace or a long truce while the armies of the Emperor were engaged with the king of Denmark.

The campaign of 1625 was conducted more effectively than those which had preceded it. By the time the army went into quarters, the whole quadrilateral of Livonia north of the Düna and west of the Ewst had been overrun by the Swedish forces; and though the troops suffered more than ordinarily from starvation and disease during the winter months, Gustavus was able, by a forced march of thirty-five miles in thirty-six hours, to crush a Polish army at Wallhof (January 1626). It was not a major victory in terms of numbers engaged, but it was one of the really significant battles of the Thirty Years War. For it gave Sweden possession of the whole of Livonia; and it made possible a step which Gustavus had already been contemplating: the transfer of the seat of war to Prussia.

The decision to invade Prussia was taken, after consultation between the king and his chancellor, some time in January 1626. The ideas behind the move are clear enough. The Vistula was the vital artery of Poland's economy: once block it, and the Polish magnate class would face a crisis, and might be expected to compel their king to make peace. If this attempt to strangle Poland should not prove successful, there were still other advantages to be expected – to the German Protestants, for instance. A campaign in Prussia would have a good chance of distracting the attention of the Imperialist commanders: the pressure on Germany might be eased by luring them on to Polish soil. Polish Prussia, after all, was a good country to fight in: it was rich, undevastated, and well able to support contending armies without their being dependent upon assistance from home – a consideration which from Sweden's point of view was becoming increasingly important. Thus the move to Prussia was directly related to German affairs: it was the first step towards Swedish intervention in the Thirty Years War.

Though the Swedish invasion had been expected for some months, no adequate forces had been assembled to meet it. Gustavus was able to advance swiftly round the southern shore of the Frisches Haff towards the Vistula, taking Braunsberg and Elbing on his way. Elbing became the administrative centre of his Prussian conquest, the headquarters of Oxenstierna and the field-chancery: it was perhaps ominous that the terms of its capitulation bound the burghers to take an oath of loyalty to Gustavus Adolphus *and his heirs*. It seemed that Elbing might be destined to follow Reval and Riga into permanent incorporation in the Swedish dominions. Within a very short time of landing, Gustavus and his army were outside the walls of Danzig. Upon the attitude of Danzig his hopes of bringing the Polish war to a speedy end depended. Those hopes were now destroyed by Gustavus himself. A little more patience in negotiation, a less hectoring style of diplomacy, and he might well have secured Danzig's neutrality, for the burghers were as anxious to avoid a breach as he was. But at the crucial moment he lost patience and issued a rasping ultimatum which the city could not accept. Instead of becoming neutral, Danzig became an open enemy; and this was fatal to Sweden's chances of a quick success in Prussia. In later years Oxenstierna was wont to say that of all Gustavus's enemies Danzig had done him the most damage.

Polish resistance now began to organize itself, and proved tougher than had been expected. The run of fighting was indeed in Sweden's favour: two victories at Mewe in 1626; two at Dirschau in 1627 (Gustavus was seriously wounded in the second of them); but nothing like a Polish collapse, either military or economic. If the Vistula was blocked, Polish corn contrived to filter out by other export routes – by Stettin, Kolberg, Königsberg, or the Courland ports. By the end of 1627 Gustavus's calculations had been thrown out of reckoning, and the narrow margin of safety which his political timetable vouchsafed had entirely vanished. Poland was far from finished; and Christian IV had failed to keep his end up in Germany. The year 1626 saw the appearance on the scene of the new Imperialist army which Wallenstein had raised for Ferdinand II. In conjunction with the forces of the Catholic League it proved too strong for Christian, who was no match as a commander for Tilly or Wallenstein. In May, Christian's freebooting coadjutor, Mansfeld, was beaten at Dessau Bridge, and with the remnant of his forces took refuge with Bethlen Gabor; in August, Christian himself suffered catastrophic defeat at Lutter-am-Baremberge. North Germany lay open to Imperialist conquest. And perhaps not north Germany only.

In 1626 the Spanish minister Olivares was busy trying to construct a league of powers friendly to Habsburg, which should consolidate the Emperor's authority in Germany and liberate Spanish forces for the war against the Dutch. Parallel with this scheme another project was developing, designed to hit the Dutch in their most sensitive spot by action against their trade: to establish a Habsburg commercial association, operating from North Sea and Baltic ports, which should engross all that eastern trade which provided the Dutch with the sinews of war. It was a plan which had grave implications for both the Scandinavian countries. It implied the revival of long-dormant Habsburg ambitions to become a Baltic power; it envisaged the occupation of north German ports by Imperialist forces, and the creation of a Habsburg navy to dominate the sea. This was something that neither Sweden nor Denmark could suffer. However they might dispute among themselves about *dominium maris Balthici*, they were at least agreed that no other contender for *dominium* could be tolerated, and above all that no other power must be allowed to keep a war-fleet in Baltic waters.

This new danger is reflected in the attitude adopted by Swedish diplomats in the negotiations for a truce with Poland which provided one of Oxenstierna's main occupations during the period when hostilities were suspended for the winter. In the discussions at the end of 1626 there appears a marked change in Swedish policy. Whereas in 1623 Gustavus had been ready to hand back all his conquests in Livonia in exchange for a real peace, by the beginning of 1627 he hardly seems to have desired peace with Poland at all. The situation in north Germany had become so critical that he felt that he dared not risk abandoning his foothold in Prussia, nor even make concessions in Livonia. Prussia was too conveniently adjacent to Germany to be lightly surrendered. If a German campaign should prove unavoidable, the customs dues levied at Prussian and Livonian ports would probably be indispensable when it came to paying for it.

By the time the next round of negotiations began at the end of 1627, these arguments had been overridden by others of greater cogency. The terms which Oxenstierna now put forward were startlingly different from those he had offered a year before. He was now ready to agree that in return for the recognition of Sweden's right to Estonia, and a truce of thirty years, all the recent conquests in Livonia and Prussia should be returned. This time it was the turn of the Poles to be intransigent. The reason for this intransigence was the same as for Oxenstierna's suspiciously sudden moderation. It lay in the swift transformation of the military situation in Germany.

By the end of 1627 Tilly and Wallenstein had cleared the Danish armies out of the Lower Saxon Circle, and had swept onwards through Holstein and Schleswig until they had reached the furthest limits of Jutland. The whole of mainland Denmark was lost; Christian IV retreated to the dubious safety of his islands, and the total collapse of Danish resistance appeared imminent. At the same time, the Imperialist troops had advanced to the Baltic upon a broad front. Mecklenburg and Pomerania were full of Wallenstein's soldiery; and his lieutenant, Hans George von Arnim, was in occupation of the island of Rügen. One by one the north German ports passed into the Emperor's hands: only Stettin, Stralsund, Rostock and Lübeck preserved a precarious independence. Already the Emperor was beginning to talk of taking permanent possession of Schleswig and Holstein. In February the tremulous waverings of the dukes of Mecklenburg brought upon them an Imperial sentence of deposition, and Wallenstein himself was installed as duke in their place. In April Ferdinand conferred upon him the title of General of the Oceanic and Baltic Seas. It was a title which sufficiently indicated a political programme. The plans for making the Habsburgs a Baltic power had suddenly acquired a menacing immediacy: in Wismar Wallenstein was already laying the foundations of a Habsburg navy. Sigismund had been making similar exertions in Danzig; and by November 1627 the new Polish fleet was sufficiently formidable to inflict a sharp defeat upon the Swedish blockading squadron off Oliva. There were plans afoot for a junction of the Polish and Imperial navies, which became a reality in 1629, when Sigismund sent nine ships to join Wallenstein's squadron in Wismar. There were even plans for naval reinforcements from Spain, and Wallenstein was considering the digging of a Kiel canal so that they might reach the Baltic without running the hazard of the Sound. Meanwhile, he aimed at making a clean sweep of the Baltic ports: 'There are twenty-eight ports in Pomerania', he wrote, 'and we must put garrisons in them all.'

These developments constituted a direct and immediate threat to Scandinavia. If Wallenstein were allowed to remain undisputed master of the Baltic shore, if his navy were permitted to gather strength, there was an end to the security of the Danish islands; for it was not to be supposed that Christian would be capable of effective resistance if the Imperialist forces should once be ferried across the Belts. The Habsburgs would then be in a position to close the Sound;

the Danish fleet would fall into Wallenstein's hands; the trade of the Dutch would sustain so severe a blow that Spain might once again make herself mistress of the Netherlands; and Sweden would be wide open to attack either from Elsinore or from Skåne. No wonder that Oxenstierna abated his demands on Poland, or that Sigismund brushed aside his offers of a truce; no wonder that in the autumn of 1627 Gustavus was making spontaneous offers of aid to Wismar and Rostock; no wonder if, in face of the threat to Sweden itself, he felt forced, almost at any price, to cut his losses in Poland. Sweden's safety, and with it the salvation of the Protestant cause, seemed now to hang upon the continued ability of Christian IV to resist.

Already by the close of 1627 Gustavus was making hasty emergency arrangements to rush assistance to Denmark. The two old enemies were driven to accept the logic of the situation. On 4 January 1628 they entered into a defensive alliance for three years: Sweden promised naval assistance; Denmark agreed to stop ship sailing to Danzig through the Sound. For Christian it was a bitter humiliation thus to be forced to accept a helping hand from his neighbour; and only necessity induced Gustavus to extend it. Each monarch entertained a reluctant personal respect for the other, but at no time was there any trust between them. The War of Kalmar was not forgotten; the national hatreds were still very much alive. The struggle between them for primacy in the Baltic remained unresolved. But for the moment that struggle was suspended in order to oppose a combined resistance to the intruder; and for a brief space they would collaborate – as the Hague allies had always hoped they might – on a basis of common interest and common fear.

·   ·   ·

NOTE

1. See Chapter 7.

Chapter 5

THE GREAT DECISION
(1628–30)

The years from 1628 to 1630 form one of the turning-points in the history of Sweden. Before 1628 it was still conceivable that she might remain a purely Scandinavian power, preoccupied with her traditional policies to east and west, pursuing against Denmark the old rivalry for supremacy inside the Baltic, trying as best might be possible to liquidate the troublesome heritage of dynastic war with Poland. After 1630 she was directly involved in the ever-widening complications of German politics, and had become a chief actor in the vast European drama of the Thirty Years War. The great-power status and obligations thus incurred, and the territorial acquisitions which resulted from the intervention in Germany, would thereafter drag her with fatal logic into policies and enterprises which were alien to Swedish traditions, but which were imposed upon her by the need for security and the inadequacy of her own resources to meet that need.

Gustavus Adolphus, though he does not seem ever to have willed these developments, was under no illusions as to the crucial nature of the decisions which he was now to take. He saw clearly that an alliance with Denmark might – and probably would – lead to a war with the Emperor and the League: already in November 1627 he had written to Oxenstierna that such a war was scarcely to be avoided, 'because of the great interest we have in preserving the state of Denmark'. On 13 November he opened the second meeting of the Diet to be held in this critical year with a speech in which the international situation was painted in sombre colours. The Estates were plainly warned of the danger of invasion: 'As one wave follows another, so the popish league comes closer and closer to us. They have violently subjugated a great part of Denmark, whence we must apprehend that they may press on into our borders, if they be not powerfully resisted in good time.' Certainly there was little confidence in Denmark's ability to resist them: by the spring of 1628 Oxenstierna was writing that when he contemplated the situation in Denmark it made his hair stand on end. To meet this threat Gustavus asked the Estates to appoint a Secret Committee to consider foreign policy, it being undesirable that matters of such delicacy should be debated in public. With this request the Estates complied; the Secret Committee was duly constituted; and so began a feature of the Swedish constitution which was to endure for a century and a half. To them, on 12 January 1628, the king expounded his view of the situation, and asked for their opinion. Should they wait for an Imperialist attack, or should they forestall it? Should they go to Denmark's assistance? And lastly, was there any need for further consultation with the Diet, in view of the fact that 'an open war between the Emperor and this country seems imminent'? The Committee's reply was decisive: neutrality in Germany was a delusion, and the Emperor had already given ample cause for war; Denmark must be rescued; no further consultation with the full Diet was necessary.

The Secret Committee's resolution of 12 January 1628 committed the nation to support an invasion of Germany whenever Gustavus should deem it necessary to launch it. But it was a resolution only in principle, a general absolution-in-advance to cover the king against recriminations if the event should turn out ill; and it would be followed in the next two years by others designed to provide further reassurance. Gustavus felt the need of it: he was painfully aware of the burden of responsibility that lay upon him. More than once in those two years it seemed just possible that war might be avoided. Nevertheless, the resolution of 12 January 1628 amounted to a conscious shift in Swedish foreign policy: henceforward, though Gustavus's attitude to Poland might continue to waver between a desire for peace and a desire for a truce, though Polish campaigns might be waged offensively or defensively, Poland had become a secondary consideration, a problem increasingly subordinate to the main centre of interest in Mecklenburg and Pomerania.

*

In the spring of 1628 Swedish anxieties about the state of affairs on the southern shore of the Baltic were powerfully reinforced by the obvious determination of Wallenstein to get control of Stralsund. Wismar, he had found, was not the ideal naval base: Stralsund would be better. Of this the Swedes were well aware: Gustavus later observed that if the Imperialists had succeeded in getting Stralsund into their hands, Sweden would have been forced to devote massive sums to the building of fortifications and the strengthening of her navy. In February 1628 Wallenstein's general, Arnim, seized the island of Dänholm, which commanded Stralsund's harbour, in April his forces began a regular siege of the town. Stralsund had old trading connections with Sweden, and as early as 1625 Gustavus had offered assistance if the burghers should need it. But he was aware that Stralsund hoped that the Hanse would provide sufficient aid to make foreign intervention unnecessary. In May 1628, though the town was now in obvious danger, he sailed away for another campaign in Prussia, taking care to leave behind him a strong army to man the Swedish defences and come to Christian's aid, if that should prove necessary. But he had no sooner set foot in Prussia than he was confronted with the news that matters in Stralsund had suddenly come to a crisis. The Hanse had given no help, and now the defence of Stralsund was on the point of collapse. Gustavus at once promised assistance; but in the event it was not he but Christian IV that saved the town from capture. Between 25 and 28 May a contingent of Danish troops was rushed to Stralsund, in the nick of time; a further detachment in the first week of July settled the issue. The advance guard of Gustavus's somewhat meagre force did not arrive till 20 June, the main body not until 17 July, by which time the danger was really over and Wallenstein was sullenly resigning himself to the raising of the siege.

Stralsund was saved; but the manner of its salvation raised delicate problems between Gustavus and his ally. Swedish and Danish troops lay cheek by jowl within its walls: some agreement would be necessary about where effective military authority should lie. Gustavus had no *a priori* views on the point: in August he wrote to Oxenstierna that if Stralsund preferred a Danish garrison to a Swedish he would be prepared to withdraw his troops, provided he could be sure that the town was really secure against another attack. As it turned out, Stralsund preferred a Swedish garrison, and in September Oxenstierna concluded with Christian IV an agreement for the gradual withdrawal of the Danish forces. But now that the Swedes had assumed full responsibility it was natural that they should insist on military control; and they compelled the burghers to agree that Stralsund's own militia should take an oath of fidelity to the Swedish commander, and to promise not to make peace without Sweden's consent. Little by little, the number of Swedish troops in the town was augmented; and insensibly the Swedish commander assumed something like the position of a Swedish governor. Whatever the formal nature of the relationship, within a year Stralsund had become in effect subject to the king of Sweden. Gustavus could not afford to risk its falling to a second Imperialist assault, and more and more he began to think of Stralsund as an eligible base for operations. By September 1629 he had come to the conclusion that the safety of Sweden demanded the permanent incorporation of Stralsund into the Swedish realm. By May 1630, on the eve of his departure for Germany, he stated categorically that the retention of Stralsund was a necessary element in that *assecuratio* (security) which was to be the real object of the German war.[1] By 1629, in effect, the Swedish empire had established its first lodgment in Germany.

All this was not seen as necessarily involving a breach with the Emperor: Sweden was still formally neutral. If Gustavus would be content to stand vigilantly on the defensive behind Stralsund's bastions, a clash with the Emperor might be avoided for some time to come. Oxenstierna was in favour of this line of action. His advice was to play for time in Pomerania and concentrate on finishing off the war with Poland. Gustavus was of a different opinion. In his view, the danger to Sweden could be met only by an offensive in the German coastlands, which should disrupt the plans for an Imperialist-Polish navy. 'What good would it be', he wrote, 'to hold Stralsund and lose command of the sea?... We are nowhere more vulnerable than in Sweden.' Oxenstierna was later to concede that on this issue the king had been right: in 1636 he told the Council that if Gustavus had not gone to Germany:

the Emperor at this day would have had a great fleet at sea. . . . and with 2,000 foot he could have taken Copenhagen and made the King himself prisoner. And if he had got hold of Stralsund, he would have had the whole coast in his grasp, and we had never been able to sit secure here at home.

But in 1628 and 1629 he had thought otherwise.

The whole question was once more thrashed out at a series of Council meetings between 15 December 1628 and 8 January 1629, with the now predictable result that they agreed that there was little hope of keeping the peace with the Emperor; that if there was to be war, it was better to fight it abroad than at home; and that the decision upon whether it should be waged offensively or defensively be left to the king. All of which implied that they no longer believed that Protestantism could be saved, nor the security of Sweden ensured, by campaigns in Poland. There was, indeed, still one more campaign there to be fought; but Poland was no longer seen as the major theatre of operations.

This appreciation of the situation, however logical it might appear, reckoned without Christian IV. The ink was scarcely dry upon his alliance with Sweden before he began to consider whether he could not escape from its obligations by patching up a peace with the Emperor. Luckily for him, his adversaries were very ready to parley. For Wallenstein, the idea of conquering the Danish islands and seizing the Sound had now lost its fascination: his mind was turning to Italy, where Ferdinand was involving himself in the War of the Mantuan Succession; and perhaps, too, to the possibility of organizing a crusade against the Turks. As to the Catholic League, it was sufficient for them to have driven the Danes from German soil: as German princes, jealous of German liberties, they felt no interest in Habsburg designs on the Baltic and the Sound. In Vienna statesmen were apprehensive of a Swedish descent upon Germany, and were not averse to driving a wedge between Gustavus and his ally. Wallenstein accordingly determined to scotch any plans for a Swedish invasion before they had time to mature: first, by making a peace with Denmark which should isolate Sweden; secondly, by sending Sigismund sufficient military assistance to ensure that Gustavus should have his hands full in Poland.

On 6 January 1629, peace negotiations between Christian and his enemies were opened in Lübeck, and it was ominous that Sweden was not invited to send representatives to the congress. Though Gustavus was thus left out in the cold, he took the opportunity to put down on paper what he considered to be the minimum terms which Sweden could accept, if hostilities with the Emperor were to be avoided. He demanded the total evacuation of Imperial troops from north Germany, the demolition of all new fortifications on the Baltic coast, the removal of the Imperial navy from the ports, and the restitution to Denmark of the territory she had lost; in return for this he was willing to evacuate Stralsund. There was not one word about the Protestant cause, or the liberation of south Germany, or the restoration of Frederick V to the Palatinate – still less to Bohemia. It was, from Sweden's point of view, a strictly practical programme. But in this year 1629 – the year in which Imperial power reached its apogee, the year when in the plenitude of his prerogative Ferdinand II issued the Edict of Restitution – it was a programme which was completely unrealizable. Only complete victory could secure it.

Meanwhile, Christian IV was finding peace a somewhat elusive blessing. Within a few weeks the congress at Lübeck had reached a deadlock. It was with the idea of breaking this deadlock that, in February 1629, Christian arranged a famous meeting with Gustavus on the frontier at Ulvsbäck. On the personal side it was anything but a success, and Gustavus had some difficulty in keeping his temper; but politically it produced exactly the effect that Christian had designed. Confronted with this apparent evidence of Scandinavian solidarity, the Imperial negotiators at Lübeck changed their tune, not without pressure from Wallenstein behind the scenes. Their demands were drastically abated, and on 27th May agreement at Lübeck gave peace to Denmark on terms of surprising lenity. Christian was indeed forced to renounce all his territorial ambitions in the Lower Saxon Circle, and to pledge himself to keep his nose out of German affairs for the future; but in return he recovered, without indemnity, all those of his lands which were occupied by the Emperor's armies. Urban VIII denounced it as a scandalous peace; the leaders of Protestant Europe heard the news of it with dismay. Gustavus however, took it philosophically: he had seen it coming. From his point of view, it was not without its advantages: by leaving his ally in the lurch, Christian had forfeited all credibility as a champion of Protestantism or a protector of the German princes, and he had also forfeited all claim to Swedish consideration. If the peace of Lübeck left Gustavus alone, it also left him with his hands free.

However, Wallenstein had undeniably been successful in accomplishing the first half of his programme; and already he had had encouraging progress with the second. The Prussian campaign of 1628 had not been among Gustavus's more fortunate enterprises: it had ended in a retreat which only just escaped being a disaster. But in January 1629, while he was at home discussing foreign politics with his Council, his commander on the spot won at Gorzno what was perhaps the biggest victory of this war. The military consequences were insignificant; but the political repercussions were considerable. Swedish prestige underwent a welcome revival; Polish self-confidence began to droop. This suited Wallenstein very well, for the Poles, who had no love of the Germans and looked suspiciously on Sigismund's *penchant* for the Habsburgs, had hitherto showed no willingness to accept a large auxiliary force of Imperialists. After Gorzno, they thought better of it; and in 1629 Wallenstein was able to persuade them to admit an army of 6,000 men under Arnim. It was just as well for Gustavus that the co-operation between Polish and Imperial commanders was anything but cordial, for in 1629 he found himself fighting against numerical odds, and he had to struggle hard to keep a hold on the Vistula delta and the coastal areas around the Frisches Haff. At Honigfelde he suffered a sharp defeat and was lucky to escape with his life; but on the whole this was a defensive campaign, and as such was reasonably successful. The Poles battered away at the Swedish strongpoints in vain. The Swedes' grip on their conquests remained unshaken; Arnim returned to Brandenburg, disgusted with his Polish allies. By the end of the summer the combatants had reached the state of military stalemate which had so often before produced a truce.

A real peace was out of the question, since Sigismund would not renounce his claims to the Swedish throne. In any case, a long truce was what Gustavus now preferred, for the tolls which he had begun to levy at the Prussian ports had become indispensable for the financing of the forthcoming campaign in Germany – too much so to be relinquished, even for a peace. The auspices for negotiation of a truce were therefore not unpropitious. At this interesting conjuncture

65

there arrived in Prussia Richelieu's roving envoy, Hercule de Charnacé. Charnacé was commissioned to do his best to disentangle Gustavus from his Polish commitment. For Richelieu, already allied with the Dutch and involved in a war with the Habsburgs in Italy, was now casting about for means to make trouble for them in Germany. He was actively cultivating Maximilian of Bavaria, in the hope of separating him from the Emperor; he had done his best to stiffen Christian's resistance; and in Gustavus he imagined he might find a tractable instrument for French policy. It was a delusion which was to vitiate his statesmanship for the next three years.

Charnacé, therefore, took upon himself the business of mediation; and a difficult business he found it. In the end, the situation was saved by George William of Brandenburg, who suggested that the Swedes should hand over to him, for the duration of the truce, most of the inland areas they occupied, and in return should be allowed to hold four of his own towns, including the ports of Pillau and Memel. This was an arrangement which would relieve Gustavus of troublesome defensive commitments, and on the other hand would *de facto* put the customs revenues from Pillau and Memel into his hands – an eminently satisfactory solution from the Swedish point of view, and at least a tolerable one from that of Poland. On 16 September 1629, therefore, the Truce of Altmark was concluded: it was to run for six years. Every river-mouth in Prussia was now in Swedish hands, save for the Danzig arm of the Vistula. And by the important Treaty of Tiegenhoff (18 February 1630), which formed a corollary to the Truce of Altmark, Gustavus made peace with Danzig upon a basis which gave him the lion's share of the customs duties collected on Danzig roads. The combined effect of the two settlements was nothing less than to make the German expedition possible. [2]

Wallenstein had attained his objective: by the Peace of Lübeck and the intervention in Prussia he had bought a whole year's respite. But he had not foreseen the Truce of Altmark. In effect, it was Richelieu's first diplomatic victory over the Austrian Habsburgs, the forerunner of his more spectacular success at Regensburg in the following year. Gustavus was free at last, for six years at all events, from the dragging war with Poland; free (as Richelieu imagined) to act as France's pawn; free to invade Germany. Yet, curiously enough, for

Gustavus the moment of emancipation was succeeded by nine months of doubt, vacillation and anxiety. The decision which had seemed so firm in January 1629 became a good deal less so on the morrow of the Truce of Altmark, as the time for putting it into execution arrived. A sombre realization of the incalculable consequences, a feeling of the weight of responsibility which would rest upon him if the venture should end as Christian's had ended, induced a nervous uncertainty which drove him to ask himself whether war might not be avoidable, and manifested itself in unwonted depression and changes of mind. In November 1629 he fortified his resolution by once more seeking the endorsement of his policy by his Council.

Once again their response was reassuring. This time the debates took the form of an academic disputation, the king himself frequently intervening; and though he put the case against his own policy with force and candour, he left little doubt in the minds of his hearers as to the decision he hoped for: much of the debate might seem to be shadow-boxing, with Skytte doing duty as sparring-partner. But really they voted as they did because the plain facts that confronted them convinced them that there was no alternative to open war with the Emperor, offensive rather than defensive, with Stralsund as its launching-pad. The speech with which Gustavus wound up the meeting made it clear that (for the moment) their solidarity had nerved him to put his doubts behind him:

That I have laid these matters before you has its cause in this: not that I have myself doubted that the offensive is the better part, but that you might now have liberty to speak your minds to the contrary, and the less liberty hereafter to dispute whether I did right or no. ... And as I hope that this measure shall conduce to the welfare of the fatherland, so I hope too, that if it prove not so, no man will impute it to me for a fault. ... What tribulation I am like to have of it I foresee right well: the difficulty that for lack of means we are not able to give every man his due reward, whence discontent, ill-will, quarelling. The doubtful hazards of war, from which I have no vain hope of glory – and of which the misfortunes of the King of Denmark afford me a sufficient example. The voice of slander, ever willing to tax this man with that offence, and that man with this; and so no glory to be expected. I have had my fill of glory, and I seek no more of it. I therefore expect of you that you should not allege that it is my object, or that I have any other object than singly the advantage and security of the country. . . . And I exhort you so to bear yourselves that either you or your grandchildren may see all this come to a good end; which God grant. For myself, I perceive that I may look to no rest until I find it in the rest eternal.

Nothing, one might think, could be more final and conclusive. Yet his mind was not at ease. Within a week of the great debate he was off on another tack, laying before the Council proposals barely reconcilable with those resolutions they had so recently adopted. The complexion of affairs was changing in ways that he could not control, and as a result the execution of his policy seemed questionable in the immediate future. What if while his armies were engaged in Pomerania or Mecklenburg he found himself stabbed in the back by Christian IV? Was it not safer, perhaps, to proceed step by step and secure his rear by means of a preventive war against Denmark? It was an idea that cropped up again in the spring of 1630; and perhaps it was only the balanced arguments and steadier nerves of Oxenstierna that persuaded Gustavus that his apprehensions were exaggerated.

He was haunted also by another difficulty. The war might appear unavoidable, but was he therefore entitled to precipitate the conflict? Was the war just? As an assiduous student of Grotius, he was fully conversant with the criteria for a *bellum iustum*: war must have not only a righteous cause, but also a righteous intent. Grotius had laid it down that one precondition for a just war was that he who waged it must first have sought to reach a reasonable agreement with his enemy. Though Gustavus spent almost the whole of his reign fighting, he was always sharply conscious of war's evils: war was a punishment from God for sin; and the ideal ruler was the peace-king. The grand exemplar of kingship was Augustus, in whose reign the temple of Janus had been closed. Yet he was equally influenced by the heroic legends of Gothic history. He saw himself as the successor to that long line of mythical kings who in past ages had burst into Europe and overthrown the empire of the Caesars; he was the descendant of Berik, and the heir of Totila. But he was also the champion of the Protestant cause, who felt himself to be doing God's work, and to be acting as God's instrument. Gothic mythology, classical history, religious fervour, the emergent principles of international law, all contended for mastery in his mind. If none ever completely obtained it, that was because none was able to obscure for long his political realism, and his determination to take care of what he conceived to be the particular interests of his country. But at least it should not be said of him that he neglected the chance of a settlement by negotiation. In November 1629, nine days after the final decision for war, he resolved upon the holding of a congress at Danzig, to see if peace were to be had from Ferdinand II on any tolerable terms. As it turned out, Gustavus had landed in Germany before the congress got down to business, and by that time it had ceased to have any serious meaning: Gustavus had by then already admitted to himself that its only purpose was procrastination or propaganda. But the proprieties had been observed; and though the ache in his conscience would return, the congress at least provided a temporary anodyne.

Meanwhile, on the assumption that the determination to invade still stood, prudence suggested that something be done to end the state of diplomatic isolation in which Sweden found herself after the Peace of Lübeck. The old alliance with the Dutch was on the point of running out, but it was an open question whether they would renew it. An organized diplomatic offensive was plainly needed; and in 1629 a succession of emissaries was sent out to take stock of the prospects. They went to England, to Holland, to France, to Switzerland, to Venice, to Transylvania; and above all they went to the Protestant courts and cities of Germany. In due course they returned, without even the vestige of an olive-branch. The Dutch were sore and sulky at the dues which Gustavus was levying in the Prussian ports. Charles I, at odds with his parliament, and ludicrously involved in simultaneous wars with France and Spain, could give only good words. Bethlen Gabor chose this inopportune moment to die. It is true that these embassies once more put Gustavus in touch with some of the Protestant powers of Germany – the dukes of Saxe-Weimar, the landgraves of Hesse – and that they made useful contacts with great trading cities such as Nuremberg: for the first time for some years it became possible to imagine the formation of a Swedish party in the Empire. But all seemed remarkably chary of committing themselves; and the undisputed leader of German Lutheranism, the Elector John George of Saxony, took the opportunity to make his attitude

69

disagreeably clear: if Swedish troops landed on German soil, he should think it his duty as a loyal subject of the Emperor to resist them in arms. It was an unmistakable warning, which should have left Gustavus in no doubt what to expect; and it foreshadowed the uneasy relations with Saxony which were to bedevil the history of the German expedition.

If the German princes held aloof, resentful of foreign meddling and already scenting the danger of Swedish tutelage, the Protestant masses exhibited very different feelings. The prospect which so disturbed the princes appeared to them as a prospect of deliverance. They awaited the arrival of Gustavus with hope; and, indeed, in an atmosphere of religious semi-hysteria. There was an old prophecy, attributed to Paracelsus, that after a period of war and disaster there would come a golden Lion from the North, who would put the (Imperial?) Eagle to rout, proceed to the conquest of Asia and Africa, and initiate a reign of peace on earth which would be followed by the second coming of Christ. Forty years after Paracelsus, Tycho Brahe had explained the import of the great *nova* in Cassiopeia as portending the end of the Holy Roman Empire and the beginning of the latter days, probably about the year 1632, and had indicated that the founder of the new order would come from the North. Amid the disasters of contemporary Germany, it was not remarkable that simple men should have recalled these predictions and found in them a source of hope and comfort. As the Swedish agents made their way through Germany, they found that men had come to believe that the golden Lion of the North was in fact the golden-haired Gustavus Adolphus. His coming may have been viewed with distrust by the Protestant princes, but to the Protestant populations he appeared as a long-foretold deliverer and an instrument of the purposes of God: almost (as Wallenstein complained) as a Messiah.

This did not count for much from a military point of view. It could not supply the place of an ally with an effective army and a long purse. By 1630 it had become apparent that the best hope of such an ally lay in France. From Richelieu's point of view, an alliance with Sweden was the logical consequence of French mediation in Poland: it was precisely in order to enlist Swedish assistance for France that Charnacé had mediated the Truce of Altmark. When the Polish war was over, Charnacé made his way to Stockholm, and in the winter of 1629–30 perseveringly dangled baits before Gustavus. But he found that Gustavus was not interested in becoming a member of that 'Third Party' in the Empire which Richelieu was trying to bring into being; least of all, since it was designed to include Bavaria. He had no intention of being France's lackey. He demanded a treaty on a footing of full equality, with the supreme command for himself, and an undertaking that France would not make a separate peace with the Habsburgs in Italy. For a moment he was tempted by Charnacé's offer of an annual subsidy of 300,000 *riksdaler*; but only for a moment. In the end he came to the conclusion that not even a substantial subsidy would compensate him for the loss of his freedom of action. The French offer was rejected; and Richelieu had been given his first intimation that Sweden could not be counted on to dance to France's piping. It was a warning which he would have done well to take to heart.

So: no allies; no subsidies; money in desperately short supply. So short, that at the last moment it seemed that the expedition might have to be cancelled. Prussia was full of German mercenary cavalry in the Swedish service, and they could not be disbanded since there was no money to pay them off. The only possibility was to find them alternative employment, and a new field of action: it was the first example of a dilemma which would recur in 1654 and 1674. The obvious answer was Pomerania, but it was a matter of great difficulty to transport them there. Oxenstierna grappled grimly with these difficulties in Elbing, to the accompaniment of despairing cries from Gustavus in Stockholm. But at last the mercenaries were persuaded to accept a compromise, and the last obstacle to the expedition was removed.

On 19 May 1630 Gustavus took leave of his people, in a speech addressed to the Council, to members of the three upper Estates and to the absent representatives of the Peasants.[3] As literature, the oration takes its place among the masterpieces of Swedish eloquence; as politics, it represents the public consummation of the union of king and people. And it is extraordinarily characteristic of the speaker's mind. His valediction to the Nobility, for instance, invoked the memory of the Ancient Goths, and urged his hearers to emulate them. The Clergy were reminded that they had the power to 'turn and twist the hearts of men', and were

71

significantly warned to make their example square with their precepts, and above all to be on the guard against the sin of pride. One aspect of the economic policy of the reign crystal-lized into a few lapidary sentences to the Burghers, for whom his wishes were 'that your little cabins may become great houses of stone, your little boats great ships and merchant-men, and that the oil in your cruse fail not'. As for the commonalty, 'my wish for them is that their meadows may be green with grass, their fields bear an hundredfold, so that their barns may be full; and that they may so increase and multiply in all plenteousness that they may gladly and without sighing perform the duties and obligations that lie upon them'. For himself,

> . . . as it is wont to be that the pitcher is borne so oft to the well that it breaks at last, so may it befall even with me, who have now in so many occasions and perils been forced to shed my blood for the welfare of the Swedish realm – yet hitherto by the gracious protection of God without forfeit of my life – and must shed it again at the last. . . . And so now, before I leave you, I would commend you all, my Swedish subjects and the Estates here present (and those absent too) in soul, life and welfare, to the most gracious protection of Almighty God, desiring that we, after this troublous and toilsome life, may by God's will meet again in the heavenly Kingdom of eternity, and may in God find life and gladness.

On 17 June the great fleet of transports put out from Älvsnabben; on 26 July they made their landfall at Peene-münde. Gustavus had arrived before them: on 26 June 1630 he fell on his knees on the Pomeranian beach and entreated the mercies of the God of battles. The great adventure had begun at last.

. . .

NOTES

1. For a discussion of *assecuratio*, see below, pp. 154 ff.
2. For the importance of these customs revenues for Gusta-vus's war finance, see Chapter 8.
3. English translation of the full text in Roberts, *Sweden as a Great Power 1611–1697* pp. 13–16.

Chapter 6

REFORMS: DOMESTIC

On 26 August 1617, Gustavus welcomed the Diet which had assembled in Stockholm for his coronation. His speech was for the most part devoted to celebrating the victory over the Russians, and to pointing out the advantages, strategic and economic, which the Peace of Stolbova had secured; but it contained also other matter of significance. The Peace, he told them,

> affords us the opportunity once more to establish that good order, and those good laws, which this country formerly enjoyed, but which of late have been much in abeyance, and through these long-continued wars as it were forgotten. The laws and statutes that we have are indeed good; but by long misrule have fallen quite out of use. Courts are indeed held, in every province and county, but it is but little justice that the commonalty gets from them; whence it comes that lawlessness prevails over law and right. Have I not set my face against such things? Indeed, as God is my witness, I have done what I could. By proclamations and beneficent ordinances I have as it were raised the law from the dead. What, then, has made them ineffective, and thwarted my intent to provide justice? What but the war, which has put obstacles in the way, and strengthened the forces of disorder?

As a description of the existing situation, this was strictly accurate. As an analysis of its causes, it was partial and defective. As a programme, it was the enunciation of a policy which had in 1617 already begun to take shape, and which was to result in some of the most solid achievements of the reign.

The early Vasas, from Gustavus Vasa to Charles IX, had

all governed Sweden in much the same way: upon a strictly personal basis, with a handful of secretaries around their person, and a corps of bailiffs to look after their fiscal interests in the country. A chancery and a treasury indeed they had, though of a less sophisticated type than others in western Europe; but their servants had no organic connection with one another, no fixed salaries, and little specialization of function. There was no central court of justice: appeals lay from provincial or county courts direct to the king himself. The Council of State was not a permanently constituted body: it met irregularly, summoned from the country to listen to the king's complaints, offer advice if asked to do so, and, if need be, put his case to the the Estate of Nobility. The Council was not a collection of ministers: in so far as there were any ministers at all, they were the king's secretaries and exchequer-clerks and bailiffs. There were, indeed, by long custom, five great officers of state: the high steward, the marshal, the admiral, the treasurer and the chancellor. But, of these, only the treasurer had specific functions and real political existence: the others were little more than empty titles. What held the whole system together was the personality of the monarch; and if the monarch had a natural taste for administration, indefatigable energy, and a shrewd business sense, it worked reasonably well.

It worked conspicuously well under Gustavus Vasa, who was superbly equipped in all these respects; it worked badly under John III, who was scholarly, aesthetic, spendthrift and lazy. Charles IX inherited a large share of his father's qualities, and he tried to run the country on his father's lines. But methods which had served well enough in 1560 no longer served so well in 1610. The business of the state had become too complex to be adequately supervised by one man, no matter how energetic. Moreover, the maladministration of John III had provoked a demand for reform. It came from the nobility, which resented the influence of low-born secretaries, and was resurrecting old theories of aristocratic constitutionalism in opposition to a monarchy which was not only arbitrary but inefficient. The nobility was coming to believe that liberties would be safer, and administration better, if they had a share in government; and in 1594 Erik Sparre produced a plan for a reorganization of the central administration which was destined not to be forgotten. He proposed the creation of five departments, each to be headed by one of the five great officers of state, with security of tenure for office-holders, and fixed salaries. Nothing came of this; but when Charles IX cut off Erik Sparre's head in 1600 he did not thereby refute his ideas. For ten years Erik Sparre's constitut-ionalism was driven underground; but it came up again in 1611. The Charter of 1611 was in one important aspect a demand for better government; and with that demand no one was more closely identified than Axel Oxenstierna.

Better government meant the more effective assertion of royal authority, and the eradication of prevailing disorders: the extortion practised by the king's bailiffs upon peasant taxpayers, the perversion of justice, the contempt for the law and the defiance of royal injunctions by powerful local magnates. It was of abuses such as these that Gustavus Adolphus was thinking when he made his speech in 1617. His long absences on campaign had revealed the urgency of the need to undertake the formalization and rationalization of the central administration. To this, the terms of the Charter of 1611 implicitly committed him; for it had pledged him to fill the leading offices in the central and local admin-istration with members of the nobility; and it had guaranteed them fixed salaries. Henceforward they would be the servants of the state, rather than irresponsible agents of the king. The Charter was thus the fulfilment of Erik Sparre's programme, save in one respect: it did not revive the five great officers of state as the leading ministers of the crown, nor did it provide five departments over which they should preside. The claim of the aristocratic constitutionalists for a monopoly of high office for the nobility was conceded; but the functions of the offices they were to fill were left undefined. It was to be the task of Oxenstierna to repair these omissions, and to translate into reality the implications of Erik Sparre's proposals.

Without some such transformation of government, the emergence of Sweden as a great power could hardly have taken place. Gustavus Adolphus, like his grandfather, was a king who addressed himself to the business of kingship with diligence; and in his quick intelligence, his range of infor-mation, his facility in mastering a variety of business, his willingness to trust his servants, he was his grandfather's superior. He had the intellectual curiosity, the desire to know

75

and do everything himself, and that knack of getting along well with all classes of men which seems to have been hereditary in the Vasas. When he was in Sweden, he was for ever on the move; and probably no Swedish monarch has known his country as well. But his absences were frequent, and for the last ten years of the reign he spent a good deal more time abroad than at home. The campaigns in Poland and Germany, the immense organizational effort which those campaigns entailed, could never have been possible to a government as personal, as loosely organized – or as unpopular – as that of Charles IX. What was needed was some system of delegation of royal authority which would enable an effective government to continue functioning when the king was away. This meant the concentration of administration in a single place, and its ordering upon clearly defined principles of differentiation, with some kind of supervisory body to co-ordinate the activities of each part of it. He had something like a prime minister in the person of Axel Oxenstierna, with whom he worked in the closest collaboration and almost unbroken harmony. But after 1626, when Oxenstierna was made governor in Prussia, he was no longer available on the spot: he did not return to Sweden until four years after the king was dead.

Moreover the government must have men fit to work it. The constitutionalists of Erik Sparre's generation may have been right in their belief that such persons were to be looked for first among the nobility; for only the nobility could provide a sizeable body of men with adequate education (ecclesiastical statesmen had no place in Sweden), and they had, besides, the advantage that they were by long tradition the custodians of the law. But they were also already the military class, the core of what was termed 'The Army Command' – a body which already aspired to the status of a separate Estate, though it never succeeded in becoming one. They served the state in great numbers in Gustavus's wars. Much as they might dislike the upstart secretaries upon whom John III and Charles IX had relied, it was impossible that the apparatus of government should function without such persons. The problem was rather how to recruit enough of them. This was a question of educational facilities. In 1611 the Swedish educational system, with its old-fashioned cathedral schools and a university stunted by poverty, was in no position to supply the raw material for an administrative revolution and a rapidly expanding civil service.

On 6 January 1612, within a week of his acceptance of the Charter, Gustavus made his first important appointment, when he called Axel Oxenstierna to fill the vacant office of chancellor. His commission was couched in terms of unprecedented amplitude: 'It is not more particularly specified what he shall do, or how he shall act, in virtue of his office, but it is left to his modesty and his understanding as he may think best, and as he may answer it to God, to Us, and to all our loyal subjects.'

His appointment marked the beginning of a process which was to transform the government of Sweden. Slowly, in the years after 1612, a beginning was made with reforms; from 1618 to 1620 the pace quickened, in the comparative calm that followed the Peace of Stolbova; by 1626 the bases of a new system of government had been firmly laid; and in 1634 they were consolidated and received statutory confirmation in the Form of Government. Most of these changes reflected Oxenstierna's personal views, and were his own personal achievement. All were based upon the principles of delegation of royal authority, regularization of procedures, and centralization of administration.

He began with the reform of justice. The Judicature Ordinances of 1614 and 1615 provided Sweden with its first Supreme Court. At its head, the high steward, whose office was now given a specific function; to assist him, four members of the Council and nine assessors: five of them were to be drawn from the nobility, as persons learned in the law, four were to be commoners. They were to function as a bench of judges, giving their decisions by majority vote; they were directed to hold sessions for five months of the year in Stockholm. For the first time justice was centred in the capital; the era of ambulatory royal justice was over, though the king's personal intervention preserved the right of a litigant to petition the sovereign for redress. Formally the new court in Stockholm was that of ultimate instance; it retained its pre-eminence even when the need for more accessible justice led to the creation of other supreme courts at Åbo (1623), Dorpat (1630) and Jönköping (1634). The effects upon Swedish jurisprudence were profound. The Supreme Court kept a full record of cases, and it had its own archive;

for the first time the development of case-law was made possible. Its existence led to the emergence of more precise rules of evidence. It opened the way to the establishment of the law as a regular profession.

Of more immediate importance to the emergence of Sweden as a great power was the reform of the treasury, which Oxenstierna initiated in 1618. The office was to be presided over by one of the great officers of state, in this case the treasurer. Again the object was centralization; above all, of accounting and audit. The new treasury was to be a board, whose decisions were to be collective. It kept its own records, its procedures were precisely prescribed, it was given judicial authority over its staff, and also in fiscal cases. The effects of the change were not long in making themselves felt. For the first time financial planning became possible: in 1623 the treasury was able to produce the first statement of national accounts; though not yet to draw up a budget; in 1624 it appointed a Dutchman, Abraham Cabeljau, as auditor-general, and with him came the system of double-entry bookkeeping. Without some such reforms it is difficult to imagine how Sweden would have mastered her financial difficulties in the years before war could be relied upon to support war.

From the moment of his appointment in 1612 to the closing months of his life in 1654, Oxenstierna held fast to the determination that the centre of government should be the chancery. For forty-two years he held the office of chancellor; and under his leadership the chancery became, and remained, *anima regis*, the soul of the state. To it alone belonged the right to promulgate the royal will, or despatch business in the king's name: all letters, orders, resolutions of other government offices, if they were acts of state, must be forwarded to the chancery, and issued by it. This gave cohesion and consistency to government. But the chancery was not merely the filter through which policy must pass, the channel of communication between government offices and the crown: it had its own special responsibilities which were extraordinarily wide. Foreign policy was its close preserve; but it dealt with all sorts of domestic affairs too: local government, domestic disturbances, communications, religion, pauperism, education. Indeed, it included everything that was not specifically allotted to some other administrative organ. Oxenstierna took it all in his stride, turning with equal competence and magisterial authority from diplomacy to commercial policies, from rogues and vagabonds to the squabbles of learned divines. The chancery, as it existed from 1612 to 1680, was essentially his creation: his successors only followed the line he had chalked out.

Within a few months of his appointment Oxenstierna had begun to organize the business of his office; but it was not until the Chancery Ordinance of 1618 that the chancery began to assume the pattern which it was afterwards to retain. That ordinance did not make it a *collegium*; for Oxenstierna was not the man to expose himself to the possibility of being voted down by his colleagues on a board. But it did fix the establishment, define the duties, and prescribe hours and wages for the staff. Something more than this, however, was made necessary by Oxenstierna's removal to Elbing in 1626. All matters of high policy continued to be concerted between the king and chancellor alone, as may be seen from the extensive correspondence between them when personal consultation was impossible, and most major administrative problems tended sooner or later to receive Oxenstierna's attention. But the routine business of the chancery must go on even though chancellor and king were absent, and its position as the nodal point of the administration must be safeguarded against encroachments. Hence Oxenstierna in 1626 drew up a second Chancery Ordinance. This time he organized the office on collegial lines: the chancellor or his deputy at its head; and to assist him, two chancery-counsellors with a subordinate staff.

By this time Oxenstierna had clearly determined on the full implementation of Erik Sparre's collegial programme. The idea of a college of war, grouped round the marshal, took definite shape in 1630. Like the treasury, it combined executive and judicial powers; for it was to function both as war office and as a court-martial. A similar development was taking place for the navy: by 1630 it too was securely established as a college under the presidency of the admiral. Both Oxenstierna and Gustavus Adolphus would have liked to extend the principle further: a proposal for a *consistorium generale*, which would have acted as a college for church affairs and for education, was defeated only by the resistance of the clergy to any participation by laymen in the determination of ecclesiastical policy. Thus by the close of the reign the pattern of collegial government had firmly established itself; and it was given definitive shape by the Form of Government of 1634, which sums up the administrative innovations of Gustavus's reign. Colleges, Council and regents were now intimately linked; the Council became a body of civil servants; the old demand of the nobility for a direct share in government was realized. At the same time, the expansion of a regular civil service opened a career to talents and quickened the pace of social mobility. Socially, no less than administratively, the Form of Government heralded the coming of a new age. Among other things, it made Stockholm indisputably a capital city; for except when there should be an outbreak of plague, the central government was now forbidden to leave it.

Without some such reform as this, Sweden could hardly have emerged at Westphalia as one of the great powers of Europe. Contemporaries abroad were impressed; and in due course Peter the Great was to take the Swedish central government as the model for his reforms. Nevertheless, it is possible that the new system has been over-praised. It took some time before it really began to function efficiently: there were sharp demarcation-disputes between the colleges; there was slackness as well as dedication in the noble members who served on them; it was long before they were adequately housed; and their whole history was a melancholy story of salaries unpaid and wages in arrears. Above all, the colleges suffered from a shortage of trained personnel. It was no unusual experience for Gabriel Gustafsson Oxenstierna, the high steward, to find himself alone in the Supreme Court save for non-noble assessors. Skytte, in charge of the accounting-and-auditing section of the Treasury, protested that he was simply incapable of coping with the work, since he was so often virtually alone. The Form of Government contained elaborate provisions for a detailed annual examination of the work of every college by the regents, who would inspect their books, keep an eye on their practice, and correct maladministration or abuses. Such an examination took place in 1636, and its results do a good deal to modify the idea that in 1634 Sweden acquired at a stroke one of the most efficient and up-to-date administrations in Europe. It was not corrupt, indeed, and it did not suffer from the current plague of venality; but it was not yet fully equal to the burdens which it had to shoulder. The effectiveness of the reforms, moreover, was to some extent blunted by Oxenstierna himself. Though the chancery had now become a college, it was not therefore a college like any other. He had no intention of relaxing its grip upon royal business. Sharp struggles with the war office and the treasury in 1645 ended with a clear reaffirmation of the chancery's pre-eminence. The result was that the colleges (apart from the Supreme Court) never really developed into independent *departments*: they were indeed staffed by ministers; their heads were men of the highest political importance; but they were something less than ministries.

If the king was to be free to lead his armies overseas, Sweden needed something more than an administration which would function in his absence: she needed also a *government* to supervise that administration and shoulder responsibility in a crisis. As long as Oxenstierna was at home he was quite equal to these things, and the king could rely upon him to do them; but after 1626, when Oxenstierna took up his governorship in Elbing, some other expedient had to be devised.

The only possible solution was to entrust the government to the Council. Much therefore turned on the relations between the Council and the crown. The Charter of 1611 had to all appearances been a victory for the Council-aristocracy: it had laid down which royal actions required the Council's advice, and which required its consent. But the strength of the Council's constitutional position was sapped by the personal acceptability of Gustavus to the aristocracy, by his close collaboration with a single adviser, and by the fact that the Council was still casual in its meeting, with only a handful of its members available in Stockholm at any one time. In the event, Gustavus ignored the obligation to seek its consent, and tended to ask its advice in terms which left little option as to what advice it should give. As he moved around the country, he might summon its members to attend him in this place or that: for the first decade of the reign there was little sign of a permanent nucleus of advisers in the capital. But after 1621 it became clear that there would have to be a quasi-regency when he was away; and as the new administration was now firmly centred in Stockholm it was clear that the Council members who formed the regency must be in Stockholm also. Gustavus never took a section of the Council with him on his campaigns, as Charles X was to do in 1656, though on occasion he summoned individual members to attend him in Germany. As the problems of foreign policy grew graver, he came to develop a new type of Council meeting, in which he elicited the opinions of the members not in the old form of written resolutions, but by debates presided over by himself and usually dominated by his own contributions.

A turning-point came in 1625, when he entrusted what was virtually a regency not to selected individuals (as on previous occasions), but to the Council as a whole, and bound them by their instructions to remain permanently in Stockholm unless otherwise engaged upon the king's business. From this moment, the Council ceased to be a loose assemblage of great magnates meeting at irregular intervals, and became in fact a government. Its powers lapsed when the king was at home; but even then its meetings became more frequent than of old. Its members, moreover, began to acquire the mental attitudes of a government, in place of the constitutional-defensive, and often critical, attitudes which had characterized them in the later decades of the previous century. This development was assisted by the Ordinance for the House of Nobility (1626), which fixed the procedures and constitution of the First Estate; for that ordinance expressly denied a seat in the house to members of the Council. Hitherto, they had been an essential element in every Diet, the natural leaders of the Estate of Nobles: now, they were severed from them, and quite soon the Nobility were thinking of them as 'they' rather than 'we' – as the Government, as the Establishment. The way was already clear for them to function, in intimate collaboration with the regents, as a regular government during the minority of Christina; and when Christina attained her majority in 1644, they continued, for the first time, to be a government under a sovereign of full age. As long as Gustavus lived they neither controlled nor initiated policy: their job was to be the king's agents, his eyes, his watchdogs; and often between 1630 and 1632 they were tremulous and apologetic in the face of outbursts of royal impatience or displeasure. Yet somehow or other they coped with their work, and Gustavus could address himself to the problems of Germany without having to be perpetually looking over his shoulder at what was going on at home.

This would scarcely have been possible, however, if reform

had been confined to the central government alone. The war effort could be sustained only if the taxpayer could be induced to provide the money and the privileged to forgo their exemptions: it depended, in fact, upon the consent of the Diet. This would have been even more difficult to obtain if the king had been incapable of ensuring good government, or if the crown's agents had shown themselves intolerably arbitrary and extortionate. The correction of abuses was an essential precondition for the intervention in Germany, and Gustavus's successive instructions for the regency governments he left behind him reveal his anxiety that there should be no distracting unrest at home. Reform of local government was, in its way, as important as the creation of the colleges. There must be effective control of the royal bailiffs; there must be a separation of executive from judicial functions. Local government areas must be made definite, and not, as had hitherto been the case, ill-defined or shifting ; and they must be in charge of permanently appointed local officials with defined functions and duties. Gustavus Vasa had exercised a strict supervision of his bailiffs, personally checking their accounts, perambulating the country to make sure that he was not being cheated too grossly, ruling the land as though it had been a collection of royal manors. Such methods were possible no longer, though Charles IX had tried to use them: out in the country, no less than in the capital, the king must now delegate his authority to a responsible hierarchy of professional civil servants.

It was left to Gustavus Adolphus to take the decisive step which would lay the foundations of a system of local government which in some important respects survives to this day. A basis upon which reform could be built did in fact exist already, in the relatively recent office of *ståthållare* (governor). But in 1611 the status and functions of the *ståthållare* were ill defined, and might vary widely. A *ståthållare* might be permanent or temporary, a regular office or an *ad hoc* appointment. He might be in effect a provincial governor, or he might be no more than the commander of a fortress: in Charles IX's time it was not unknown to have two *ståthållare* in the same castle. (Kalmar at one time had no less than seven.) Gustavus removed these ambiguities. The *ståthållare* was firmly established as a provincial governor, and nothing else. The area over which he ruled was precisely defined: by 1621 Sweden had been divided into clearly demarcated administrative areas; and the process was completed by the Form of Government of 1634, which fixed their number at twenty-three, the former *ståthållare* now being designated *landshövding*. By and large, those provinces, as then established, form the basis of Swedish local government still.

The new governors ruled in the king's stead: it was their duty to represent the crown's interest in their provinces, and especially to exercise that control over the crown's bailiffs which Gustavus's other preoccupations rendered impossible. A memorandum of 1620 subordinated the bailiffs to the governors, not only in adminstrative but in financial matters. Instructions to the bailiffs henceforward went through the governors, and not direct, thus eliminating confusion and cross-purposes. Their accounts were now to be rendered to the provincial treasury and audited there, before being sent on to the treasury in Stockholm. A general ordinance of 1624 consolidated these changes, and formed the basis for a famous Instruction of 1635 which laid down office procedure, fixed the establishment, prescribed duties, and expressly forbade the governor to act in a judicial capacity. The Instruction marked an epoch in the history of local government: it placed the *landshövding* in much the position within his province (excepting only in regard to justice) as that occupied by an *intendant* in the time of Louis XIV. Within the provinces, the old counties (*härader*) remained, each with its sheriff (*härads-hövding*) and its county court (*häradsting*), where the standing jury of the county (*häradsnämnd*) assisted the sheriff to dispense justice. And lower still down the social scale the parish council and vestry still vigorously defended the rights or prejudices of the parishioners. Thus the reform of 1635 did little to qualify the fundamentally democratic structure of local government.

Thus, both in local and in central government, Gustavus's reign saw the coming of a new ideal of business-like administration, delegated by the crown to full-time civil servants. If that ideal were to be realized, there must be an adequate corps of competent persons available. The earlier Vasas had partly surmounted the difficulty of finding administrators by importing them from abroad; and most of the rest had perforce received their training in Germany, since they could not get it at home. In the long run, the success of Gustavus's administrative revolution would depend upon Sweden's being able to produce the men to operate it. Underlying the administrative problem lay an educational problem. In a speech to the clergy in 1620 Gustavus complained that 'the land is become barren and unfruitful of useful folk, so that despite the hardness of the times we are in greater straits for men than money': there was not a single good town clerk or bailiff in the country, and local government officials often could not even write their names. Education was still education for Holy Orders; it was dominated by the study of theology and the biblical languages. The results were deplorable: in 1623 Oxenstierna was embarrassed because he could find no Swedish diplomat whose command of Latin was such that he could be entrusted to conduct negotiations fluently with the Poles. Latin there must be, therefore; but, in addition, Gustavus insisted that education should be expanded to include the more 'modern' subjects: law, history, politics, mathematics, science. His solution was the creation of a new type of school, the *gymnasium*. The first was founded at Västerås in 1623, six more followed before 1632, and a further four had been established by 1643. They provided a secondary education broader and deeper than that previously offered by any Swedish school – Västerås, for instance, taught geography, history, science and law.

The university needed reform even more. Uppsala had been virtually refounded in 1593, after more than half a century of inanition; but for the next quarter of a century it was crippled by penury and torn by internal dissensions. Its European prestige was low; national self-respect, apart from any other considerations, demanded that something be done to improve it. In Gustavus Adolphus it found the patron it needed. There must be more professorial chairs, and a wider variety of subjects; there must be better endowments. In 1620 he raised the number of chairs to thirteen; in 1622 to eighteen, establishing for the first time chairs of Swedish law, medicine, mathematics, history, and politics. Two years later, in 1624, he gave it that magnificent donation which really assured its future: 317 manors from the Vasa family estates, to be held free of all taxation for ever. At a stroke the financial situation was transformed: after 1624 the university's income was more than eight times what it had been in 1613. Uppsala began to attract students as never before – there were perhaps a thousand when Gustavus died in 1632 – and among them were now sons of the nobility who had hitherto sought a university education in Protestant Germany. The university had now, by the king's generosity, its own printing press; and as Gustavus pursued his victorious career overseas, he did not forget to endow it with the spoils of war: the libraries of Riga, Braunsberg, Würzburg, and Mainz did something to fill the gaps on the bookshelves of Uppsala. The motive underlying this royal concern for higher education was expressed in the university's constitution of 1626, which laid down that half of the scholarships for poor students which the king had made available should be reserved for boys who intended to enter the service of the crown. That concern was exemplified still more clearly in his foundation of the University of Dorpat in 1632. Here there was from the beginning a deliberate concentration on the production of graduates fit for the administration of the Baltic provinces, to which end the curriculum included courses in French, Lettish, Estonian and Ingrian, a knowledge of German and Swedish being assumed.

If the objective was clear, the success was dubious; at least in Gustavus's time. In 1627 the professor of history at Uppsala had only four students; in 1629, out of a total of sixty-two freshmen, only five read law, and only two medicine. There was no instruction in modern languages at all: Uppsala had to wait for a *lektor* in French until 1637, and for a *lektor* in Italian until 1640. In 1627 Johan Skytte (the university's chancellor) discovered that it had no mathematical instruments of any sort. In 1632 it proved impossible to find in Uppsala any suitable candidates to be sent out to Germany as secretaries to generals in the Swedish armies: all studied theology, and none politics. But it would be unreasonable to expect a dramatic change in the space of a single decade. Gustavus died too soon to see the harvest of his policies, but the generation after his death had cause to thank him. Little by little the situation changed: by the middle 1650s the complaint began to be, not that too few undergraduates read politics and law, but too many. The market began to be glutted with aspirant civil servants. Graduates now entered the new colleges, the new municipal administration, the new provincial governments, the nascent profession of the law; they provided the solid body of administrative competence without which the Swedish empire would have fallen into confusion. The king's service became a career open to talents, and the man of ability could look forward with some confidence to ultimate ennoblement as a reward for his labours. For the first time in Swedish history, education became a powerful agent of social mobility, and (some historians would add) of social control. And it is to Gustavus Adolphus that the credit for these achievements is due.

His reign was thus a period when the institutions of the State were given an orderliness, consistency and effectiveness, such as they had never had before. This was true not only of the executive, but also of the legislature. Despite the 'over-many Diets' to which Charles IX had had recourse as a weapon against his enemies, or a buttress to his authority, the position of the Diet in 1611 was still in many respects undefined, It was *a* representative body; but it was not necessarily *the* representative body, for it was still open for the king to negotiate with individual Estates, or with provincial gatherings, or with those representative cross-sections of his subjects who put in an appearance at the great winter markets. The number of Estates was still uncertain: the free miners of the Bergslag, the 'Army Command', the bailiffs, were all possible candidates for estatehood. Procedure was unformulated and often rudimentary (the Peasants customarily assented to propositions by shouting), and meetings lacked order. The Charter's requirement that the king should obtain the assent of 'those concerned' by no means necessarily implied the consent of the Diet. Yet by 1634 there had been an important advance. The Form of Government of that year stated that the resolution of the Diet was binding law, to be altered only by another Diet; and it had become an accepted convention of the constitution that new taxes must usually be granted with the Diet's consent: 'King and Estates *together* constitute the sovereign authority of the realm.' And the composition of the Diet had been fixed on lines which were to endure till 1866.

A landmark in this process was the Ordinance of 1617. Like the contemporary reforms of treasury and chancery, it was Oxenstierna's work: one more example of his passion for order and precision, though it was very much in Gustavus's spirit. For if it finally fixed the number of Estates at four and laid down rules for the conduct of their business, it placed the king in a strong position to exercise a personal influence on parliamentary proceedings. Whereas the old method of transacting business between crown and Diet had been by written Propositions from the crown and Resolutions upon them, the Ordinance of 1617 provided for joint sessions of all four Estates in the king's presence, and for impromptu debates between himself and their spokesmen. It provided also that if the resolutions of the Estates were discrepant, the king should adopt 'that which seems good to him'. Almost all the Vasas, from Gustavus I to Charles X, had a gift for popular oratory which enabled them to establish a personal *rapport* with their subjects. In Gustavus Adolphus this gift was highly developed; and the Ordinance of 1617 was designed to enable him to exploit it to advantage. He felt the need to solidarize his subjects behind his policies, the need for a national consensus expressed in reciprocal pledges to stand or fall together. Certainly his oratory, and the power of a personality which could both awe and charm, did much to coax his subjects into making the sacrifices which he demanded of them.

In the event, the device of joint sessions proved a clumsy one, and the grand public debates envisaged in 1617 never really established themselves as parliamentary practice. It was easier, and not less effective, to operate through smaller bodies; and in the 1620s the custom developed of calling together small meetings of representatives of some or all of the Estates, or meetings of the three upper Estates without the Peasants. The peasantry bore the main fiscal burden; but it was argued that since in the national emergency the privileged nobility were waiving their exemption from taxation, the peasants' consent might be taken for granted, and their representatives dispensed from the expensive business of parliamentary attendance. In 1627 came another innovation, destined to be of high importance for the future, when Gustavus set up the first Secret Committee drawn from the three upper Estates. It was called into being to take cognizance of matters of foreign policy too secret to be communicated to the Estates at large; but it was to become in the next century a body omnicompetent (save in regard to finances), overshadowing the Diet itself.

These developments posed a potential threat to the future of the Diet as a true parliament, as the melancholy history of seventeenth-century German Estates reminds us. But in fact the Swedish Diet had already established itself too firmly as a part of the machinery of state for the threat to materialize. In

1632 it still fell far short of the level attained by an English parliament: it had no monopoly of legislation, since much (especially in the economic field) was still done by royal ordinance; no initiative other than by way of petition; and not until 1675 would it make any attempt to control foreign policy. The very idea of parliamentary privilege was unconceived; and elections to the three lower Estates were in greater or less degree influenced by the crown. But still it was a parliament in the making; and the Secret Committee would have many successors. The Ordinance of 1617, and the Ordinance for the House of Nobility in 1626, had provided it with a basic organization on which to build; when Oxenstierna returned home in 1636 he would find it expedient to take a leaf out of his master's book, and cultivate the arts of the parliamentarian. The historian Fredrik Lagerroth once wrote of 'the confidence between king and people' which existed in Gustavus's time, and remarked that such confidence was 'possible only in a primitive society and in the extraordinary historical situation'. There is much truth in this. It was in the Diet that that confidence was created, and it was one of the major assets with which Gustavus plunged into the adventure of the German war.

Chapter 7

REFORMS:
NAVAL AND MILITARY

The domestic reforms were essential to Sweden's emergence as a great power, but it would be absurd to suggest that they were responsible for it. An improved system of local government could not decide the issue in Livonia or Prussia; the new *collegia*, whatever their merits, can hardly be credited with the Peace of Westphalia; the battle of Breitenfeld was not won on the playing fields of Västerås. The Swedish empire was based on victories in the field, on the fact that for many years Swedish armies were better than those of their adversaries, on the accident that produced two generations of exceptionally distinguished commanders who from 1630 to 1660 made Sweden the greatest military power in Europe. So much is obvious; what is not so obvious, but hardly less important, was the part played by the navy.

The Swedish empire, from start to finish, was a maritime empire, linked together (but also sundered) by the sea. The command of the Baltic was both the precondition of its coming into being and an essential element in its survival. Without a powerful fleet, Sweden could not hope to protect her own coasts from Danish attack – as the experience of the War of Kalmar had made plain. The attainment of something like naval parity with Denmark was a necessary condition for an expansionist foreign policy. It was achieved by 1624; but the Danish fleet was still there, guarding the Sound, dividing the Swedish west-coast and east-coast squadrons from one another, hanging over Sweden's overseas line of communications. Though Sweden might now feel relatively secure from Danish attack, the change did not lessen the need for a strong navy; rather it increased it, for foreign policy was now directed towards lands on the other side of the sea, and without the navy it could not be conducted at all. The navy must take troops to their destinations, guard convoys, ferry military supplies to bridgeheads, maintain a blockade of enemy ports, with one eye always on what might be afoot at Copenhagen or Malmö.

It was no easy service. The Baltic is a narrow sea, no point in it more than sixty-seven sea miles from land; but it is a stormy and treacherous sea, subject to fogs, and was at that time largely uncharted and unlighted. There was always trouble with ice; for the seventeenth century was a very cold century, and great stretches of the sea were regularly frozen. This put the Swedish navy at a recurring disadvantage, since the Danish fleet could always get to sea from its more southerly bases a month or so before the Swedes were free of ice at Vaxholm or Älvsnabben: it was for this reason that Charles XI shifted the main Swedish naval base to the new town of Karlskrona, in the far south. But whatever the difficulties, the Swedish navy was simply essential: without it, Riga could not have been conquered, Stralsund could not have been saved, Breitenfeld could not have been won. The fleet was both a barrier against invasion from Poland and a guarantee against rash enterprises by Denmark. It enabled Gustavus to put his troops down at whatever place he might choose to land. It was an indispensable adjunct in the collection of those tolls upon Baltic ports which by the end of the 1620s had become a mainstay of Swedish war finance. Its astonishing feats of endurance in maintaining a blockade of the ports of Prussia and Mecklenburg (in some cases until as late in the season as December and January) were unparallelled in seventeenth-century naval history, and effectively killed the maritime plans of the Habsburgs.

That it should do any of these things would have seemed very unlikely in 1611. Charles IX had cared a good deal for the navy and had built up a fleet of more than a hundred vessels, but his efforts were thwarted by incompetent administration, timid commanders, and the superior weight of metal of his Danish opponents. During the War of Kalmar the Swedish east-coast fleet put up a miserable performance, while the west-coast fleet had to be scuttled when the Danes took Älvsborg. The lesson was not lost upon Gustavus and Oxenstierna. Both had a vivid appreciation of the importance of a strong navy for their country: as Oxenstierna once put it, 'In the fleet (under God) stands the safety and welfare of our fatherland.' Gustavus had said as much on more than one occasion. He is the only king of Sweden ever to have commanded a ship at sea;[1] and he is said to have astonished his officers by his expert knowledge of how to work and fight it. Certainly he had a sure grasp of how a fleet should be used as an element in strategic planning, and an Elizabethan realization of the fact that the best use that can be made of a navy in warding off a threatened invasion is to bottle up the enemy's fleet in his ports and if possible destroy him there. He had no idea of tactical innovations (in which, indeed, he seems to have lagged behind contemporary English and Dutch practice); and his experiments in ship-design were not altogether happy – as the fate of *Vasa*, which turned turtle on her trials, sufficiently demonstrated. The only significant naval engagement of his reign – the skirmish off Oliva in 1627 – presented the Poles with the only naval victory in their history. But it remains true that his reign gave Sweden the navy she needed in order to play her part in Europe.

Gustavus built many ships: by 1630 his navy was almost as big as Charles IX's had been in 1611. In everything but numbers it was superior: bigger ships, heavier guns, standardized calibres, a regular supply of recruits from the coastal areas, hard training which made the crews efficient, the creation of a profession of naval officers. Above all, the typical characteristic of all Gustavian reform: stronger and more efficient administration at the centre. The emergence of a true admiralty in the years after 1620 was the sign of this; and its chief instrument was Klas Fleming, who in 1620 was appointed chief assistant to the admiral, Karl Karlsson Gyllenhielm. Fleming came to office with virtually no experience of naval affairs; but he soon turned himself into an expert, and he became one of the greatest naval administrators in Sweden's history. More than any other man, he ensured that Sweden should have the navy she needed; his death in battle, at the moment of victory over the Danes in 1644, fittingly closed a career which had made Sweden, rather than Denmark, the greatest naval power in the Baltic. His most remarkable achievement was probably the organization of the expedition to Germany in 1630. On this occasion a main body of 15,000 men in a hundred transports, with a heavy covering fleet, set sail from the Stockholm archipelago, while seven other contingents were simultaneously embarked from points all round the Baltic. All were landed at or near their point of disembarkation at approximately the same time – an example of precise planning and administrative efficiency which must be unique for the seventeenth century.

The navy, then, did all that was required of it: it made the campaigns possible, and it sustained them when they had begun. But only the army could provide the victories; and in 1611 it would have seemed incredible that it should be able within twenty years to overwhelm the hardened veterans of continental warfare. It is no longer possible to maintain, as Swedish military historians of half a century ago did, that Gustavus Vasa created the first Swedish standing army in 1544, and that this was in effect the first national standing army based on conscription to appear in any country. In his time, and during the reigns of his sons, the Swedish infantry was provided primarily by calling up the militia, in fulfilment of that obligation to defend the country against attack which lay upon all subjects of the crown. Such militia levies had, however, the disadvantage that they were bound to serve only in wartime, and only within Sweden's borders: as late as Charles IX's time militia levies which had been sent to fight in Estonia mutinied on the ground that the law did not oblige them to serve abroad. Already it had become necessary to supplement them by some form of conscription. As to the cavalry, it was provided, in theory by the knight-service owed by the nobility as the price of their exemption from taxation, in reality mainly by voluntary enlistment. Conscript armies did not enjoy a good reputation among contemporary writers on the art of war, and the poor performance of the Swedish army against Danish mercenary forces during the War of Kalmar suggested that they were right. Certainly that war had revealed serious defects in the Swedish system. The conscription of the infantry was badly organized, and it was tardy in providing recruits. The training of new levies was unsatisfactory. The nobility were grossly negligent in providing their quota of heavy cavalry, and they defeated all efforts of Charles IX to enforce their obligations upon them: in 1611 they provided a total of twenty horsemen. There were scarcely any permanent peacetime *cadres*, no real organization into regiments to provide a geographical basis for recruiting, nor had the tactical units been fixed with sufficient attention to the system of fighting. The administrative machinery was ineffective; the country was far from being self-sufficient in the matter of armaments; artillery was cumbrous, handicapped by too many different types of gun, and in general old-fashioned; and Charles IX happened to be a bad general.

Not the least of his difficulties lay in the fact that his reign coincided with the emergence of a new type of tactics, of which Maurice of Orange had been the innovator. In the second and third quarters of the sixteenth century the battlefields of Europe had been dominated by the Spanish *tercio*. The *tercio* was a solid block of pikemen and halberdiers, originally 3,000, later 1,600, strong, with a surrounding girdle of shot. It was essentially a formation for defence, a fortress against which attacks splintered and collapsed; but it was also capable of lumbering offensive action which steam-rollered the enemy by sheer weight of numbers. Its main defects were that it was incapable of tactical improvisation, and that it made poor use of the musketeers which surrounded it, since those at its flanks and rear had little opportunity of firing. The reforms of Maurice of Orange were designed to eliminate these defects. Maurice arranged his armies, not in great clumps, but in two or three lines, each covering the gaps in the line to its front; his tactical unit was the battalion of 550 men; his formations were shallower; his shot had a clear field of fire; and it was easy for him to reinforce threatened portions of his line by transference of units from one sector of the battlefield to the other. But for both Spaniards and Dutch the sixteen-foot pike was essential: a rampart within which or behind which the shot could take cover if attacked by enemy cavalry. The coming of the pike had indeed denatured cavalry all over Europe, except in Poland; for the pike outranged the cavalry lance, and thus inhibited those frontal attacks which had been typical of cavalry tactics in previous ages. In this situation, cavalrymen were driven back upon the device of riding to within a few yards of the pike-hedge and discharging their pistols at it, in the faint hope of blowing a gap in it into which they might subsequently charge. They thus sacrificed the impact of man and horse which are cavalry's essential characteristics. Everywhere tactics tended to become defensive, battle came to be the sign of an incompetent commander, warfare became a kind of glorified chess. And this was true as much of Maurice's linear formations as of the *tercios* of Spinola. Contemporary opinion was sharply divided as to the merits of the rival schools; but in some respects the Dutch school was clearly superior: in the matter of training and drill, in the use of firepower, and in the larger number of officers and NCOs which its more numerous units required.

Charles IX was an adherent of the Dutch school, and in the course of his Polish war he embarked on the risky enterprise of remodelling the traditional Swedish style of fighting on Dutch lines. The results were disastrous. It was not possible in wartime to retrain the officers and men in the new methods. His infantry offered a passive but successful resistance to his attempts to re-arm them with the cumbrous and unhandy pike, with the result that when (as at Kirkholm in 1605) they came up against Polish cavalry which charged home with cold steel they were able to offer no effective resistance: at Kirkholm the Poles killed three times as many Swedes as their own total force. Thus in 1611 the Swedish army, on top of all its other deficiencies, was halting uncertainly between its traditional border-warfare type of fighting, and the new Dutch school which it was both unwilling and unable to assimilate.

Gustavus Adolphus did not repeat his father's mistake: until the Russian war was over he contented himself with making the best of the material at his disposal, without too many unsettling innovations. But whatever the style of fighting, it needed an adequate supply of men; and the first problem was therefore to ensure a satisfactory flow of recruits. As to what sort of recuits, that was a matter on which he took a year or two to make up his mind. The experience of the War of Kalmar seemed to suggest that native conscripts could never expect to fight on equal terms with professional mercenary soldiers; and there were plenty of mercenaries in the Swedish army during the Russian war. But by the time that war was over he had come firmly down on the side of a national conscript army. It was cheaper; it had patriotism as a stiffener to morale; its relationship to himself would be as that of subjects to sovereign, so that its duties would be a matter of obedience to order, and not of the terms of an agreement capable of differing interpretations: there would be no nonsense, for instance, (as there frequently was with mercenary troops) about refusing to dig. Not least important, his men would use weapons which he prescribed for them, and not those which they happened to dislike least.

He began, then, with the reform of conscription. The 'Ordinance for Military Personnel', which Gustavus drew up personally – probably in 1620 – laid down in precise detail the procedures which were to be followed. In every parish all males over the age of fifteen were to be grouped into 'files' of ten men (or in the case of the peasants or the nobility, 'files' of twenty men), and from each file the king would draft as many as the security of the state might seem to require. The conscripts were not selected haphazard. The new model conscription commission included not only a military officer, but also the local sheriff, the jury of the hundred-court, and the parson of the parish. Thus the law, the local community and the church were available to temper military requirements. Gustavus intended a selection process which would reconcile the country's needs with the needs of the community; and for this the heavy weighting of the commission with men of local knowledge provided some security. The really indispensable man was the parish priest. For the clergy as a rule kept parochial records of baptisms, marriages and deaths; and they knew, better than anybody, who had attained the age of fifteen, and who had not. Thus they – and the standing jury of the hundred also – became in some sense the king's collaborators. And this was true not only in regard to conscription. The first decade of the reign saw many 'inquisitions' – investigations into maltreatment of peasants by the king's bailiffs, or by local nobles, fraudulent noble claims for exemption from services, peculation by the king's servants, evasion of taxation. The shortfall in the yield of Älvsborg's ransom provoked an especially stringent and thorough investigation of this sort; and its effectiveness depended largely on the co-operation of the local popular instances, and especially of the clergy, who on this occasion and afterwards provided the crown with an indispensable basis of reliable statistics.

Gustavus realized this very early. Among the rural population illiteracy was still so widespread that it was not unusual for the parson to be the only man in the parish who could read; and it fell to him, therefore, to communicate the decisions of the Diet to his flock, to broadcast royal proclamations from the pulpit, and – not least – to animate his hearers by royal propaganda. And just as the clergy provided much of the local knowledge required in order to lubricate the machinery of the conscription, so too they were used to provide the information required for the raising of taxes. The new taxes of the 1620s were all either in origin personal taxes, or soon in fact became so: the tax to redeem Älvsborg had fallen on everyone over the age of fifteen; by the end of the reign the Mill Tax had been converted into a personal tax payable by every person over the age of twelve. And just as the clergy had been the main source of information for the new type of conscription, so now they were bound to keep official lists of the taxable members of their congregations, and these lists were to be preserved not in the diocesan, but in the royal archives. This was clearly a very different matter from the keeping of lists of tithe-payers (or defaulters), and accounts of the yield of Easter offertories. The clergy had become the crown's unpaid civil servants. They did not relish the job. They complained, loudly and often, of the burden of 'clerking and summing' which had been laid upon them, to the prejudice of the proper discharge of their spiritual functions. And they were painfully aware of the odium they incurred among their parishioners by the invidious part they were forced to play in the assessment of taxes. Their burdens were indeed to be a little eased by the privileges granted to them by Christina in 1647, but they grew heavier than ever after Charles XI's Church Law of 1686, when for the first time they were obliged to keep a record of the movement of population into and out of their parishes.

The Ordinance for Military Personnel was much more than a successful regulation of the unsatisfactory arrangements which it supplanted. It was a social landmark. It heralded the advent in Sweden of the military state; and it stamped a pattern upon Swedish society which was to endure until 1720 – indeed, in the view of some historians, for longer than that. The military state is seen by those historians who in recent years have discussed it as a specific, distinct type of society in which human and material resources are systematically organized and regimented to subserve the state's overriding military demands. Most men in the seventeenth century would have agreed that it was the duty of a monarch to provide for the security of his subjects from attacks by a foreign power; and the military state can be seen as the logical acceptance of this responsibility. Much has been written on the military state in Prussia, or in Petrine Russia; but it seems that the first fully-fledged example of it is to be observed in the arrangements for which Gustavus Adolphus was responsible. It is not to be confused with what may be called a *militaristic* state, that is, one in which militarism is a matter of personal prestige, of social intercourse and manners, of brilliant uniforms, of the right to wear the sword in society – a state, in fact, where the military purpose may be subordinate or half forgotten, and the decorative, narcissistic considerations are all-important – just such a state as (ironically enough) Sweden was to become after 1721. The military state which Gustavus founded never allowed itself to be distracted from the purpose for which it was created, and for which it continued to exist: at first, self-protection against potentially hostile neighbours; later, the provision of resources for the offensive war that Sweden's predicament seemed to enforce; finally, under Charles XI, a total integration of human with material resources which should leave Sweden able to maintain a credible – and formidable – posture while resting on her arms. But it by no means implied a military *government*. Swedish statesmen, from Oxenstierna and Skytte to Johan Gyllenstierna, were almost all civilians. The expansion of the civil service, which was one result of Oxenstierna's reforms, created a bureaucracy which by Charles XI's time eclipsed the military in importance. The Swedish nobility, though they participated on a large scale in their country's wars, were not bound – as were the nobility in Prussia – to send their sons to the *Kadettenhaus*: a spell as an in-service trainee in the Supreme Court might well be a more solid investment than a cornetcy in a cavalry regiment. Certainly the way to the top did not lie only through the profession of arms: over the whole century 60 per cent of members of the Council were civilians; and during the two regencies, when the political predominance of the high aristocracy was most marked, only six military men entered the Council, as against twenty-six civilians. It is true that when in Charles XI's time society was carefully stratified by the Table of Ranks, the military came off very well; it is true likewise that at meetings of the Diet the Estate of Nobility showed a large majority of military members; and it cannot be denied that a typically militaristic ethos permeated the aristocracy. But though society might show militaristic traits, they were never in any danger of weakening or displacing the essentials of the military state, for the civilians who ran it kept them firmly in mind.

Not the least important of such characteristics was the state's unremitting control of its subjects. As Sven A. Nilsson noted, it was a state in which there could be no escape into anonymity: 'the state became a power which in an almost terrifying way kept an eye on its people from the cradle to the grave' – an anticipation (as Nilsson candidly adds) of that 'constantly-refined system of population-registration which in our own day numbers us all'. The welfare state, with whatever reluctance, must reckon the military state as among its ancestors. It is no wonder that it was Sweden which in 1752 produced the first reliable census. There has, however, been a tendency among some historians to view this system of control as extending beyond its purely military purpose. It was control, they assert, for control's sake. The state's interest in education, which is so marked in Gustavus, is seen as being motivated by a determination to discipline and control those that received it. The endeavours of the bishops to enforce church-attendance and a knowledge of the catechism, their concern with standards of morality, their hostility to the grosser forms of what is termed 'popular culture' (which might mean something a good deal less innocent than dancing round the Maypole) – all this is seen as having little to do with religion, and very much to do with a desire to strengthen episcopal authority. So too, the standing jury of the hundred, the popularly-elected vestries, the 'parish meetings' (in which all members of the congregation participated, including nobles and women) – these are no longer perceived in some quarters as examples of genuinely popular structures: they are dismissed as being simply local élites who became the willing tools of the crown. The expansion of the civil service was likewise not only a matter of utility or necessity: it was a device to extend the ambit of the state's control, and was designed with that end in view. All this pushes the thesis of 'control' a good deal further than the evidence warrants. Granted, for instance, that it is possible to discern some sort of symbiosis between state and Church, it is balanced by the intimate association of parson and people, and by the Church's courageous championship of the rights of the peas-antry. It was no improper thing for bishops and parsons to uphold the Christian principles to which *ex professo* they were committed. The 'control' thesis is challenged also by the survival, in vigorous activity, of the popular local instances and jurisdictions; and this remained true even when they were afforced by civil servants with a professional legal training. For tradition, custom and the sense of community continued to be a vital part of that 'rule of law' which had been firmly implanted in Swedish society since the Middle Ages: the advent of the professional lawyers, or the royal appointees, might serve to complement the custom of the country, but only rarely subverted it. In short, these developments are not satisfactorily explained by viewing them as manifestations of the crown's thirst for power, or as an aspect of a conspiracy of the élites to dominate the lower orders in their own interest. In Sweden, as in so many other countries in this century, the growth of the power of the state contributed essentially to what Elias has called 'The Civilizing Process'; and the fact that in Sweden this type of development happened to occur in a state which had become a typical military state implied no paradox.

From the purely military point of view the Ordinance for Military Personnel was a reform which applied only to the foot: the problem of the cavalry proved less tractable. Like his father, Gustavus made great efforts to compel the nobility to do knight-service; and like him he failed. Even in 1630, a peak year, the total number of horse provided by this means did not exceed 375. He had therefore to fall back on inducements to volunteer, and this proved to be a better solution. The cavalry he obtained was light cavalry, and its horses were smaller than the great chargers of Germany; but by the time he had finished he had made it the equal of any cavalry in Europe, and the superior of most. Thus, long before the beginning of the German war, the problem of recruitment had been solved.

The scope of that war was too vast for Sweden's manpower, and mercenaries were necessary from the beginning. In 1630 they accounted for perhaps half the Swedish army; in 1631, perhaps for three-quarters; in 1632, when the armies under his command reached 149,000, for nearly nine-tenths. There was no difficulty about recruiting them, for soldiers of fortune were only too willing to serve with a general who had the knack of victory. Yet the kernel of the armies of the

Swedish empire was always Swedish: the native troops formed an élite within the army, reliable when mercenaries turned mutinous, entrusted with the holding of key fortresses and vital positions, not to be squandered recklessly, less burdensome financially to the state. This last advantage was a consequence of the method of payment which was resorted to after 1620. Every soldier derived his pay from the revenues due to the crown – whether by way of rent (on crown lands), or of taxes (on freeholds) – and in peacetime he was quartered on a farm, giving aid to the farmer in return for his keep, while the farmer deducted the soldier's pay from his liabilities to the king. Officers were given farms of their own, the fiscal obligations of the farm being offset against the pay due. In wartime a proportion of the pay was in cash, but in the case of native troops the king was able to get away with monthly advances of a fraction of what was due to them; the deficiency being partly made good by the monetary contributions, *quarter* and *commis*, levied upon the country in which the army happened to be operating. This method of automatically functioning army finance (which applied only to native troops) remained an essential feature of the military administration for as long as the empire lasted.

One element in the new regulations for conscription was the provision of precisely defined recruiting areas corresponding to the provincial divisions of the new local government. This implied the creation of military adminstrative units on a provincial basis; that is, of provincial *cadres*. The first move towards provincial regiments was a scheme devised by Oxenstierna as early as 1616; but the system did not become effective until after 1621. It entailed the establishment of some fixed relationship between the provincial regiment and the tactical unit in the field: the one must be easily adaptable to the other, without any odd fractions of a provincial regiment being left over when it came to drawing up an order of battle. This was rare in early seventeenth-century armies. It necessitated a basic decision on what the size of the tactical unit should be. Soon after 1620 the decision was made: the basic unit for the foot was to be the squadron of 408 men, plus officers and NCOs. Two squadrons were together to form a field regiment; and each provincial regiment was to furnish three field regiments, or six squadrons. Thus the administrative and tactical units were firmly related to one another,

101

which had the double advantage of simplicity of administration and the preservation of provincial *esprit de corps*. Before the end of the reign, Swedish provincial regiments had been born which have survived until our own day. The same process was applied to the cavalry, which in 1623 received its allocation of recruiting areas and had its tactical unit established as the squadron of 175 horse: in 1628 the union of two squadrons formed the first (Västgöta) cavalry regiment, which still exists. So too with the artillery: the first artillery regiment dates from 1629.

These changes, and especially the decision on the size of the tactical unit, had far-reaching tactical implications. And it was mainly tactical considerations that determined the direction of the great programme of rearmament which had been carried to completion by 1630. Gustavus here took a firm line. The infantry were rearmed with the pike, despite their objections; the shot now had the musket as a standard weapon, and were provided with a lighter type of weapon than was usual in other armies; the cavalry, though still equipped with pistols, were also given swords, and Gustavus was determined that they should use them. As regards the artillery, the reign was a period of constant experiment and improvement. Gustavus was himself an expert gunner, and he was quite clear as to what he wanted; simplification of types; increased mobility, which implied less weight. He had his way in both particulars. By the end of the reign, guns were conveniently classified by the weight of shot they fired: twenty-four, twelve, or six pounders. A long series of experiments, under the king's personal supervision, led to the production in 1629 of the so-called 'regiment-piece'. This was a three-pounder: it required only one horse to move it, or it could at need be handled by two or three men; the ball was wired to a cartridge, which gave unprecedented rapidity of fire. It gave Sweden a decisive advantage. The regiment-piece was produced as a high-priority weapon: Gustavus took over eighty of them to Germany in 1630, and many others followed. When added to the exceptionally high standard of fire-drill which he managed to instil into his musketeers, the regiment-piece made the Swedish armies in Germany superior to all adversaries in concentrated and mobile fire-power, and gave Gustavus an advantage in gunnery which was rammed home by the extraordinarily high number of pieces (9.4 per thousand men in 1630) which were available in his German campaigns. He had another important asset in Sweden's resources of iron and copper, for Sweden was able to produce armaments at home more cheaply than they could be imported. He was thus able to insist on the standardization of calibres and windage. By 1632, Sweden, perhaps alone of European countries, was self-supporting in the matter of armaments.

The new weapons, and the new tactics they were intended to serve, demanded intensive training in their use. Maurice had been the first commander of modern times fully to appreciate the importance of drill, as a matter of weapon-training, for tactical flexibility in battle, and as an essential constituent of morale. Gustavus continued and developed the Maurician methods. He cared less than Maurice did for the intricate evolutions of the parade ground, being more concerned for what was practicable in battle. But he brought his native recruits to a level of disciplined efficiency which the critics of conscript armies had always alleged to be attainable only by experienced mercenaries; and in every interval of peace, or every breathing-space on a campaign, he was unremitting in practising his men in the kind of manoeuvre they might be called upon to execute in battle. The mercenary forces he enlisted were put to school under Swedish officers to relearn their trade according to Swedish notions, and they speedily learnt it well. It was more difficult to get them to conform to Swedish standards of discipline. These had been laid down in the Articles of War of 1621, drafted personally by Gustavus and revised by Oxenstierna. They were based upon many early codes of military law, but differed from all of them in that they were devised with a purely native army in view, and were thus not a matter for negotiation between the king and the military entrepreneurs. They were direct orders from the sovereign: they explicitly stated, for instance, that soldiers must dig when commanded to do so. And they provided for a regular heirarchy of courts-martial, culminating in the college of war. Under the strain of privation, or in the elation of victory, the Swedes in Germany undoubtedly committed atrocities (especially in the later stages of the war) which rather take the gilt off their traditional reputation as a godly army; but it was only rarely that they mutinied. Internal discipline was, and remained, very high.

All these reforms and innovations were made with clearly formed tactical objectives in mind; and all are important because they contributed to that tactical superiority which was the decisive reason for the Swedish victories in Germany. The ideal tactics are those which succeed in combining hitting-power, mobility and defensive strength; and judged by this standard neither the *tercio* nor Maurice's linear formation could be considered satisfactory. The opportunity was thus wide open for a commander who could avoid the defects of both schools, enable each arm of the service to exploit to the full its peculiar characteristics, and combine them so as to produce an effect transcending what each could achieve in isolation. Gustavus saw the opportunity, and he took it.

On the face of it, his battle orders were based on the Dutch school: two or three lines, with reserves; small units; a high proportion of officers and NCOs. Until about 1627 they were disposed primarily for defence, since his cavalry was still no match for the Polish horse. But from the beginning there was a difference: Maurice's lines were ten deep; Gustavus's only six, since he argued that if they were deeper the men would not hear the word of command. So too with the cavalry: by the time of Lützen it was drawn up no more than three deep. And it was intended to operate very differently from the cavalry of the Spaniards or the Dutch: the Poles had taught him better things. It was still armed with the pistol; but its real weapon was to be the sword, and its method of fighting was to be not pistol-popping but hand-to-hand encounter: in short, it was to use its natural advantage of mass, speed and shock. To do this effectively it needed to find a gap in the bristling pike-hedge that confronted it. By 1627 Gustavus had begun to attach musketeers to his cavalry, to blow holes in the opposing lines or squares: the first example of this comes at Wallhof (1626); it occurs again at Dirschau (1627). The idea was simple enough: the musketeers discharged their volley into the enemy ranks; the cavalry charged into the wreckage; and by the time they were ready to ride back from their charge the musketeers had had an opportunity to go through the slow process of reloading their weapons and were ready for the next volley.

The same principles were applied to the foot. Gustavus's squadrons contained a distinctly higher proportion of pikes than Maurice's; partly because he had not forgotten the lesson of Kirkholm, and realized that the shot needed strong pike protection against cavalry at the vulnerable moment when they were reloading, but also because he envisaged a very different function for the pike than that which was assigned to it in other contemporary armies. For him the pike was to be a battle-winning weapon, an offensive weapon thrusting at the enemy's heart. But if the pikeman were to do this successfully, he must (like the cavalry) be provided with an opening; and that opening could be made only by missile weapons. For the foot, as for the horse, close co-operation with the shot was the precondition of success: the combination of arms was essential. It was therefore necessary to achieve the maximum concentration of fire upon the right objective at the right moment. Maurice had aimed at continuity of fire; Gustavus, by rigorous training, was able to achieve it. But this was not enough: what he wanted was not a rolling fire but a shattering and demoralizing blast. And so he exploited the salvo, whereby the musketeers in alternate platoons or alternate ranks fired simultaneously, instead of firing successively as in Maurice's armies; and thus (to quote Sir James Turner),

> . . . you pour as much lead in your enemies bosom at one time as you do the other way at two several times, and thereby you do them more mischief, you quail, daunt, and astonish them three times more, for one long and continuated crack of thunder is more terrible and dreadful to mortals than ten interrupted and several ones.

This might mean that for some minutes, until they had reloaded, they would be virtually defenceless; but they would in the meantime have made such havoc in the enemy's ranks as to afford an opening for a push of pike, and the ensuing *mêlée* would give them the time they needed to recharge their muskets. Thus, both in cavalry and foot, battle tactics depended upon intimate and disciplined co-operation between firearms and cold steel, and this in turn upon careful training. There was to be a rhythmical alternation of discharge and charge; and the role of the shot was not to win victories, but to prepare the way for that hand-to-hand encounter which alone could win them.

This new style of fighting would in any case have been

105

sufficiently daunting to Gustavus's opponents, even though it had been pressed no further; but to the combination of foot and horse, pike and musket, he added a third element: the artillery. Before the Swedish irruption into Germany, artillery had had a largely static function. It fired from ravelins or hornworks; it battered fortifications from more or less protected emplacements; or, in the open field, it was planted at the front of the battle order, to make what practice it could before it was overrun by the enemy: artillery was used in this way by both sides as late as Breitenfeld. In existing conditions this was the only way in which it could be used, since it was so ponderous as to be virtually immobile in battle. But Gustavus transformed the role of the artillery; and this in two ways. First, by making it lighter it was possible to shift it from one position to another during the course of an engagement; it was so shifted, more than once, in the course of the battle of Lützen. The effects of the change were most brilliantly displayed at Torstensson's great victory at Janków in 1644, which was won mainly by the unprecedented speed with which the guns were moved to enable them to give the maximum assistance in the combat. Secondly, the artillery was for the first time linked in intimate co-operation with both infantry and cavalry; and this was made possible by the invention of the regiment-piece. Its function was to intensify the missile shock which was achieved by the salvo of the musketeers; and this its high manoeuvrability and rapid rate of fire enabled it to do. And not infantry only; for regiment-pieces, like musketeers, were also attached to the cavalry, and for them, as for the foot, provided the openings they needed for victory.

Thus Gustavus, alone among commanders of his age, succeeded in effecting a real combination of all arms of the service. It was, admittedly, an imperfect combination, especially in regard to the cavalry, since horsemen moved much more quickly than musketeers, and still more quickly than the men who had to handle the regiment-pieces. This meant that until within fifty yards or so of the enemy the cavalry's pace was reduced to little better than a walk, and the final cavalry onset, when it came, was nearer a trot than a gallop. It seems too that the lessening of the weight of guns was achieved only at the cost of their endurance. The combination was effective, moreover, only if the conditions were appropriate: at the Alte Feste, for instance, where the steep and broken nature of the ground forbade the manhandling of regiment-pieces, it failed; and at Lützen shortage of pikes gave the Swedes a harder battle than they had had at Breitenfeld. Still, it represented something superior either to the Spanish or the Dutch schools, and it was decisive in Germany: already by the time of Lützen Wallenstein was trying to imitate it. It depended for its success, to a great extent, on the high state of training of the individual units, the relatively high numbers of officers and NCOs, and the spirit of individual initiative which Gustavus succeeded in fostering.

Nevertheless it is clear that no system of military administration, however efficient, no system of tactics, however revolutionary, can succeed in the hands of an incompetent commander; and no explanation of Sweden's military ascendancy can ignore the fact that for two generations the country was able to produce commanders of exceptional quality. And Gustavus was the best of them. He was a general of much and varied practical experience. The itch to know everything and do everything himself, which was almost as marked in him as in Peter the Great, made him a master of every branch of the service. He was an enthusiastic drillmaster and trainer; he was an expert gunner; Monro admired him for his skill in 'recognoscing' (in which, indeed, he was often too venturesome for his safety); and he had a European reputation as a constructor of earthworks and field fortifications: at Werben, Nuremberg and Naumburg he demonstrated his mastery of the spade. There is no doubt that he derived a feeling of exhilaration from personal participation in the *mêlée*: this was not a commander who led his regiments from behind. In addition, he had other qualities which set him above his contemporaries. Unlike them, he saw battle as the logical end of manoeuvres; for only battle could produce that annihilation of the enemy which would bring total victory. If the early months of his campaign in Germany were marked by caution, that was because he must have a firmly held base area from which to operate, and because he could not hazard what was virtually his only army in rash enterprises. But after Breitenfeld it is clear that he sought battle, and that his strategy was designed to culminate in battle. Its objective was annihilation of the enemy, something very different from Wallenstein's

107

gouty strategy, and still more from the siege warfare of Maurice. And when the chance of battle came, Gustavus displayed a tactical audacity which made contemporaries gasp: no other general of his age would have attempted the passage of the Rhine at Oppenheim – and still less that of the Lech, in the face of Tilly's entire army drawn up in a carefully chosen position. The assault on Wallenstein's camp of the Alte Feste must appear extraordinarily bold even today, when one considers the difficulties it had to encounter. Add to these qualities his determination to share the hardships of his soldiers ('He is *commiles* with every man', as Sir Thomas Roe remarked), the authority which he derived from his regal as well as his military office, a personal charm and accessibility which neither derogated from the awe with which he was regarded nor was impaired by his violent but transient fits of rage, and lastly, that elusive quality which inspires men to feats of which they had not believed themselves capable. It was no wonder that Robert Monro, after long service in the Swedish armies, should have described him as 'the Captaine of Kings, and the King of Captaines', or that Alexander Leslie should write of him as 'the best and most valorouse commaunder that evir any souldiours hade', for Monro and Leslie had come under the sway of that dazzling fascination which Gustavus could deploy when he chose. It is perhaps more significant that Napoleon, who was not too generous with his compliments, should have included Gustavus in the small band – not more than six or seven in all – of the commanders whom he considered to be truly great.

. . .

NOTE

1. Charles XIII might be held to be an exception to this generalization, but his naval exploits antedated his accession by a couple of decades.

Chapter 8

THE SINEWS OF WAR

In 1621 the Swedish armies in Livonia numbered 17,800 men.
Eight years later, in Prussia, the numbers had risen to 26,500.
By November 1630, Gustavus had 42,100 under his command
in Germany; by December 1631, when the victory at Breitenfeld had brought men flocking to his standard, the figure was
83,200. Thereafter the numbers steadily increased, as his
operations came to embrace one part of Germany after the
other; and on the morrow of Lützen the forces at Oxenstierna's disposal reached the enormous total of 149,000. In
addition, there were strong native forces at home, in the Baltic
provinces, in Prussia, and in the navy. But of the 149,000
in Germany at least 82 per cent were mercenaries; and
mercenaries were terribly expensive. Besides the immediate
cash outlay which was required at the moment of enlistment
– the so-called muster-money – the cost of a mercenary foot
regiment at this time was of the order of 1,080,000 *riksdaler* a
year; that of a single cavalry company, about 300,000 *rdr*. The
official estimate of the cost of the German armies for 1633
(which was certainly a gross understatement) was 4,377,732
rdr.[1] What this meant to Sweden can be appreciated when it
is recalled that after 1613 it took six years of the most stringent
taxation, aided by loans from the Dutch, to raise the 1,000,000
rdr which Christian IV had exacted for the ransom of Älvsborg. In the face of figures such as these, the new system
whereby the native conscript army was automatically provided for by the allocation of specific land-revenues must
appear as a device of little more than marginal importance.

How was it done? How were these huge armies paid for?
How could Sweden, which had almost sunk under the burden

of the ransom for Älvsborg, possibly sustain an effort of this order of magnitude? It might be supposed that the answer to the problem is to be sought in the fact that Gustavus, like most contemporay monarchs, ran deeply into debt. At times this was so: in 1629, for instance, the debt was just under three millions. But this is a modest sum compared with the war budget for 1633. On the whole, the wars which made Sweden a great power were financed out of income; though not out of domestic income.

From the point of view of war finance, the reign falls into three clearly marked divisions. In the first period, which runs to 1627–28, Sweden is able to pay for the war without intolerable strains by reliance on conventional financial devices. In the second period, which runs from 1628–31, these devices prove inadequate; and though other resources are made available as a result of the victories in Livonia and Prussia, the financial situation becomes desperate, so that in 1630 it looks for a time as though the whole German enterprise is in danger of collapse. In the third period, which begins after Breitenfeld, the burden is firmly placed on the shoulders of Germany itself, so that at the time of Gustavus's death there seems no reason why Sweden should not continue to fight indefinitely, without being in any danger of overstraining her exiguous resources.

The war in Livonia, and (after 1626) in Prussia, was an undertaking more onerous than any upon which Sweden had ventured in the past; but for some years there was no reason to suppose that its demands could not be met by energetic measures by the government and increased sacrifices by the people. The most obvious way to meet them was by increasing taxes and reforming the fiscal system. In 1611 the ordinary revenues of the crown consisted mainly of taxes on freeholds, rents from crown lands, a royalty on precious metals (in which was included copper), and customs dues at the ports. After 1620 every effort was made to increase the yield of all of them; in particular, a long-overdue reassessment of land values did something to improve the revenues from the taxes on land. Moreover, 'aids' granted for specific purposes, and extraordinary taxes granted for a single occasion, tended to become permanent parts of the ordinary revenue. But the difficulty was that, apart from customs revenues, the major part of these taxes was paid in kind: in butter, iron, tar, hides, fish, copper, and a score of other commodities. The system had its advantages: among other things, it made the crown's revenues less liable to erosion by that price revolution which embarrassed monarchies elsewhere. Since many revenues were assigned to crown servants by way of wages, it placed in their hands the task of converting a portion of these commodities into cash; while for such revenues as were not assigned in this way the crown maintained a system of warehouses and marketed its store to the best advantage as opportunity offered. But it was not a handy system for fighting an overseas war: you cannot pay an army with butter or tar. An immediate need was therefore to convert these commodity revenues into cash revenues. One obvious method was to farm them. The first farm of taxes (for a single district) was effected in 1618; and it soon became a cardinal point of financial management: in 1621 Gustavus announced his intention of farming the entire revenues of the crown. Until 1629, a great part of the crown's income came to it in cash from the tax-farmers. Whereas in 1621 the revenue in cash amounted to 138,500 *rdr*, by 1624 it had risen to 588,000 *rdr*. The system brought the usual disadvantages from the point of view of the taxpayer; and by 1629 the extortions of the tax-farmers had produced such popular discontent that the government began to dismantle it. By 1635 all farms of direct taxes had been abolished. But in the meantime the device had greatly eased the burden of administration, and had produced the stock of coin which was indispensable to military operations.

Another obvious method was to pledge crown lands, or sell them outright, or to make over crown revenues in return for immediate payment of lump sums in cash. Alienations of this sort became common under Christina (though most of them, it should be noted, occurred *after* the war was over), and they lay at the root of the acute constitutional crisis of 1650: in the sequel they made necessary the resumptions of 1655 and 1680. Gustavus certainly initiated this policy, but in his reign it really made little headway in Sweden and Finland, though alienations on a massive scale occurred in the Baltic provinces.

It soon became apparent that the yield of the ordinary revenues, even when farmed on reasonable terms, was inadequate to meet the rising scale of war expenditure. There must be new, extraordinary impositions; and between 1620 and 1625 a reluctant Diet was induced to grant three such taxes. The first, in 1620, was the Stock and Land Tax, a direct tax assessed on the number of stock held or the acreage of land cultivated: it thus fell both on pasture and tillage. Moreover, in 1627 the nobility agreed that it should be paid by their tenants, not at half-rates (in terms of their privileges) but at full rates. The other two taxes infringed noble privileges even more directly, for they were to be paid not only by the nobility's tenants, but by the nobility themselves. This significant innovation began with the Little Toll of 1622, which was a toll on all consumable goods brought to market; and the consent of the First Estate to it had to be purchased by extensions of their privileges in other (mainly social) directions. The Mill Toll, of 1625, was a toll on all corn brought to be ground at the mill. It was a bad tax, for it made the grinding of corn at home in hand-mills illegal, and it entailed the principle familiar from the French *gabelle* – of assessing each household for tax on the basis of what the government considered it ought to consume, rather than what it did consume. It was avowedly a tax for military expenditure. Assented to with reluctance, it had a chequered and unhappy history; and it was eventually transformed into a direct tax in cash.

These extraordinary taxes were of great importance, in that they permanently breached the fiscal immunities of the nobility. In absolute terms they were quite productive: by 1632 the Stock Tax and the Little Toll were together yielding about 227,000 *rdr* a year, or about 10 per cent of the total, and down to about 1628 they formed a considerable proportion of the cash resources available to the crown; but in comparison with the swollen military expenditures of the close of the reign they were quite insignificant. The armies that fought at Breitenfeld and Lützen would need far more substantial resources than these.

Nevertheless, it may well be asked how it came about that the nobility, which had so plainly had the upper hand in 1611, could be brought to acquiesce in arrangements which pinched their pockets and infringed those privileges which had so lately been guaranteed. In part the answer is provided by the structure of Swedish society and the character of the nobility's most eminent members. In Sweden there was nothing like the feudal nobility of France, with its formidable local power-bases from which it could threaten or organize rebellion, or maintain a passive resistance to the crown. There were no great castles in noble hands which were places of strength: Per Brahe's Visingsö, Jakob de la Gardie's Läckö – or, a generation later, Karl Gustav Wrangel's Skokloster – were magnificent palaces, but they would have been incapable of serious resistance to any monarch who was determined to take them. The really important castles – Kalmar, Älvsborg, Stegeborg, Uppsala (and of course Stockholm) were in the crown's hands, and would remain so. An insubordinate nobility could not in Sweden recruit its forces by playing on provincial particularism; for despite local dialects and costumes Sweden was a strikingly unified country and the last attempt at political action by a particular province had been crushed long ago by Gustavus Vasa. Secondly, the nobility was broadly speaking in sympathy with the crown's policies – at least, as long as Gustavus was alive. It shared his apprehension of the dangers threatening the country from the Counter-Reformation; it was undoubtedly animated by a genuine patriotism, and prepared to make sacrifices for the sake of the country; and (not least) the great majority of the nobility – men whose circumstances were by no means brilliant, and whose style of living might not differ much from that of their tenants – saw in the king's wars an even chance of bettering themselves. Finally, the king's need of money led him, as it had led his father, to make grants of land, and the revenues from the land, to members of the aristocracy, in the expectation that they would do him good service. In exchange for an immediate supply of much-needed cash, he would pawn his revenues, or sell them on attractive terms. And to deserving persons he might also make outright gifts of land, and of the revenues it yielded. The crown thus offered, or seemed to offer, an offset against the increased burden of taxation and the erosion of noble privileges. But the appearance was in fact deceptive. Whereas by 1632 sales or pledges of crown land amounted to about 6 per cent of the king's *ordinary* revenue, and outright gifts to a further 7 per cent, this by no means balanced the yield of the *extraordinary* revenues arising from the new taxes of the 1620s to which the nobility increasingly found themselves liable. And as they were to find, privilege once lost could only rarely be recovered; but rights and revenues alienated by the crown might one day be resumed by it – as had happened during the first years of the reign, and as was to be demonstrated most painfully by the partial *reduktion* of Charles X, and the clean sweep of Charles XI after 1680.

One argument for the alienation of crown lands and revenues was that the personal concern of their new owners would lead to better cultivation, higher productivity, and hence increased indirect revenues. The better exploitation of the nation's resources, whether in land or not, was certainly one of the basic principles underlying Gustavus's economic policies. His object was to mobilize the country's resources for war, in order that Sweden might be self-sufficient, not least in armaments. The best prospect in this regard lay in developing Sweden's industrial potential. For this the prime requisite was capital, in which Sweden was hopelessly deficient. It was necessary therefore to attract capital from abroad, and Gustavus set himself to do it by providing inducements to foreign investors; with success, for Sweden was at that time an attractive field for investment. There were abundant mineral resources awaiting exploitation, and unlimited water-power and timber for fuel. There was a large pool of available labour to be had at attractively low wages, no important native vested interest to cause difficulties, and no religious persecution for Protestant entrepreneurs.

The result of this combination of favourable circumstances was a considerable influx of foreign capitalists and businessmen, mostly concerned in the metallurgical industries. They came from Liège, or from Amsterdam, or in a few cases from Germany: men with names which were already famous, or were destined to become so – Anton Monier, the de Besche brothers, the Siegroths, and above all, the great merchant and armaments-king Louis de Geer, with his widely ramifying European connections; and many of them settled permanently in Sweden. To them Gustavus leased mines and foundries and forges. They brought with them Walloon workmen, skilled in iron, who formed self-contained communities which retained their individuality for two generations; they brought new techniques in iron manufacture, notably 'Walloon-smithing'; and they founded the first large-scale iron industry in

Sweden. As a result of their efforts, Sweden had by the end of the reign become a large exporter of bar-iron and a considerable exporter of cannon; and it was these foreign workmen who made the Swedish armies more or less self-sufficient in the matter of armaments.

It was one of Gustavus's most cherished convictions that a country could not be wealthy without flourishing towns: the fact that towns in Sweden were few and small, he thought, was one reason for the country's poverty. As he looked at the nations of western Europe, it seemed to him that their wealth was concentrated in urban communities: kings who were well supplied with towns were well placed for borrowing money from rich burghers, and could swell their exchequers by heavier taxation. It was his policy, therefore, formulated in the Trading Ordinances of 1614 and 1616, to concentrate all foreign trade – 'active' as well as 'passive' – in a limited number of staple towns, and to forbid it to all others; at the same time ordering that no domestic retail trade should be permitted anywhere else. This latter was a bait which he was in no position to offer. Market towns in Sweden were few, insignificant and very widely scattered, and for those who lived in the country the sale – or very often the barter – of their produce was necessarily conducted at some convenient spot in the countryside. It was a practice which all the Vasas had attempted to suppress, by successive ordinances of great stringency: those who resorted to it were guilty of the notorious crime of *landsköp* (rural retailing). But the edicts and the prosecutions had invariably proved futile: for the countrymen *landsköp* was a necessity of life. Gustavus soon found, as his predecessors had found, that his policy in this respect was unenforceable. The solution, he concluded, was simply to create more towns, and so give the peasant or the rural craftsman outlets for their goods. He therefore set about founding new towns, especially along the coast of the Gulf of Bothnia, where hitherto there had been virtually no towns at all, and he tried to persuade or compel the local populations to migrate to them. Any increase in the number of towns had an important fiscal aspect also, after the introduction of the 'Little Toll' (1622), which was a duty upon all goods brought to market in a town, payable at a customs-hedge specially erected to collect it. But this proved no solution to the problem either. The influx into the new towns was minimal; *landsköp* continued as before; the new towns served no need and made no economic sense; and until the nineteenth century most of them led a languishing and precarious existence: at the end of his life Gustavus himself described them as 'idle, rotting and tumbledown', and a member of the Council dismissed them as 'thieves' kitchens': the best of them were no more than fishing hamlets. In the south, indeed, the new town of Borås proved a paradoxical exception. It throve on the ruins of his policy; for its privileges in fact gave it a monopoly right to practise *landsköp*; and for the next two centuries the Borås pedlars made their small fortunes, and served wide areas of Sweden, by supplying little necessities which would otherwise have been less easy to obtain. Nevertheless, the king's enthusiasm for towns could register one great success: Gothenburg. The town had been founded by Charles IX, but had been destroyed during the War of Kalmar. Gustavus refounded it, on a site selected by himself, once Älvsborg had been recovered in 1619. It was designed to be Sweden's great port for those exports to western Europe which he was so anxious to encourage; and it did indeed become the natural outlet for the increasingly important iron of Värmland and the Bergslag. It was provided with generous privileges; and it started under favourable auspices by attracting (with royal encouragement) Dutchmen and Scots, who brought with them the commercial acumen of their homelands. They were, regrettably, Calvinists, but this he was prepared to overlook (as the Charter entitled him to do in such cases); and in practice they enjoyed full religious freedom. In effect Gothenburg was, and long remained, a Dutch colony.

This exception notwithstanding, the towns did not escape the government's characteristic attempts to rationalize, order and make uniform, in the interest of ensuring the efficient discharge of their functions. Among the flood of reforms which is so conspicuous in the years after 1617 was a great statute for the towns, drawn up by Oxenstierna in 1619. It would have remodelled and made uniform the structure of municipal government; but in the event the difficulty of any general application deterred the king from sanctioning it. He tried, nevertheless, to effect its object by applying it piecemeal, and five towns were remodelled on Oxenstierna's principles; but thereafter the preoccupations of war prevented any further progress. But if municipal government escaped

116

wholesale reformation, the gilds did not: the commission appointed in 1621 to revise their regulations and eradicate their abuses, and the regulations which the commission drew up, provide a typical example of the king's desire to organize the economy into forms which could be easily supervised and directed. And one persistent problem of town government was dealt with in 1624, when Gustavus pressured a reluctant Diet to approve his personal draft of the first really comprehensive Poor Law in Swedish history. Finally, he made a start with an improvement in Swedish communications, without which the development of the economy must remain hamstrung. The first important canal linking the great lakes of central Sweden was the result of his initiative; his journeys round the country led him to insist on considerable improvements in the roads; in 1620 came the first Swedish postal system, completed by Oxenstierna in 1636: an innovation whose importance would be emphasized when Sweden moved into Germany. And in 1617 Sweden's first analogue to a Navigation Act gave tariff reductions or exemptions to Swedish armed merchantmen, especially if manned by Swedish crews.

The same concern for increasing his revenues through expanding the country's trade inveigled him into other ventures, less sound and less successful than the foundation of Gothenburg proved to be. It led him, for instance, to swallow a scheme, propounded to him in 1626 by that restless individual Willem Usselincx, for a Southern Company, designed to be an imitation of the Dutch East India Company: it was to make its profits by supplying commodities to the (unfortunately imaginary) continent of Magellanica. Not surprisingly, it did not thrive. He tried his hand, too, at royal monopolies, in the hope of fat profits: a salt monopoly, which began in 1627, and had failed hopelessly within two years; a monopoly of grain exports from the Baltic region which for a time did rather better, thanks to the goodwill of the Tsar. In 1630 it brought in 108,500 *rdr*, though by 1632 the profits had fallen to 22,882 *rdr* – figures which are a sufficient comment on Porshnev's attempts to argue that Gustavus's successes in Germany depended on the aid of Russia.

More important for supplying the sinews of war than any of these devices was the development of the export trade in

117

copper. Copper, wrote Oxenstierna in 1630, was 'the noblest commodity which the Swedish Crown produces or can boast of'. It was obtained almost entirely from one great mine at Falun, worked by hundreds of free miners, each with his carefully defined share. Unlike iron, it did not require large resources of capital for its working. What it did require, in Gustavus's opinion, was an efficient marketing organization, for there was in the early 1620s an exceptionally favourable market-opportunity. The European demand for copper was rising; partly for armaments, but especially for minting, for these were the years when Spain was operating on a vellon currency, of which copper was a main constituent. It happened, too, that copper was in short supply. The wars in Germany cut off the Transylvanian mines from their markets, and there was no other serious competitor until, in the second half of the decade, the Dutch began to bring consignments from Japan. Finally, one of Gustavus's imported experts, Govert Silentz, around 1620 introduced a new fining process into Sweden which greatly improved the quality of Swedish plate copper.

To this opportunity Gustavus responded by the creation, in 1619, of the Swedish Trading Company. The company was given a monopoly of the marketing of copper; it was to pay a fixed price to the miners, and a duty to the crown on every ship-pound of copper that came into its hands. The leading shareholders were Monier and de Geer. To begin with, it was a success; and for some years after 1619 it made a vital contribution to the royal revenues: the amount payable in duties was estimated at 327,000 *rdr* for 1625–26, and 337,000 *rdr* for 1627. By that time it was running into difficulties. First, because Gustavus raised the rate of duty to a level which the company could not afford to pay, and insisted on a minimum selling price for copper which after 1626 proved unattainable; secondly, and this was decisive, because Spain went off vellon and returned to a silver currency in 1626. The result was a fall in the price of copper which knocked the bottom out of the company's finances. Copper did recover somewhat after 1631; but what mattered was that it had crashed in the previous four years. It was this that caused the first real crisis in financing the war. Until 1627 it had been conceivable that Gustavus might succeed in paying for his foreign policy by the means we have been describing; after 1627 it was utterly impossible. Domestic resources were no longer adequate; it was necessary to find other means.

In this emergency salvation came in three ways. First, Gustavus took to minting the copper he could not sell overseas. The new copper coinage professed to be an intrinsic coinage: every piece should be worth its face value. But as the price of copper fell, the new coins had to be weightier and weightier if they were to be acceptable at all, and in the end they attained monstrous proportions: special sledges had to be constructed to transport the higher denominations, and thieves are said to have shrunk from the prospect of loading themselves up with such exhausting booty. Moreover, the less copper that could be sold abroad the more had to be put into circulation at home, with the predictable consequence of adding inflation to the king's other problems. On the other hand, the cost of the armies could in part be met, the inhabitants of occupied territories could be fobbed off, at a relatively economical rate, however much they might dislike it, since they were in no position to complain. Livonia and Prussia found themselves deluged with a flood of ponderous copper; and it continued to flow into Germany, even though the worst of the financial crisis might, after Breitenfeld, be over. In 1632 Gustavus ordered that the entire output of the Falun mine for that year should be minted into copper *Kreutzer* and shipped to Germany to defray transactions with the civilian population – all of which led one historian[2] to the rash conclusion that the real reason for the Swedish entry into the Thirty Years War was the need to find a vent for unsaleable copper: a theory which has found few adherents. But it remains true that in the financial crisis of 1629–31 copper was still of importance. It would be absurd to maintain that copper won the war; but not unreasonable to suggest that it helped to save Gustavus from losing it.

The second resource which made it possible to surmount the crisis was the exaction of contributions from occupied Prussia. It was an idea which occurred to Gustavus as early as 1628. In a letter to Oxenstierna of 1 April of that year he wrote that the only resource now was to 'strengthen the army by ruining the enemy'; and added, in an oft-quoted phrase, 'if we cannot say *bellum se ipsum alet* [war pays for itself], I see no way out of all that we have engaged in.' He had in fact already begun to apply this principle: in the winter of 1627–28 the occupied areas in Prussia were made to yield no less a sum than 700,000 *rdr*, which very nearly paid the cost of the army that exacted it. This was a rate which it proved impossible to maintain; but the importance of the Prussian contribution may be seen from the fact that the army-estimates for 1628 provided for Sweden's paying 310,000 *rdr* against Prussia's 253,000. In the event, Prussia did in fact provide about 250,000 *rdr* this year. In the crisis year of 1630, as the result of extraordinary efforts, Prussia and Livonia between them were made to produce 758,000 *rdr*.

But the occupied area in Prussia, rich though it was, was too small to meet the ever-growing demands upon it. Some other source of revenue had to be found. What helped to save the situation in the bad years from 1628 to 1631 was the ship-toll at the Baltic harbours. A Swedish squadron stationed in Danzig Roads had begun to collect tolls from ships of all nations visiting the port as early as the summer of 1626. In July 1627, as a result of strained relations with George William of Brandenburg, tolls began to be collected at Pillau also, and Pieter Spierinck, an enterprising Dutchman, was given the job of supervising them. At Spierinck's suggestion, the system was extended to cover all the harbours in Ingria, Estonia and Livonia; to which were added, in 1628, Courland and Memel, and, later, Stralsund. The effect was that virtually the whole trade of western Europe to Eastland was now mulcted by Swedish customs officers, backed where necessary by the Swedish fleet. The action aroused bitterness in the English, but especially in the Dutch, for whom the Eastland trade was of the first importance. But Oxenstierna, remarking that he had never yet heard of a merchant's being killed by high customs dues, was not prepared to make concessions to appease Protestant powers who had shown themselves so unready to give Sweden effective assistance.

The results were impressive: in 1629 the tolls produced 584,000 *rdr*; and it was confidently estimated that they would produce about the same amount in 1630. It was of crucial importance that they should; for 1630, with the huge cost of newly recruited regiments, and all the expense of transporting the army to Germany, was a critical year. In fact, the estimate proved disastrously wrong. With the Swedish invasion of Germany obviously impending, neutral merchantmen were avoiding the Baltic that summer; an unusual drought so lowered the waters of the Vistula as to be a hindrance to navigation; an outbreak of plague frightened off many who might otherwise have ventured. The yield of the tolls dropped to 361,000 *rdr*; with the result that the whole German expedition was imperilled. Copper seemed to have failed; the tolls had apparently failed too. And in this situation Sweden and Finland were called upon in a single year to provide 2,368,000 *rdr* in cash.

It was impossible to suppose that they would be capable of such an effort again in 1631; if the German campaign were not to perish of inanition, war must somehow be made to support war. This would be possible only if Gustavus could occupy large areas of German territory fairly quickly. And for this his army was not large enough. If it were to be made larger, he must recruit more mercenary regiments – at a million *rdr* a year per regiment! No territorial expansion without more financial resources; no more resources without the conquests which only a larger army could effect. Financially and militarily, the autumn and winter of 1630–31 was probably the darkest and most critical moment of the whole reign: the unpaid mercenaries were on the verge of mutiny. Before long, things improved: the Treaty of Bärwalde, concluded with France in January 1631, promised Sweden an annual subsidy of 400,000 *rdr*; the tolls picked up again in 1631 and yielded 553,000 *rdr* (they reached 660,000 *rdr* in 1632); but these developments came too late to tide Gustavus over the crisis.

Somehow or other he contrived to live through it and keep his army together to win the battle of Breitenfeld. From that moment the financial picture was transformed. Money for new mercenary regiments came in without stint, and for as long as he lived he was never really in financial difficulties again. The change had been heralded as early as August 1630. At the end of that month Gustavus had imposed an agreement upon Pomerania to contribute 200,000 *rdr* to the Swedish war chest, and in addition to supply quarters and provisioning to the Swedish army. It was the beginnings of the system whereby the financial problem was finally solved. The example of Pomerania was followed by friendly (or frightened) German princes, some of whom were allowed to collect the contributions themselves rather than leave the

Swedish quartermasters to do it for them; and a similar system was imposed upon occupied enemy territories. And so evolved a regular financial administration, whereby each unit of the army was allocated a territory for its maintenance. It was all admirably organized, with a proper accounting system. It was operated, on the whole, with good order; and if it was stringent, it seems also to have been fair. Contributions were in cash, and this fact entailed the consequence that the Swedish occupying forces could not afford indiscriminate plunder: trade must go on, markets must be held, towns must be spared, or the territory would never be able to pay the contribution that was required of it. Contributions on this methodical basis were not a Swedish invention: they had been organized by Wallenstein. But the Swedes took over, improved, and extended Wallenstein's practice; and till as late as the reign of Charles X contributions formed a normal and essential feature of Swedish war finance. Their relative importance may be judged from the fact that in the closing years of the war the small territory of Bremen-Verden annually provided more money than the sum of the subsidy paid by France.

The French subsidy, though it became more important later on, was relatively insignificant in 1632; the Dutch subsidy was both trivial and shortlived; the contribution of Saxony, at 40,250 *rdr* a month, was more important than either. In addition there were the ransoms paid by captured towns to avoid plunder: Munich, for instance, was made to pay the swingeing sum of 300,000 *rdr*; Landshut and Freising got off with 100,000 *rdr* apiece. And finally there were the loans, of which the most substantial was the 100,000 *rdr* from Nuremberg.

But all this was only the tip of the iceberg. As Sven Lundkvist has shown, the exactions in kind – for quarter, food, fodder, fuel – were in the early 1630s vastly more important. The amounts collected were startling. The friendly town of Erfurt, in addition to paying a contribution of 14,000 *rdr* a month, between September 1631 and April 1632 provided commodities valued at 354,848 *rdr*. Between 25 June and 26 August 1632, when the Swedish army lay encamped in Nuremberg, the city's supply of bread alone amounted in value to 495,340 *rdr*: compared with this, Richelieu's annual subsidy of 400,000 *rdr* was unimportant. Statistics such as these make the treasury's estimates and budgets for war expenses virtually meaningless. For 1633, for instance, the war budget was estimated at 4,377,732 *rdr*: the true figure Lundkvist guesses to be anywhere between twenty and thirty millions.

This enormous escalation in the cost of war, and the success in meeting it, radically altered the whole financial situation from the point of view of the Swedish authorities at home. After 1630 the war practically financed itself. This appears most clearly from the amounts of cash which it was necessary for Sweden and Finland to pay in order to keep it going. The following table shows the decline in the burden on the Swedish taxpayer – or at any rate, the decline in the amount demanded for the German war:

Year	Cash provided by Sweden and Finland (in *rdr*)
1630	2,368,000
1631	1,147,278
1632	476,439
1633	128,573

These figures refer, of course, only to sums sent to Germany – there were still heavy burdens to be borne to maintain the navy, the fortresses, the troops at home, and the armies in Livonia and Prussia. But these were burdens which it was not beyond Sweden's ability to carry. After 1633, certainly, it became a maxim of Swedish policy, more than once enunciated by Oxenstierna, that the German war must pay for itself. It did not always do so: the Imperialist recovery after Nördlingen (1634) and the disaster of the Peace of Prague (1635) deprived Sweden of those large areas of German territory which were essential to the maintenance of the system. Hence the anguish of Oxenstierna when the Prussian tolls were given up by the truce at Stuhmsdorf (1635); hence the difficult back-to-the-wall campaigns of Banér in the late 1630s; hence the new importance of the French subsidies in 1638 and afterwards. But though it was never altogether possible to dispense with assistance from home, there were times when the Swedish armies came within measurable distance of it. And the memory of those times imprinted itself on the next generation of Swedish statesmen: they never forgot – least of all Charles X – that though their country might be unable of its own resources to support an army adequate to ensure security in an emergency, security might nevertheless be had if they were prepared to take the calculated risk of hiring enough mercenaries without being able to pay them – provided (and this was essential) that they got them on to enemy soil quickly, and occupied enough of it to make possible a repetition of Gustavus's feat of making war sustain war.

But the sinews of war, after all, were not either then or afterwards simply a convenient metaphor for money. In stark reality those sinews were implanted in 'men of like passions with ourselves', men subject to strains which could in the end become unendurable, men liable to be weakened by scanty rations, men liable to fall victims to disease. The wars which Sweden fought from 1621 to 1632 made dreadful inroads upon her population. Year after year came levies of conscripts: in 1621–22 14,000 men were sent over to Livonia; between 1626 and 1630 levies averaged somewhere between 10,000 and 15,000 a year, with a peak in 1627. In 1630–31 Sweden and Finland sent 25,000 recruits to Germany. The percentages of losses were formidable: of the 14,000 troops shipped to Livonia in 1621–22, 6,000 never returned; of the 25,500 who went to Germany in 1630–31 more than half were dead two years later. The total losses for the decade 1621–31 amounted to probably not less than 50,000: this out of a population of just over a million. All armies of the period suffered comparable losses: in the Flanders campaign of 1635 the French army lost 18,000 men by disease, out of a total of 26,000. But France had a much greater supply of manpower to draw on. Relatively few of the Swedish losses are accounted for by men who fell in battle. They fell victims to the 'camp fevers' – typhus, typhoid, dysentery, plague – which ravaged encampments and winter quarters. The king's own family, and those attending him, were not exempt: his brother, Charles Philip, died of typhus in 1622; in the winter of 1625 Gustavus wrote to Oxenstierna 'Lars Nilsson and Peder Erson are both sick, which means that I'm secretary and chamberlain. I need only to be orderly, and I'll be the whole staff.' Thus the prudent policy of conserving the Swedish elements in the army by setting them to garrison occupied towns or hold vitally important positions often meant in practice condemning them to death: had they been active in the field, life-expectancy might well have been higher.

Such losses had their effects at home. In practically every year of the late 1620s there were disturbances, minor risings, resistance to the conscription; and among the conscripts desertions were notorious. The instructions which Gustavus left for the government in Stockholm during his absences regularly included directions for measures to be taken in the event of trouble; the clergy were urged to bring home to their parishioners, by doomsday sermons and frequent 'days of prayer', a sense of their Christian and patriotic duty to support the fainting Protestant cause. Inevitably the drain of manpower had perceptible economic consequences: for lack of labour farms became unproductive, and in the worst event might become 'waste', to the detriment of the crown's revenues. When in 1627 Gustavus forced the nobility to agree to the conscripting of their tenants on the same terms as applied to the rest of the population, their estates suffered severely from a shortage of hands – Oxenstierna's own estate at Tidö being no exception: indeed, in that year the king expressly ordered that the new levies should be taken 'in the first place' from the peasants of the nobility. In 1628 the chancellor's brother, Gabriel Gustafsson Oxenstierna, was writing to him that 'the common man wishes himself dead'; two years later he informed him that 'the country is so drained of men through these last four stringent levies that it seems to be on its last legs; and if this were to continue for another year or so we might indeed say that we have conquered lands from others, and in doing so have ruined our own'. Admittedly, Gabriel Gustafsson was constitutionally inclined to take a gloomy view of things; but in these instances he was not far from the truth. By 1632 there was a noticeable surplus of women over men. The shortage of manpower on the land might on occasion be met by reorganizing the village economy in such a way as to make it possible for women to take over the main burden of providing subsistence, as has recently been demonstrated[3] in regard to the Norrland village of Bygdeå; and the representatives of the local community on the conscription commissions might contrive to so arrange matters that the conscripts taken were those whose absence would do least damage to the community's welfare. But it is far from certain that Bygdeå can in these respects be considered typical of many others.

When Gustavus fell at Lützen the worst was probably already over. After 1632 levies became less frequent and less stringent. Oxenstierna's policy was now to leave the war to be fought by the Germans; and Sweden's objective had become to get out of it on tolerable terms. The mortality from disease was diminished by arranging for regiments to be given in rotation a spell of home leave. The regency made efforts to reassure discontented elements by personal contact and salutary persuasions. But from 1621 to 1631 'the sinews of war' had been subject to strains such as they were never to experience again until the reign of Charles XII.

. . .

NOTES

1. Statistics for this chapter are mainly borrowed from Einar Wendt, *Det svenska licentväsendet i Preussen, 1627–1635*; Sven Lundkvist, 'Svensk Krigsfinansiering, 1630–1636'; and Sven A. Nilsson, *De stora krigens tid.*
2. Friedrich Bothe.
3. By Jan Lindegren.

Chapter 9

THE PATH TO THE SUMMIT

In the summer of 1630 the fate of the Holy Roman Empire hung in the balance, and upon which way the beam should tip depended the destiny of the German people, and hence perhaps the destiny of Europe. The victories of the armies of the Emperor and the League had by 1629 placed Ferdinand II in a position in which there was a good chance of establishing his authority more effectively than any of his predecessors for a hundred years. But his very success had called forth a reaction, in the name of those 'German liberties' which served as a stalking-horse for the particularism of German princes. Faced with the prospect of an Empire which was a reality and a Germany united by force, allies, neutrals, and enemies among the German princes united to defend their concept of the constitution. The principle of Imperial unity was confronted with the principle of disintegration, and at the Diet of Regensburg the electors – the Catholic Maximilian of Bavaria, no less than the Lutheran John George of Saxony – joined forces to administer a sharp check to the Emperor's assertion of his sovereignty. They declined to elect his son as King of the Romans, and forced him to dismiss his general, Wallenstein. At the moment when Gustavus landed on Usedom, German politics had once more been brought into an uncertain equipoise.

The equipoise was destroyed by foreign intervention: the intervention first of Sweden, and later of France. The victories of Gustavus threatened the overthrow of the Habsburgs, and led to the organization of the politics of disruption under Swedish patronage. When death had removed Gustavus from the scene, German patriotism for almost the last time rallied to the Emperor at the Peace of Prague in 1635. Then French intervention in alliance with Sweden prevented the Emperor's exploiting the opportunity, and forced Germany to accept a peace which was made palatable to the princes by its recognition of anarchy as a constitutional principle. By 1648 it was clear that Germany must renounce any prospect of being a nation-state like England, France, Sweden, or even Spain.

It was not in these terms that Gustavus saw the German situation. His only interest in the clash of principle in the Empire was its possible effects upon his enterprise. The dismissal of Wallenstein, and the reduction of the armies of Emperor and League which followed it, greatly diminished the initial dangers of his campaign. That thousands of Imperial troops were locked up in Italy, fighting to keep France's candidate out of the succession to Mantua, was another uncovenanted piece of good luck. But the political situation was more difficult to assess, and at bottom more intractable, than the military. The Diet of Regensburg had seemed to foreshadow the emergence of a 'third party' in Germany, a party prepared to stand neutral between the Emperor and his adversaries. Much depended upon the strength and resolution of those princes who were inclined to this position: in particular, upon George William of Brandenburg and John George of Saxony, whose electorates might be made a barrier against Imperial power in north Germany.

It was conceivable, in 1630, that a 'third party' might take shape which would do Gustavus's work for him, and by pushing back the Emperor from the Baltic shore give to Sweden the political and religious security he was seeking. If this should happen, he might be prepared to withdraw from his German campaign altogether, retaining only an outpost in Stralsund; alternatively he might hope to share the burden of defending north Germany with neutral states anxious to restore peace to this area. Twice in the autumn of 1630 he made offers to John George on these lines. They met with no response, for John George was a patriotic German who hated foreign intervention. He was the greatest Lutheran prince in Germany, and as such regarded Gustavus as a competitor for the leadership of German Protestantism. By tradition and principle he was disposed to support Imperial authority so long as it was not abused. He was also short-sighted, procrastinatory, and a lover of peace: not a man to do Gustavus's errands for him. As for George William of Brandenburg, caught in a cross-fire of Swedish and Imperialist menace, with scarcely the simulacrum of an army and an electorate already drained by Imperialist requisitions, his only assets were a flaccid tenacity and a certain influence on John George. From a 'third party' with such leaders not much was to be expected.

Gustavus could hardly hope to attain his objectives without German allies. Potential collaborators existed in north and north-central Germany, among princes less determinedly neutral than Saxony and Brandenburg: William V of Hesse-Cassel, or the Welf dukes of Brunswick, or the dukes William and Bernard of Saxe-Weimar; but at the moment of the Swedish landing they were in no condition to stir. Some were willing but impotent, some were extruded from their territories, some were too timid to take risks. For the moment he had not a single ally in Germany; nor, for that matter, outside it. He waded into the morass of German politics unassisted and alone.

This political isolation entailed military difficulties which in turn reacted unfavourably on the political prospects. The prime objective of the expedition was the eviction of Imperialist armies from the Baltic coastlands; but if those lands were to be secure the Imperialists must be defeated in battle and pushed as far away as possible. For this Gustavus at first lacked the resources. His army was too small for victory, but it was too big to be fed in the area it occupied. The speedy enlargement of his original bridgehead was an urgent necessity. But every expansion entailed a drain of troops into garrisons at the expense of the field army; and every forward move was likely to mean an infringement of somebody's neutrality, and the alienation of sympathy by the enforcement of requisitions. It was precisely this sort of violence which had united the German princes in hostility to Wallenstein. Hence measures which might be militarily unavoidable might prove politically counter-productive.

In the period which immediately followed the landing, military needs took precedence over all else. At whatever political cost, Stettin must be secured and held against possible Imperialist attacks; the bridgehead must be extended on either side of the Oder. As soon as possible, the Imperialists must be evicted from Gartz and Greiffenhagen, and the way be opened for a possible advance up the Oder against Habsburg Silesia. Even this programme proved far from easy to carry out. The Imperialist forces in Pomerania were neither large in number nor impressive in quality, but Gustavus for some months dared not risk a major engagement for lack of cavalry. He made a beginning with the clearing of eastern Pomerania, but not until Christmas 1630 did he dislodge the Imperialists from Gartz and Greiffenhagen, and not until February 1631 was he able to bring the greater part of Mecklenburg under his control.

It was during this trying period that Gustavus acquired his first allies, and we can see the gradual crystallization of a policy (or rather, policies; for there was more than one) in concluding treaties with the German states. The first ally of all was the city of Magdeburg, which concluded a treaty with Sweden on 1 August 1630. Magdeburg had triumphantly survived a protracted siege by Wallenstein in 1629. Even before the German landing Gustavus had his agents there, and it was they who now induced Magdeburg formally to defy the Emperor. Gustavus heard the news with exultation: the revolt, he wrote, would be 'a signal-flare of rebellion for the whole of Germany'. If Magdeburg could make good its revolt, Gustavus would have at his command not merely one of the great cities of Germany, but a bastion and a crossing-place on the Elbe of high strategic importance, affording him access to the Lower Saxon Circle and the restive Protestant princes of that region. The natural assumption had been that when he came to Germany his best line of operations against the Emperor would lie up the Oder and through Silesia. The revolt of Magdeburg opened the way to other possibilities which might complement a campaign in Silesia. From this moment his strategy is influenced, and finally dominated, by the need to break through to the Elbe and fulfil his pledge to his new ally. Fortunately there seemed to be no great hurry. The siege of Magdeburg was for many months not much more than a loose blockade; the reports about available supplies of food, arms and gunpowder were reassuring; morale was high. It did not appear probable that he would be called upon to make good his word to send aid before his armies had been sufficiently expanded to enable him to do it without undue risk.

Some three weeks after the treaty with Magdeburg, Gustavus concluded with Pomerania an alliance of a very different character. Soon after the landing on Usedom he had ferried a portion of his army across the Haff direct to Stettin. There he compelled Duke Bogislaw XIV to sign a treaty.[1] It put a Swedish garrison in Stettin; and it assured to the Swedish army such supplies as Pomerania could still provide, with a cash contribution of 200,000 *rdr*. Here, then, begins the system of regulated and orderly quartering upon German territory to support the forces of the deliverer. The treaty was important to Gustavus not only for its military but for its political implications; and above all as a possible means of exerting pressure on his brother-in-law, George William of Branden-burg. Bogislaw was elderly, childless, and not likely to live much longer. When he should die, his prospective heir (though not the only possible claimant) was George William. Gustavus therefore inserted into his Pomeranian treaty a unilateral reservation to the effect that if, at the time of Bogislaw's death, George William had not ratified it, and had not also given effective aid against the Imperialists; or if the succession were in any way disputed (as it was certain to be); then he would take Pomerania into his 'sequestration and protection' until such time as he should have been compen-sated for his war expenses, the disputed succession should have been cleared up, and the next duke should have ratified the treaty. Whatever happened, he could not afford to see Pomerania pass into neutral or unfriendly hands.

In the autumn of 1630 he extended his diplomatic activity to the princes west of the Elbe, and especially to William V of Hesse-Cassel. On 11 November he concluded with the Hessian representatives the so-called Contingent Conven-tion.[2] It marks the beginning of a new development in Swedish policy. Whereas Gustavus's relations with Stralsund and Pomerania had been designed to give him permanent security in this area after the war, he was now about to weave a pattern of treaties to last only for the duration of hostilities, and shaped to meet short-term military needs. Such a treaty was the Contingent Convention. Like the Pomeranian treaty, it gave him quarters for his troops, control of fortresses and the supreme command. Unlike that treaty, it involved the virtual subjection of one party to the other: Hesse was to be in Gustavus's 'protection' for as long as the war should last; the alliance was to be an offensive league, aimed explicitly against the Emperor; William V was committed to fight for Sweden's 'safety and welfare', and to go on fighting 'until we have achieved our aims'. In short, the treaty entailed a surrender of Hesse's sovereignty for the duration of the war. These were rigorous terms. Yet if Gustavus was to venture across the Elbe in pursuit of victory over Tilly's armies, he could clearly not afford to take any chances.

William V declined to ratify the Convention for the present. What restrained him was a rekindling of the hope of forming a strong 'third party' in Germany: a solid Protestant bloc which could stand on its own feet between the Emperor and the King of Sweden. Many German Protestant princes saw in the Swedish invasion a unique chance to extort reasonable treatment from the Emperor; few or none wished to see themselves reduced to the status of Swedish clients. If they could form a league with an agreed policy and an army capable of inspiring respect, they might simultaneously restore the political balance in Germany and render the Swedish intervention superfluous.

Their prospects of doing this depended essentially upon John George of Saxony, and their best hope of influencing him lay through the Elector of Brandenburg, to whom it seemed that only a Protestant league offered any chance of rescuing him from his forlorn and dangerous situation. It was in fact George William who persuaded John George to summon a congress of Protestant states to Leipzig in February 1631. It was a great gathering of princes and their representatives, Lutherans and Calvinists meeting together in unwonted harmony. But though they contrived to avoid the more provocative forms of theological polemic, they failed to reach a satisfactory solution to their political problem, largely because John George was not prepared to accept a league such as they had desired. He conceded the principle that the participants should so far defy the Emperor as to arm, but he destroyed the impact of this by insisting that it should be done piecemeal. Unlike the Weimar dukes, or William V, he was not prepared to contemplate an armed clash with the Emperor if Ferdinand should prove intransigent. He saw the Leipzig Congress rather as a warning shot across the Emperor's bows than as a programme for resolute action.

The Leipzig Congress was thus a disappointment to almost all those states that attended it, and scarcely less so to

Gustavus Adolphus. If it had produced a league of Protestant princes willing to defend themselves, it might have realized one of the objectives with which he came to Germany; and he had made it clear that he would be very willing to enter into a defensive alliance with such a league. Its failure drove him back on a policy of separate negotiations with those Protestant princes who were prepared to engage in them; any treaties which emerged from such negotiations would reflect the disparity of power of the parties. A Protestant league would have been able to get far better terms from him than those which he was able to impose on the Welfs, or the Mecklenburg dukes, or John Frederick of Bremen.

The Leipzig Congress left him where he had been in November, with no other German allies than Magdeburg and Pomerania. In one other respect his position had improved in the interim, for in January 1631 he had obtained, by the Treaty of Bärwalde, the alliance of France, on terms which amounted to a diplomatic defeat for Richelieu.[3] The alliance was to last for five years; France was to pay Sweden a subsidy of 400,000 *rdr* a year; Gustavus promised toleration to Roman Catholics in such territories as might be occupied by his army, and bound himself to maintain 30,000 foot and 6,000 horse in Germany. But the treaty also stipulated that Sweden should regard Bavaria and the League as neutrals *provided* they themselves observed neutrality. Gustavus made it clear that he understood this to mean abstention from all open or clandestine activity against Sweden or her friends and allies. But among those allies was Magdeburg, which Tilly was already investing; and among those friends was certainly to be reckoned Hesse-Cassel, which was in danger of attack by Tilly's forces.

It was an object of French policy to drive a wedge between the Emperor and Maximilian of Bavaria, and to turn Bavaria into a French client state; and Richelieu had persuaded himself that he could hire a Swedish sword without compromising this object. Sweden and Bavaria should be yoked in double harness to serve French designs, and together offer such effective resistance to the Habsburgs as to make French intervention in Germany unnecessary. The terms of the Treaty of Bärwalde made this programme impossible. So far from securing France against the possibility of a conflict between Sweden and the League, it went a long way towards

making that conflict inevitable. From this moment, Richelieu's German policy collapsed. His subsidies came too late to
make much difference; their amount was inconsiderable in
relation to Sweden's total war expenses; and at no time did
Gustavus show the slightest sign of being influenced by the
interests of his new ally. For France, the treaty was a major
miscalculation; for Sweden, its main value was as a help to
morale at a somewhat trying period.

At the very moment when Gustavus and Charnacé were
concluding their alliance at Bärwalde, Tilly came to take
command of the Imperialist forces at Frankfurt-on-Oder. His
coming presented Gustavus with his first really dangerous
adversary. It inaugurated a period of manœuvre; Tilly seeking
to pen Gustavus into the coastal area, Gustavus seeking to
break out of it, and to keep Tilly running round from one end
of his beach-head perimeter to the other. But essentially the
object they were contending for was Magdeburg. Tilly had as
yet by no means made up his mind to press the siege to an
issue, but he believed that Gustavus must sooner or later
make an effort to relieve the city, and he hoped to trap him
into giving battle in unfavourable circumstances. Gustavus
on his side calculated that if he could keep Tilly busy by
diversions Magdeburg would be safe.

In February Gustavus took the initiative by his campaign
into Mecklenburg; in March Tilly replied by pouncing on the
exposed Swedish position at Neu-Brandenburg: Gustavus's
order countermanding his instruction to the garrison to resist
to the last man failed to get through to them, and when the
town fell most of the defenders were massacred. Yet in the
days immediately following this reverse Gustavus was presented with the best chance he was ever to have of saving
Magdeburg by beating Tilly's army in the field. He had
reacted to the fall of Neu-Brandenburg with extraordinary
promptitude and concentrated forces considerably superior to
those which Tilly had at his disposal. But the chance was
missed. For once in his life Gustavus hesitated, called a
council of war, and accepted their advice not to risk battle. It
was a serious error. By the end of March Tilly had finally
made up his mind to take Magdeburg at all costs; by the
beginning of April many of the outworks had fallen. The news
was wholly unexpected, and it came upon Gustavus like a
thunderclap. He met it in the only way that lay open to him:

by launching a diversion. On Palm Sunday (3 April), in an operation which dispensed with all the formalities of siege-warfare, he took Frankfurt-on-Oder by storm, his ill-paid troops committing scandalous excesses upon the friendly population of that Protestant city. This was regrettable enough, but at least the exploit seemed likely to have the effect intended: Tilly broke up with his army from Magdeburg. But the very brilliance of the operation against Frankfurt in the end nullified the intention which lay behind it. The attack was so swift, the success so complete, that Tilly never had a chance to intervene: before he had marched very far towards Frankfurt it was irrevocably lost, and there was nothing to be done but to accept the fact and return to Magdeburg. The diversion had been so successful that it had failed to divert.

Failing a diversion, the only remaining way of saving Magdeburg was now a direct advance to the Elbe. Militarily, it entailed grave risks: if he forced his way to the city, Gustavus might well find himself confronted at the end of his march by a superior army; and if he were beaten, he would be isolated at a great distance from his base, with a line of retreat of dubious security. Politically, too, the problems were baffling. The only hope was the direct route, to the crossings of the Elbe at Dessau or Wittenberg, for the relatively safe route through Mecklenburg to the lower Elbe was too long: Magdeburg might fall before he arrived. But the direct route lay through the territories of George William and John George. In Brandenburg, the route was guarded by the electoral fortresses of Küstrin and Spandau; and Gustavus judged it essential to his security that these fortresses be under his control. What he really needed was a firm alliance with George William, preferably on the Pomeranian model; but the most that George William was prepared to offer was an alliance on the Leipzig terms (i.e. an alliance not directed against the Emperor), with pass and repass through Küstrin and Spandau for the Swedish army. At the beginning of May, in desperation, Gustavus marched his army upon Berlin, well knowing that the Elector was in no condition to offer serious military opposition. George William fell back upon passive resistance, and the fear of alienating other Protestant princes restrained Gustavus from measures of violent coercion. In the end he failed to extort an alliance: the best he could get was a

Swedish garrison in Spandau and the Elector's order to his commandant in Küstrin to consider himself under Swedish command. With this he had to be content, and the army advanced as far as Potsdam. But there still remained the problem of inducing John George to permit it to march through Saxon territory; and on 6 May Gustavus sent a last urgent appeal to the Elector to give him leave: in vain. On 10 May Magdeburg fell to Tilly's army. In the confusion that followed, the city was swept by a great conflagration which laid much of it in ashes; and 20,000 persons were killed or consumed in the flames.

The blow to Gustavus's reputation was severe: he had so emphatically pledged his word to relieve Magdeburg that his failure to do so seemed a betrayal. But he had not known before 21 April that the city was in any real danger, and even the defenders had not discovered until the first days of May that catastrophic shortage of powder which was the real cause of their inability to continue their resistance. When the true state of the situation became known to him, Gustavus had to balance the possible loss of Magdeburg against the possible destruction of his only army if he should march directly to its relief. It was not until 3 May that George William offered terms which provided a reasonable basis for discussion; and if Gustavus then bickered on matters which do not seem of the first importance, the delay made no difference to Magdeburg's fate. In the end he was, after all, prepared to risk his entire army in a desperate attempt at relief. If he had reached Magdeburg he would assuredly have faced very superior numbers; and he would probably have been beaten. So probably, indeed, that it may well be that only the intransigence of John George saved him from disaster. There was only one moment when an advance upon Magdeburg might have been attempted without undue risk, and that was in the six days after Neu-Brandenburg; but at that time Gustavus had no reason to suppose that the city was in any danger, and many reasons to enforce a policy of caution.

On the morrow of the sack of Magdeburg, Gustavus's prospects must have seemed dark indeed. Militarily, his position was hazardous; politically, it appeared desperate. He had suffered one of his two allies to be overwhelmed, with consequences which became apparent when William of Weimar stopped his military preparations and relapsed into neutrality. He had been baffled by the feeble resistance of George William; he appeared to have been outmatched by John George. Such Protestant league as might now take shape would be a league destined to ineffectiveness by John George's negative leadership. The subsidies under the Treaty of Bär-walde had scarcely begun to come in. The problem of supporting such forces as he had was still far from solved. The fall of Magdeburg had even nullified his agreement with Brandenburg, inadequate as that was; for the arrangements about Küstrin and Spandau had been valid only for the duration of the Magdeburg campaign. The end of that campaign accordingly ushered in an acute crisis in his rela-tions with George William which was not resolved until 11 June, and then only upon a basis far from satisfactory. He did indeed compel the Elector to agree to allow his dominions to be divided into ten quartering areas, each of which was to contribute 30,000 *rdr* a month to the Swedish war chest; but he failed to coerce him into an alliance, to obtain any assurances about Pomerania, or even to get control of Küstrin.

In these discouraging circumstances a policy was indispens-able; and at the very moment of Magdeburg's fall one of his experts on German affairs, Dr Steinberg, was drawing up the blueprint of what that policy must be, in the document which goes under the name of *Norma Futurarum Actionum*.[4] The basic thought underlying it was that something better must be contrived than John George's emasculated Protestant league; and that he must not be allowed to retain his position of leader of evangelical Germany. There must be a 'new evan-gelical Chief', and that Chief must be the king of Sweden. Around the new Chief must be gathered a league of states bound to him by ties of military obedience and political clientage for the duration of the war, advising him by a standing 'council of war and state'. Such a league would undoubtedly abridge the political and military independence of its members; for it would subject German princes to the 'absolute direction' of a foreign sovereign. But it implied no long-term political objectives, and certainly was not intended as a plan for the creation of a Swedish empire in Germany.

Only military victory could afford any chance of translating the programme of the *Norma* into reality. And, as it turned out, military victory was not so far away. The sack and burning of Magdeburg left Tilly sitting on a heap of ashes and wrecked all the plans he had built upon its capture. Impossible to feed and house his armies in the ruins: it was essential to move them elsewhere without delay. Away in the south of Germany – in Württemberg, in Baden – Protestant princes were arming under the terms of the Leipzig Congress, and their arming threatened to block the return of Imperial troops from Italy, where the Mantuan war had just been concluded. Nearer at hand, William V of Hesse-Cassel, undaunted by the catastrophe of Magdeburg, was preparing to take the field. Tilly turned to attend to these matters. Instead of a menacing Imperial force impending over him from Magdeburg, Gustavus unexpectedly found something like a temporary military vacuum.

He proceeded, with little delay, to fill it. At the end of June he moved out of Brandenburg; on 2 July he took Tanger-münde. He was now across the Elbe in force; into a new supply area, into central Germany: it was significant that for the first time his armies had marched off the maps which he brought with him from home. On 10 July he moved down the river to Werben; and here, in a great loop of the Elbe, he constructed a huge fortified camp. His hope was to force a pitched battle on Tilly before the Imperial troops from Italy arrived: the Protestant risings in south-west Germany, iso-lated and unsupported, had been crushed with little trouble. Tilly himself was ready for battle. But when he came up against Gustavus's field fortifications at Werben he experi-enced something of the same sort of shock as Masséna was to experience when he came up against the lines of Torres Vedras. His cannonading made little impression on the defenders; in the skirmishes outside the camp he could show no advantage, and his cavalry suffered a sharp defeat in a significant engagement near Burgstall. On 29 July he aban-doned the hopeless enterprise and ignominiously withdrew.

It was a marked turning-point. Until Werben, it had seemed that the best that Gustavus might hope for was to be able to maintain himself in the Baltic coastlands. But with the advance to the Elbe, and the successful maintenance of himself astride it, the situation had altered: more room for manœuvre, better hopes of supply and recruiting, a nearer approach to the areas where allies were most likely to be found, and a corresponding stiffening of the morale of princes whom the fate of Magdeburg had discouraged. The tide began, slowly but perceptibly, to flow in his direction. The exiled dukes of Mecklenburg were restored by Swedish arms to the capital from which Wallenstein had evicted them: it was an event which had great symbolic significance, even though its military importance might be small. Duke John Albert accepted a command in the Swedish army; Duke Bernard of Saxe-Weimar followed his example. William V, who alone had retained his nerve after Magdeburg, and who had probably been saved from annihilation by Tilly only by Gustavus's sudden advance to Tangermünde, cast aside his last hesitations, and on 12 August accepted the Contingent Convention: he was to prove the most enterprising and the most constant of all Sweden's German allies. But though all this was encouraging, it did not provide Gustavus with the additional forces that he needed if he was to meet the armies of the League on equal terms. Only one Protestant prince could do that: John George of Saxony.

By the beginning of August John George was faced with the fact that his policy was in ruins. The Leipzig allies had been crushed in south Germany; the viability of the Leipzig policy had been shattered by the fate of Magdeburg; the more courageous or desperate of the Protestant princes no longer hoped for any leadership from him. Worst of all, he could no longer believe that his tactics of moderation would avail to exempt him from the operation of the Edict of Restitution or the exactions of the Imperial armies. Despite his protestations that the troops he was raising were for defensive purposes only, Tilly was now brusquely demanding their disbandment. John George's situation was now so alarming that he swallowed his pride and opened negotiations with the Swedish invader. On 14 August Tilly despatched an ultimatum to Saxony; on 25 August his troops crossed the Saxon frontier. Gustavus was ready for the emergency. Four days later his advance guard entered Wittenberg, and was received with enthusiasm by the inhabitants. On 2 September John George at last concluded an alliance with Gustavus 'for as long as the danger from the enemy shall continue'. He accepted the king's absolute direction only for such operations as should be agreed between them; otherwise, he would pledge himself only to conform to Gustavus's plans 'as far as possible'. He also retained his own army and his own generals, among

139

whom was one – Hans George von Arnim – of more than respectable talents, who was to prove a thorn in the side of Sweden for some years to come. It was an agreement extorted by necessity, and it was repugnant to the feelings of both contracting parties. John George found himself yoked to Gustavus's chariot wheels; Gustavus found himself saddled with an ally over whom his control was by no means assured, and to whom the alliance had guaranteed an undefined, and therefore dangerous, measure of military independence. Each party was suspicious of the other. Yet upon this treacherous and insecure basis Gustavus's German policy was henceforth doomed to be founded; for the Saxon alliance, once obtained, could not with safety be abandoned.

For the moment, it gave him a respectable numerical superiority over his adversary, at least on paper. When on 7 September 1631 the two sides drew up their forces near Breitenfeld for that general engagement which all now desired, the allies had some 42,000 men (24,000 Swedes; 18,000 Saxons) against Tilly's 35,000. But the event proved that what mattered was not numbers but tactical ability and morale. For within a short time after the opening of the battle the Saxon horse had been swept from the field; the *tercios* had made mincemeat of the Saxon foot; and with some few inconsiderable exceptions the whole Saxon army was broken, scattered and in panic flight, leaving the Swedish left wing naked and unprotected, exposed to devastating attack on the flank by overwhelming numbers. In this situation, the tactical reforms which Gustavus had initiated first revealed their true value. Gustav Horn, commanding the Swedish left, met the situation by swiftly forming front to his flank, summoned reserves from the centre, and launched a furious attack with every man at his disposal – cavalry, musketeers and regiment-pieces all collaborating together – upon the tight-packed masses of the victorious *tercios*, before they had had time to recover themselves from their efforts against the Saxons. Simultaneously, on the other wing, the new Swedish cavalry tactics halted, and finally defeated, the utmost efforts of Pappenheim, generally accounted the finest cavalry commander of his time. Soon the Swedes were victorious on both wings, the Imperialists lost their heavy guns, the Swedish centre moved forward. When night fell, the invincible Tilly was a wounded fugitive, and the army of the League was totally overthrown. All in all, its casualties may have amounted to 20,000 men, including 7,600 dead on the field, and a total of prisoners which eventually reached 9,000. The Swedes lost no more than 2,100. It was the hand of God, the fulfilment of the prophecies, the dawn of a new age of Swedish greatness. Contemporaries did not underrate the importance of what had happened. Ferdinand II was so shattered by the news that he contemplated flight to Graz, or even to Italy. Military men everywhere were forced to rethink their precepts, for at Breitenfeld Europe witnessed the triumph of a tactical revolution. The art of war would not be the same again.

On the morrow of Breitenfeld Gustavus Adolphus had all Germany before him. Tilly had fled with the remnants of his army north-westward, and there was not another force in Germany (or at least, in the immediate neighbourhood) which seemed capable of offering serious resistance. Within limits, he could go where he would; the question was only, which way to choose? Between 14 and 16 September he discussed the possibilities with John George. They appeared to reduce themselves to three: either he might strike direct for Vienna through Silesia; or move to the rich lands of the Main and Rhine; or pursue Tilly relentlessly into the Lower Saxon Circle and complete his annihilation. The advance on Vienna was soon ruled out, and rightly so: its capture would have decided nothing, and what was needed was the destruction of the enemy's army, not the taking of his capital. John George was given the task of advancing up the Oder into Silesia. By allotting him a separate command Gustavus might hope to avoid disputes with his ally, while at the same time removing him from the temptation of meddling in central Germany. For himself, he decided to move towards the Rhine in two stages: the first, which should suffice for this year, into Thuringia, where he could command the vital communications centre of Erfurt; the second, which he intended to reserve for the next campaign, to Franconia, the Main valley and the Rhineland. By choosing this option he would be in a position to rally potential allies, or come to their aid; he would have good quarters for an army which since Breitenfeld had been swollen by mercenaries who had changed sides; and he might hope to keep Tilly isolated in north-west

Germany, and drive a wedge between him and his bases in Bavaria.

It was an intelligible choice, both on military and political grounds; but it may well be that it was a mistaken one. It left the Lower Saxon Circle unsubdued and vulnerable, and this was to cost him dear later; above all, it left Tilly in peace to regroup his shattered forces unmolested. The sequel was to suggest that it might have been better to follow him in hot pursuit and complete the business which Breitenfeld had begun. For the moment, however, all went well. By the third week in September Gustavus was safely in Thuringia, and on the 22nd his forces liberated a somewhat unwilling Erfurt, which henceforward became Sweden's main bastion in central Germany. It had all been so easy that there now seemed no good reason to stop: why wait till next year to 'infest' the rich bishoprics of Franconia? The advance therefore continued, in unbroken triumph: by early October he had reached the upper Main; on 4 October Würzburg surrendered. Three days later, by a daring feat of arms which much impressed contemporaries, his troops stormed the episcopal fortress of Marienberg, making a vast haul of booty, including a rich store of books which was sent home to strengthen the meagre holdings of the university library at Uppsala.

But now his progress was halted by a most disagreeable interruption. Tilly, left to his own devices, had recovered himself with extraordinary swiftness. He had gathered the scattered Imperialist units in the north-west; he had effected a junction with the army of Charles of Lorraine; and by the middle of October he was once more at the head of 40,000 to 45,000 men. With this force he was now bearing down on the middle reaches of the Main, and cutting across Gustavus's line of advance. By the 25th he was threatening Ochsenfurt. Only a day's march separated him from Gustavus at Würzburg; if it should come to a battle, the Swedes would find themselves heavily outnumbered. Luckily for Gustavus, Tilly had orders to take no risks; his threat to Ochsenfurt had been no more than a feint, and he continued on his way to winter quarters in southern Germany without any attempt to bring his enemy to battle. But it had been a fortunate escape.

With Tilly safely heading south, there was now no reason why the advance down the Main should not be resumed. Gustavus, whose nerve had been shaken for a moment by the

Ochsenfurt affair, quickly recovered his confidence. He was already thinking in terms of the liberation of southern Germany next year and revolving in his mind plans for a concentric advance upon Vienna. The cautious strategy of the early months was abandoned. The success of his new tactics, the ever-increasing size of his armies, the vast new resources which were now available for recruiting and supply, seemed to make anything possible. He entered Frankfurt on 17 November, a resplendent figure in his scarlet 'Polish coat' astride a great Spanish charger, unopposed, assured, radiant with victory. The end of the astonishing campaign was in sight. It was at Mainz that he intended to establish himself for the winter.

Before he could do this he must cross the Rhine, for Mainz lies on the west bank; and the Rhine was a formidable obstacle. But nothing now seemed formidable to him. A characteristically audacious personal reconnaissance, a brilliantly organized little operation to follow it, and he was across the Rhine at Oppenheim. Worms capitulated to him on 7 December; Mainz, from which the Elector had prudently fled while yet there was time, opened its gates five days later. In a single campaign Gustavus had marched his armies from the Oder to the Rhine, he had defeated in a classic victory the man who was esteemed by many to be the ablest general of his age, he had broken free of those financial and logistical shackles which for so long had impeded his progress, and he had set himself indisputably at the head of Protestant Europe. As he kept Christmas at Mainz, the future of Germany appeared to be in his hands. And Sweden, for the first time in her history, had become a great power.

.   .   .

NOTES

1. English translation of the main articles in Roberts, *Sweden as a Great Power*, pp. 140–1.
2. English translation of the principal points in ibid., p. 141.
3. English translation in ibid., pp. 136–8.
4. English text in ibid., p. 142.

Chapter 10

THE PLENITUDE OF POWER

In the winter and spring of 1631–32 Gustavus Adolphus stood in a position such as no other Swedish monarch – not Charles X, not Charles XII – was ever to enjoy in the future, and certainly had not enjoyed in the past. His astonishing military successes enabled him to bully the princes of Germany, ride rough-shod over neutrals, and towards allies assume a brusque intransigence and an asperity of language such as Richelieu, for one, had not been used to encounter. His vast new armies, his confidence in his ability to defeat his enemies, permitted him to adopt a tone of menace to his old enemy, Christian IV. Nor did his involvement in the politics of Germany inhibit him from manœuvres designed to shake the throne of the Polish Vasa. His diplomacy took on a wider range; his political horizons expanded to include virtually the whole of Europe. From Constantinople to Amsterdam, from Switzerland to Lithuania, his agents were active, disseminating the story of his invincibility, dilating on the exploits of the ancient Goths, painting in flattering hues the wealth and the economic potential of his backward dominions, spreading their nets for recruits, provisions, subsidies, alliances, to lend weight to the great military projects he was formulating for the coming year.

As German princes and French envoys sought to persuade him to adapt his measures to conform to their wishes, he shed those restraints which had hitherto enforced the cloaking of his distrust for the one and his contempt for the other: no need now to keep a bridle on his tongue or dissimulate his feelings. For it seemed now that there was no power – not in Germany, nor perhaps in Europe – which was in a position to

144

dispute with the master of the greatest accumulation of military force on the Continent. He was indeed for a moment incontestably the greatest man in Europe; and it seemed that he was destined to be its master. He had been the architect of his own fortune. Since the landing at Peenemünde he had perforce grown accustomed to relying on himself, for there was no other upon whom full reliance was to be placed, until Oxenstierna at last disengaged himself from his governor-generalship in Prussia and joined him in Mainz in the new year. In the absence of Oxenstierna's emollient diplomacy, the volcanic Vasa temperament found vent in sharp speeches to lukewarm friends, nervous neutrals, or allies whom he considered to be trying to lead him by the nose. His own exertions had placed him in a position in which he might reasonably hope not only to attain the immediate objective with which he had come to Germany, but also to realize larger, more distant aims.

Meanwhile he kept his court in Mainz like some new Emperor, the incontestable focus of the diplomacy of Europe. Here his agents busied themselves with drafting alliances, hither came diplomats from all quarters. They came from George Rákóczy, the new ruler of Transylvania now that Bethlen Gabor was no more; they came from the Khan of the Crimean Tatars; while to their overlord, the Sultan, Gustavus sent an embassy of his own. The purpose behind these approaches was to open a second front against the Habsburgs, if it could be done on reasonable terms. Experience proved that it could not: the Sultan and his vassals were too shrewd and too preoccupied with their own concerns to run Gustavus's errands for him. Nevertheless the contacts with south-eastern Europe established a connection which remained for three-quarters of a century: Charles X and Charles XII would not forget it. Nearer at hand, the Swiss proved equally elusive. Gustavus was disposed to feel that the Swiss had a duty to abandon a neutrality which they had hitherto (very much to their advantage) contrived to preserve; or at least, that it should be a neutrality weighted in his favour. Peaceful, prosperous and unravaged, the Swiss cantons appeared admirably adapted to provide him with recruits and supplies, if only they would listen to his exhortations. But the Swiss, contemplating at close range the miseries of Germany, felt no inclination to extend them into their own borders; and even the Protestant cantons were deaf to the tactless appeals of the agent whom Gustavus sent to persuade them.

He had better success with Russia, for here the ties of common interest were stronger. Since the Peace of Stolbova, relations between the two countries had grown comparatively cordial, for each saw in Poland an irreconcilable enemy. The Tsar had been willing to give Sweden concessions in regard to the export of Russian grain which had for a time a very real value; and Gustavus on his side was prepared to be obliging if by doing so he could keep Poland preoccupied. Whereas the Truce of Altmark would not expire until 1635, Russia's truce with Poland was due to come to an end in 1632. Already the Tsar was preparing for that day, in the hope that a renewal of the war might lead to the recovery of Smoleńsk. Gustavus was very willing to facilitate its outbreak. As early as November 1630 he had agreed in principle to a request from the Tsar to act as his recruiting agent in Germany – not least because his estimated profit on the transaction would have been of the order of 127,000 *rdr* a month. In 1632 Alexander Leslie was given his permission to raise 5,000 foot in Swedish-occupied Germany to reinforce the Russian armies. In March 1631 Sweden, first of all nations, established a permanent Resident in Moscow. A month before the battle of Lützen these complaisances brought their reward, in the shape of a Russian declaration of war against Poland; if Gustavus had lived only a little longer it seems likely that there would have been a Russian–Swedish alliance. Sigismund III was nearing the end of his life (he died in April 1632), and his death would pose the question of the succession, since his attempts to secure the election of his son Ladislas in his lifetime had stranded on the constitutional susceptibilities of the Polish nobility. It seemed politic to patronize their enthusiasm for their liberties, and desirable to contrive that Polish patriots should be set at one another's throats by a disputed election. Swedish agents therefore approached influential magnates in Lithuania and Poland who happened to be Protestants, and Gustavus went so far as to put himself forward as a candidate for the Polish throne. It seems unlikely that he was very serious about it, but his Protestant friends in Poland were not serious about it at all. In the event, Ladislas was elected without difficulty; as he deserved to be, for he was a good candidate. Still, though this gambit failed, the encouragement of Russia did not; and Gustavus could devote himself to the problems of Germany without having to keep one eye on the Vistula.

As it turned out, it was not the Vistula but the Elbe that threatened to distract his attention; not the dynastic rival in Warsaw, but the unsleeping enemy in Copenhagen. Christian IV felt himself eclipsed by Sweden's successes in Germany, but he was not prepared to remain in the shadows without a struggle. Denmark was now too weak, and the Danish council too pacific, for there to be any real possibility of that stab in the back which haunted Gustavus's imagination. But Christian's busy diplomacy was a constant source of uneasiness. He attempted, though for the present without success, to supplant Sweden in the favour of the Tsar: here begins a long-continued Danish policy, which was to bear monstrous fruit in 1699. He intrigued in the politics of the Lower Saxon Circle, in the hope that his son Frederick might be chosen as the Circle's captain-general; he was deep in negotiations with Wallenstein for the purchase of portions of Mecklenburg, which Wallenstein was all the readier to dispose of since they were no longer in his possession. In the spring of 1632, Pappenheim, the Imperialist commander in the Lower Saxon Circle, came near to concluding a bargain which would have restored to Christian the long-coveted dioceses of Bremen and Verden. Gustavus reacted strongly to this provocation, and if the crisis had not solved itself would have been prepared to halt his advance upon Bavaria and turn all his forces north-wards to launch an attack upon Jutland. If such an attack had come, Christian was certainly in no condition to offer effective resistance: the days when Denmark had been the dominant power in the Baltic were gone for ever. It was by way of 'putting a bridle upon the Jute' that in June 1632 Gustavus concluded an alliance with Christian's dynastic rival, Frederick III of Holstein-Gottorp, and so laid the foundation for that connection between Sweden and Gottorp which was to be one of the corner-stones of Swedish foreign policy for the next three generations.

But these were matters of peripheral interest. Much more important were relations with France and Spain. The advance to the Rhine had brought Sweden to the fringes of the great

Franco-Spanish struggle: as yet an undeclared war, in which each side confined itself to acting as an auxiliary to the enemies of the other. Gustavus had not hesitated to attack Spanish forces, at Oppenheim and afterwards, and any extension of his grip on the middle Rhine might well lead to further encounters. It seemed to him at times that war with Spain lay in the logic of the situation; and the Spanish council of state was of a similar opinion. He did not shrink from the prospect, though he certainly did not desire it: trade with Spain was still a consideration, even after the demonetization of vellon. The Council in Stockholm, however, viewed the prospect with alarm; and Philip IV's advisers, on reflection, decided that Spain could not afford another enemy. A direct confrontation was in the end avoided by both sides.

Nobody would have been better pleased than Richelieu if it had really come to war; and this, perhaps, was one good argument for peace. For Gustavus's relations with his French ally were not such as to encourage him to put himself out in order to serve French interests. The presence of large Swedish forces on the left bank of the Rhine was anything but welcome to France, for this was a region which the cardinal hoped to make a French sphere of influence. The Elector of Trier was a French client. The passages of the middle Rhine were destined, in Richelieu's long-term political strategy, to serve as French look-outs into Germany. Lorraine was the bolt-hole for Gaston of Orleans, and other plotters against his authority, and it must be French troops which reduced its duke to order, not Swedish. There was no escaping the conclusion: on the Rhine, France and Sweden were rivals; Gustavus was an unwelcome intruder. In August 1630 Father Joseph, discussing the expediency of an alliance with Sweden, had written: 'Il faut se servir de ces choses ainsi que de venins, dont le peu sert de contrepoison et le trop tue.'[1] By the beginning of 1632 the cardinal might well begin to ask himself whether he had not inadvertently taken too strong a dose.

Certainly his ally showed remarkable indifference to French susceptibilities, and no sign whatever of compliance with French wishes: the Treaty of Bärwalde had served only to emancipate Gustavus from the need to consider Richelieu's feelings. The cardinal's policy for Germany showed no sign of catching up with the march of events: at the beginning of 1632, as at the beginning of 1631, its object was the formation of a 'third party' under France's patronage, and, as before, that party was to include both Bavaria and Saxony. Spain, after all, was jealous of Maximilian's influence in Vienna, and hoped to replace the League with a Habsburg alliance: here, surely, was France's opportunity. John George's treaty with Sweden, and the exhilarating effects of Breitenfeld, ruled out Saxony as a French client for the moment; but Bavaria at least might be accessible to French persuasions. This policy depended for its feasibility upon whether France could induce Maximilian to declare himself neutral, and upon whether Gustavus would be prepared to recognize his neutrality. At Bärwalde he had promised to respect it, provided Maximilian's conduct agreed with what might be expected from a neutral, but the events of the last twelve months had effectively disposed of any fantasies of that sort. Bavarian troops, Bavarian money, a Bavarian general, had fought (and lost) the battle of Breitenfeld. If Maximilian could be induced to desert the Emperor it would no doubt be extremely convenient; but in Gustavus's opinion it would be still more surprising. He did not trust Maximilian an inch; nor did he trust Richelieu much further.

The event was to prove his caution fully justified. From the month of October 1631, a succession of French diplomats laboured to devise some arrangement which would detach Maximilian from Ferdinand and protect him from Gustavus. By the end of the year they were able to report that the prospects looked promising. Not, indeed, in Munich; but the weaker members of the League – bishops such as Würzburg, Worms, and Osnabrück, ecclesiastical electors in the danger-zones of Mainz, Cologne and Trier – were persuaded to agree in principle to neutrality. The League appeared to be breaking up. But this miscellaneous episcopal jetsam was scarcely worth the salving: what mattered were the views of Maximilian and Gustavus. Gustavus's armies occupied a choice collection of fat German dioceses, which supplied them with necessary maintenance. Not even as the price of Bavarian neutrality was he prepared to evacuate them until the Emperor should have been finally defeated. French attempts at persuasion were curtly rebuffed; tactless French suggestions that he should withdraw from the west bank of the Rhine (including Mainz, which he was rapidly turning into a great fortress) and seek territorial compensation in north Germany served only to provoke the angry retort that he had come 'as *protector*, not as *proditor* [betrayer], *Germaniae*'.

Maximilian's simulated complaisance to French appeals had never been more than a feint; and when the Swedes intercepted one of his letters to the Emperor his duplicity became patent. By March 1632 Bavarian neutrality, in Oxenstierna's words, was 'sunk'. Gustavus was prepared so far to humour his ally as to make no objection to the entry of French troops into Trier and the imposition of a French *diktat* upon Lorraine, for these proceedings brought France closer to real involvement in the struggle against the Habsburgs. But he had not the slightest intention of allowing Richelieu to deflect him from the path which his interest dictated. The cardinal's diplomacy foundered on a stronger will and a greater force than his own. Gustavus had no desire for a quarrel with France; but with all the resources of central Germany to draw upon he was not prepared to commit political errors for the sake of a trumpery subsidy of 400,000 *rdr*. If Richelieu was too weak to fight, if he elected to wage war against the Habsburgs at second hand, he must take the consequences of his debility. By the late spring of 1632 France's German policy had become a fiasco. By the summer, though the alliance still held, there was scarcely a pretence of friendship.

Still less was Gustavus disposed to listen patiently to the bleatings of English diplomacy. As Richelieu found it difficult to disabuse himself of the notion that Gustavus's function was to subserve the interest of France, so Charles I and his ministers cherished the delusion that his prime duty was to restore Frederick V to the Palatinate. Sir Henry Vane was sent to Germany in the autumn of 1631 to preach on this text, and for months thereafter trailed irritably in the wake of the Swedish armies, emitting remonstrances which were otiose, and propounding projects which were visionary. Gustavus had long since taken the measure of English statesmanship. He would have been willing to enter into an agreement with England upon any terms which had some element of practicability, but from a monarch without hope of parliamentary supply such terms were scarcely to be expected. The large subsidies guaranteed for the duration of the war, the substantial military aid, the absolute command of any English auxiliary force, the formal alliance for a term of years which he demanded: these were things that Sir Henry Vane had not the power to promise.

Nor was the case much mended by the arrival of Charles I's unfortunate brother-in-law, Frederick V, who appeared at Mainz in February 1632 in the Micawberish hope that something might turn up. Gustavus treated him kindly, and punctiliously insisted that he be accorded the honours of royalty; but he was careful to evade precise commitments, and adamant in his refusal to permit the immediate restoration of Frederick to his forfeited electorate. That restoration was, no doubt, among the objects which the German expedition had been intended to secure, and Gustavus was probably sincere when he assured him that he should have his own electorate again once the war was over. But it did not make sense that he should have it now. The Rhineland was far too important as a base, as a supply area, as the springboard for the next campaign, for it to be entrusted to the feeble hands of the Winter King. Until September 1632 Frederick accompanied Gustavus on his marchings up and down Germany, intermittently pleading his cause. But the best offer he could obtain was too bitter a pill for him to swallow: absolute Swedish military control of the Palatinate for the duration of the war; toleration for Lutherans; restorations of his lands as they had existed *before* his acceptance of the Bohemian crown; and, worst of all, explicit recognition that he held them by the grace of the Swedish crown.

By Christmas 1631 the Swedish armies were in control of half of Germany; and upon the effective organization and administration of the occupied areas the Swedish war-potential essentially depended. That administration had had to be improvised as the armies advanced, with such material as lay to hand; and, until Oxenstierna came to Mainz early in 1632, most of the work was done by Gustavus himself. It was a remarkable achievement for a man who was also simultaneously commander-in-chief and virtually his own foreign secretary. Gradually, as winter turned to spring, something like a central government for Swedish Germany was organized in Mainz: here was the chancery, the standing council, the exchequer for German finance, a judicial authority. Hence proceeded those regulations of tolls and customs, those allocations of contributions and quartering areas upon which the army depended, based on a systematic survey of the occupied lands. It was this government which saw to improvements in communications, the reorganization of postal services, the creation of a propaganda press; which promulgated a new Church Ordinance for Lutheran Germany, and took care that Lutherans were tolerated (and Catholics not persecuted) in Calvinist territories. For these activities, as for the local government, Sweden had no resources of trained personnel to spare. There was therefore a brisk recruitment of Germans who aspired to a career in the Swedish service, whether military or civil. German princes took advantage of the opportunity. By doing so, they put themselves in a delicate situation: at once servants of the Swedish crown and immediate vassals of the Emperor. Oxenstierna found them difficult to handle; and soon after Breitenfeld it became expedient to gratify them with donations of conquered territory, if only as an easy solution to the problem of adminstering these lands: when Gustavus fell at Lützen a great part of occupied Germany had been alienated in this way to provincial governors, meritorious generals, or querulous princelings. But such donations always reserved sovereignty to the Swedish crown, and safeguarded its right to levy contributions. The supply of the army was not to be imperilled; and for the duration of the war, at least, the donation-holders must 'depend' on the king of Sweden.

Thus necessity and force of circumstances produced what was *de facto* a Swedish empire in Germany. It had not been foreseen in 1630; nor was it consciously willed in 1631. Two months after the king's death, Oxenstierna commented that Gustavus, in going to Germany, 'intended to safeguard his kingdom and the Baltic Sea, and to liberate the oppressed lands; and thereafter to proceed as things might fall out: to begin with he had not intended to go as far as he did'. But whatever his original intentions, he could not evade the consequences of his victories; and if those victories continued, the commitments would grow wider still: how would it be if by Christmas 1632 he had overrun south Germany as he had overrun the north?

One thing at least was clear: if his grip of the situation were not to relax, if by a gigantic military effort the war were to be brought to a victorious conclusion next year, the German Protestant rulers must accept the necessity for disciplined co-ordination of effort under his leadership, and resign themselves to something like subjection to his orders. They must bind themselves to him, by alliances or conventions, for so long as the war should last. The more so, since he had little faith either in their capacity or their goodwill. He bitterly resented what he felt to be their ingratitude, and was contemptuous of their hankerings after an inglorious neutrality: 'It is a fight', he had said to a Brandenburg envoy, 'between God and the Devil . . . *tertium non dabitur.*' He was determined that they should 'depend' upon him, and was prone to demand that the treaties of alliance which he prescribed for them should include specific and rather humiliating references to their 'gratitude'. The Protestant princes, not surprisingly, were affronted. The stringent terms which he sought to lay upon them threatened them with reduction to the status of vassals, and implied the subversion of their constitutional status as members of the Germanic body. The dukes of Mecklenburg, for instance, were confronted with a demand that they should 'recognize' Gustavus and his heirs; or alternatively that they should declare their independence of the Empire – which would in fact have made them little better than Swedish puppets. The Welf duke of Brunswick-Wolfenbüttel was required 'thankfully to recognize' Gustavus for all the lands recovered to him in consequence of the Swedish victories, save for those which would pass on failure of heirs to his cousins of Lüneburg; and in January 1632 was pressed to agree to hold some of them as a Swedish fief. Resistance to these pressures was passive, but ultimately successful: the treaty with Mecklenburg was toned down; that with Brunswick-Wolfenbüttel was not concluded at all. But undeniably the king's demands had feudal overtones of the same disturbing kind as so alarmed Frederick V. And even William of Hesse, most loyal of all the allies of Sweden, was given back the eccesiastical lands which he had lost by the Edict of Restitution only on condition that if his line became extinct they should pass to the Swedish crown.

What lay behind this rude disregard for German susceptibilities? It seems to have been (or at least, to have appeared to Gustavus to be) a logical consequence of the principles which had led him to Germany. The object of the expedition had been security, and that implied the handing over to Sweden of bastions on the southern Baltic shore. In October 1629 he had mentioned Wismar as one such possible bastion (no doubt because it was the base for Wallenstein's fleet). Already by May 1630 he had made up his mind to keep Stralsund after the war was over, since he could not run the risk of its falling into his enemies' hands. Very soon after landing he came to the conclusion that a couple of isolated strongholds was not enough: the terms of his alliance with Pomerania were designed, among other things, to ensure that the whole duchy should be safeguarded from being used as a base for attacks upon Sweden. Shortly before he left for Germany, when Oxenstierna sent him a memorandum on the objectives of the expedition, Gustavus remonstrated with him for omitting the most important of them all: *assecuratio* (security). But since the need to obtain security had been imposed upon him, and since his country's resources were strained to the utmost to obtain it, it seemed to him reasonable that he should seek compensation for his efforts, and indemnity for the sacrifices his country had been obliged to make.

From the beginning, the search for *assecuratio* was matched by a demand for *satisfactio* (indemnity). At first indemnity was thought of as a cash payment: the price of liberation, or the penalty of defeat. The Pomeranian treaty, for instance, stipulated that Pomerania should remain in Swedish hands until the cost of the war had been paid. It was not long, however, before *satisfactio* began to change its character. Already by the autumn of 1630 Gustavus was thinking of an indemnity in the form of cessions of territory: the Contingent Convention with Hesse, for instance, provided that he should keep all the lands conquered by the Swedish armies. No doubt many such lands had recently passed into the hands of the Emperor or the League as a result of the defeat of the Protestant princes, or as a consequence of the Edict of Restitution, and it might seem just to restore them on reconquest to their previous owners. But Gustavus did not think so. It was not only that he felt strongly that he was entitled to some reward from those whom he had liberated. It was also that he had (he believed) an indefeasible right according to the principles of international law, as they had recently been laid down by Hugo Grotius. Grotius was quite clear on the point: the lands were his, *jure belli* (by the laws of war); and the defective title of those he had evicted made no difference to his right. As early as August 1630 Gustavus had told the scandalized Pomeranians '*jure belli* you are my property'; and though at the time this was probably intended only as a warning, it was not so long before it became a declaration of intent. By the end of 1631 he was stating flatly that Pomerania – the whole of Pomerania – was to be retained as indemnity. Thus, what had once been thought of as security had been transmuted into indemnity; and the claim for reward, for gratitude for services rendered, had been ominously reinforced by claims *jure belli* which, as his armies advanced, might be extended until they included the best part of Germany.

By the summer of 1632 he made the implications quite explicit: the German states, he announced, could be divided into six categories, ranging from open enemies to effective allies; and against five out of the six he considered himself to have claims which were good in international law. This meant, in practice, that he had claims against everyone except William V and John George. No doubt, as he was careful to explain, he had no intention of insisting rigorously upon his due: his purpose was no more than to make plain – especially to waverers and weaklings – exactly where they stood, if he should be disposed to be demanding.

But the rigorous legalism of his interpretation of his rights, the truly monstrous dimensions which they seemed to give to the idea of indemnity, the quasi-feudal subordination of his allies which seemed to be implied in his attempts to force treaties upon them, were no very good cement for a common front against the Emperor. Nor did they provide a permanent basis for the peace of Germany. What form was security now to assume? The problem had been in the mind of Gustavus at least since May 1631, when the *Norma Futurarum Actionum* was drafted; but it acquired special urgency as a result of the efforts of George of Hesse-Darmstadt, from October 1631 to February 1632, to prepare the way for a general peace in Germany. George of Hesse-Darmstadt was a young man of good intentions but deficient political realism; a Lutheran, but also a loyal Imperialist. However, George approached Gustavus with a view to finding out upon what terms he would consent to treat for peace. The king's answer, in January 1632, was as stiff as it had been to Richelieu: all Imperialist forces must quit the Lower Saxon Circle; Sweden must retain the dioceses of Mainz, Würzburg and Bamberg. No progress was possible along this line.

But the negotiations set Gustavus thinking about the

155

general question of post-war security, and at the end of the year he was discussing the problem with William V of Hesse-Cassel. Though there was as yet no precise formulation of a programme,. he had made up his mind that the situation could be rendered permanently safe only if there were some sort of continued Swedish presence in Germany after the war was over. Already in his negotiations with Mecklenburg he had adumbrated a kind of Swedish protectorate which should extend beyond the conclusion of peace. In the *Norma* he had outlined a project for a league of Protestant princes under Swedish direction, to last for as long as the war continued. The two lines of thought now converged in a plan for a standing Protestant alliance under Swedish leadership, which should act as a watchdog for the political interests of Sweden, and the religious interests of Protestantism. He was already referring to himself as 'supreme head of the evangelical electors, princes, and Estates of the German nation'. To William V he suggested that he should stand forth as *protector religionis* – a suggestion which William V, who had no reverence for the institutions of the Empire, greeted with enthusiasm. In the following months the concept took on firmer contours: in June 1632 Gustavus told the citizens of Nuremberg that what he wanted for Germany was a free association of Protestant states, maintaining a permanent war organization, but also a civil organization. He made no specific claim to the command of the former: indeed, he hinted that it might be given to William V, or even to John George, if either of them were willing and able to assume it. But it is doubtful if he really had any idea of abdicating military leadership to anyone else; and certainly he made it quite plain that the civil organization must be under Swedish direction. Just what form it would take was still obscure: there must be some kind of *parliamentum*, some forum for consultation on matters of common concern, and perhaps (he suggested) some association might be devised roughly on the model of the United Provinces.

As yet, these were no more than general ideas, statements of principle or tentative suggestions; but in the last two months of his life they acquired solid substance. In a letter to Oxenstierna of 24 October 1632 the King cast his thoughts into a firm institutional mould;[2] and between 24 and 26 October, in the course of his last meeting with his chancellor, the final touches were given to a scheme of government for southern and western Germany. There was to be a Swedish-controlled military and civil organization for the Swabian, Franconian and Upper and Lower Saxon Circles; a congress of representatives of these areas was to be held at Ulm in December to launch it. Over that congress Oxenstierna was to preside, and to him was to be given the command-in-chief of all the forces raised in this region. The immediate purpose was military: the levying of more troops (it was hoped that the four Circles would provide the enormous number of 130,000 recruits for next year), and the establishment of regular arrangements for their pay and maintenance. To supervise these military matters there was to be a formal council presided over by Philip von Solms, a German prince in the Swedish service. But such measures necessarily carried political implications. The four Circles were therefore to be provided with administrative machinery not only for the collection of funds for a common war chest, but for other purposes also: for education; for the securing of religious liberty to Protestants, and the prevention of the persecution of Catholics; for building a system of church-government for Lutheran communities; and so forth. Though the expression was not used on this occasion, there was clearly going to be a regular civil government; and the amplitude of the powers conferred upon Oxenstierna makes it obvious that it was intended that he was to rule the four Circles as a viceroy in all but name. He was to take care that the king of Sweden should step into any rights formerly enjoyed by the Emperor; he was to try to persuade the states to renounce obedience to Imperial authority; he was to sound them out on the idea of reforming the Imperial Chamber of Justice; he was if need be to act on his own initiative in matters of foreign policy. And the unmistakable underlying assumption was that the whole arrangement was to continue for the foreseeable future.

Here then at last was what they had been fumbling for: a security system which was not simply a cession of territory, but a general nexus of guarantees bound together by Swedish leadership, continuing for as long as there might be any recurrence of those dangers which had brought Gustavus to Germany. Admittedly, it was as yet only a partial solution; an instalment, rather than a final settlement. It did not as yet apply to north Germany. It left out the two states which it

157

was essential to include, for Gustavus was not so sanguine as to suppose that Brandenburg and Saxony would willingly adhere to it at present. But if it should prove effective, they might change their minds later. For south Germany, at all events, the scheme had obvious attractions; for here the princes and cities were in particular danger if there should be any revival of Imperial power, and the more ready, therefore, to welcome a measure of organization and collective security imposed from above. At least it provided a nucleus around which other states might rally; it was a first step on the right road. What Gustavus was really looking for, as the final *assecuratio*, was a sort of miniature NATO for Germany, with Sweden in the role of the United States; provided, of course, that the cost of vigilance should not be expected to be borne by the Swedish taxpayer. If the Protestants of Germany wanted him to act as captain of the local fire brigade, they must pay for the service.

Unfortunately, it was far from clear that they wanted any such thing; at least in general, and on such terms as these. A month after Gustavus died the Ulm Congress did indeed meet, and the organization for the four Circles was set up. But the terms of Oxenstierna's instructions show that, too late, the king had realized the unwisdom of his previous handling of the German princes. Oxenstierna was ordered to exercise the greatest tact, to treat the representatives with amenity, to show consideration for their feelings: though there was to be no concession on matters of substance, there was to be a conscious improvement in manners. No doubt the new tone did something to explain the success at Ulm, but it could not eradicate the memory of much verbal brutality in the previous eighteen months. Nor could it allay a real unease at the constitutional implications which the new *assecuratio* might carry with it.

It is impossible not to ask how far a league of this sort was really reconcilable with the Imperial constitution. Certainly some of the princes were ready for a reform of Imperial institutions: William V was frankly iconoclast, and even so conservative a ruler as John George conceded that some alterations might be considered. Comparable associations of states had existed before without disrupting the Imperial fabric: the League of Schmalkalde, for instance, or the Protestant Union, of lamentable memory. But this was to be a league directed and controlled by a foreign monarch, who had repeatedly attempted to force upon the princes terms which threatened to infringe their constitutional status by reducing them to his feudal inferiors: on the most benevolent interpretation, to reduce them from immediate to mediate subjects of the Emperor. They might be willing to go along with him in his suggestion that the college of electors be recast so as to achieve a balance between the religions, or to acquiesce in a reconstruction of the Imperial Chamber of Justice on the same lines, if only to safeguard themselves against losing the peace after winning the war. But they could hardly wish to see him as Elector of Mainz (a suggestion which was for a moment canvassed at Swedish headquarters); and it must have occurred forcibly to them that princely liberties were unlikely to be much safer if they exchanged Habsburg tyranny for Vasa domination.

Gustavus much underrated the genuineness of their concern and the real force of their objections. In a Protestant league under his direction he saw nothing inherently repugnant to the laws of the Empire. He was not greatly interested in reform of the Empire as an end in itself: he told the burghers of Nuremberg that he had no wish to prescribe new laws for the *Reich*. But on the other hand he had no patience (and his advisers even less) with princes who (as Oxenstierna remarked) had 'centuries of constitutional nonsense in their heads', for such scruples might stand in the way of efficient military collaboration. One way out of the constitutional difficulty, no doubt, would be that he should himself become Emperor, and so regularize the anomalous relationship between himself and his allies and clients. The idea was generally current in 1632, and some of his servants (though not Oxenstierna) spoke of it almost as a solution which must sooner or later be adopted. Undoubtedly the possibility was in his mind: in an angry outburst to Adolf Frederick of Mecklenburg in January 1632, at a time when that prince was proving especially tiresome, he flung out the remark 'If I were Emperor, then would your grace be my prince'; but this was not much more than a manifestation of his exasperation.

It could hardly have been a serious political programme: first, because he was consistent in his determination to hold Pomerania as an Imperial fief; secondly, because such hold as he had over his German allies depended not only on his

159

defence of them against the effects of the Edict of Restitution, but (even more) on the fact that he was their coadjutor in the struggle against the over-mighty power of the Emperor. If the German princes were to free themselves from such Imperial obligations as happened to be inconvenient to their private dynastic policies, it was to Swedish arms that they must look for aid. A Swedish Emperor, from their point of view, made no political sense – especially at a moment when his power appeared more formidable than that of the Habsburgs had ever been since the time of Charles V. William V might have reconciled himself to the substitution of Gustavus for Ferdinand, but John George certainly would not. And however little John George was to be relied upon, he was still Sweden's most powerful ally among the German states. Lastly, whatever might be thought of Richelieu's German policy hitherto, the election of Gustavus as Emperor (on the unlikely supposition that sufficient electors could be found to support him) would present the cardinal with a gratuitous opportunity for forming that 'third party' which he had so far failed to bring into being. It would mean the end of the French alliance. On the whole, it is unlikely that the idea of his election was ever more than one possibility among many, and not a possibility which can have had many attractions for him.

Yet if he was proof against this delusion, he allowed himself to fall victim to another. Throughout 1632 it became increasingly evident that he was not interested in any compromise peace. On the contrary, he became obsessed with the dream of total victory. He would 'clip the wings of the Imperialists so that they shall not fly again'; he would accept no peace which did not secure him, not only against the Austrian but against the Spanish Habsburgs. Oxenstierna, apparently, shared that obsession: in October 1632 he was writing that the only peace that could be acceptable was a peace 'with our foot on their neck and a knife at their throat'. Both believed that they must finish the business once for all, with a victory so decisive and a settlement so buttressed by long-term guarantees that Sweden would never need to have to do the work over again. The Council at home, more immediately aware of the strains imposed on the country, more pragmatic and limited in outlook, less entangled in the dilemmas of German politics, found it hard to share these views. The event was to prove only too plainly the justice of their fears.

But to the king and his chancellor, grappling with uncooperative allies and friends whose fidelity they suspected, and profoundly convinced that no reliance was to be placed on the good faith of papists – to them any compromise seemed a pitfall to avoid. For the time being, they were sure, there must be in Germany what was virtually a Swedish military dictatorship; after the war, a settlement which would permit them to devote their attention to their country's traditional interests. And in the immediate future there must be total victory.

It was no doubt a logical programme, and it is not easy to see a flaw in the chain of reasoning which led them to it; but it was logic at the expense of common sense. Already it was questionable whether total victory, in a military sense, was really attainable. But total victory was the goal to which they had now committed themselves; and in the campaign of 1632 Gustavus would make his last effort to achieve it.

. . .

NOTES

1. 'We must make use of these things [i.e. negotiations] as one uses poisons; which serve as an antidote if one takes a little of them, but are fatal in excess.'
2. English translation of the essential points in Roberts, *Sweden as a Great Power 1611–1697* pp. 145–6.

Chapter 11

FINALE

The tactical innovations for which Gustavus was responsible were so successful, their impact on the art of war so immediate and long-lasting, that it is easy to forget that he was not only a master of tactics, but also a strategist of impressive stature. Clausewitz considered him a learned, cautious, systematic commander; but it seems unlikely that he would have persisted in this judgment if he had had the researches of recent Swedish military historians at his disposal. For though the conquest of Germany was indeed a systematic business – a deliberate organization of successive base areas, a step-by-step advance in which each forward move was solidly underpinned – there was also in it a striking element of boldness, a vastness of scale, an ability to think in large categories, and a conscious striving after a victory of annihilation, which was certainly unique in the first decades of the seventeenth century.

In the early months of 1632 Gustavus Adolphus found himself at the head of six distinct armies (not counting John George's 20,000 Saxons), all of them of respectable proportions, and at least one of them (that under his own command) a good deal more than that. They were disposed in a vast arc, from Silesia to the upper Rhine. Apart from the field armies, his troops were garrisoning nearly a hundred German towns and cities: altogether, they may have numbered something like 100,000 men, to which was to be added some 16,000 at home or in the Baltic provinces. It would, indeed, be impossible for him to concentrate so large a force on a single battlefield: local commitments, wide separation, slow communications, all put obstacles in the way. Since this was so, and since he aimed at decisive superiority at the critical time and place, it was logical to seek to recruit yet more troops, so that he might bring overwhelming force to bear without denuding his other armies. He set as his recruiting target for the winter the enlistment of a further 108,000 men, which would have given him a total strength of 210,000. Germany – even those still-unravaged areas upon which it would be necessary to draw – could hardly support such numbers for long. Total victory might demand concentrations of this order of magnitude; but if so, decision must come quickly, before shortage of supplies, and the indiscipline and mutinies which would be its consequence, caused the whole military edifice to crumble.

Of this Gustavus was well aware; and his strategy was designed accordingly. His plan for 1632 was to finish the war by a great right-handed sweep which should culminate in the crushing of the Habsburg armies within the hereditary lands, and afterwards in the capture of Vienna. The Saxon armies in Silesia and on the Bohemian frontier were to form a pivot on which the main operation was to swing. He would in the first place overrun Bavaria; and as the immediate fruit of its conquest he would occupy Swabia, which would form the last of his base areas, and by its unspoiled resources provide him with the maintenance which he needed for his great new armies. The new Swabian base would be firmly integrated into the territory already under his control: to use his own phrase, it would 'link up the Rhine with the Danube'. It would close the exits from the Alpine passes: just as his lodgement on the Rhine had set a barrier to any intervention from the Spanish Netherlands, so the occupation of Swabia would bar the way to the arrival of any reinforcements from Italy. Once secure in Swabia, he would be able to use Bavaria south of the Danube as the springboard for the final assault upon Vienna from the west. And all the time the great arc of armies would keep up such a pressure on Imperialist forces in other parts of Germany as to make impossible the concentration of superior, or even of equal, numbers against him in the decisive battle which from the beginning he envisaged as the ultimate objective of the campaign.

How was it possible for him to contemplate, and in great measure to carry out, a strategic concept of such breathtaking grandeur? Neither superiority in tactics, nor efficient

163

organization, could alone provide the answer. But there was one decisive factor which distinguished his German campaigns from those which Spain and France and the Dutch were waging in the 1630s. This was the almost total absence from central Europe of towns and cities which had modernized their defences in accordance with the new style known to contemporaries as the *trace italienne*: that is, with angled bastions, ravelins, hornworks, deep ditches, and so forth; and which made a war of rapid movement almost impossible in Flanders. It was too dangerous to leave a strongly fortified city in one's rear, and technically too difficult to reduce it quickly: hence a war of protracted sieges, where battle occurred mainly between besieging forces and the armies sent to besiege the besiegers. None of these obstacles impeded the movements of Gustavus: he could sweep from Breitenfeld to Mainz, from Mainz to Munich, without wasting time on towns which he could obviously capture as soon as he had leisure or inclination to attend to them. On the only occasion when he came up against a city strongly fortified and provided with the latest improvements – at Ingolstadt – he showed no disposition to besiege it. Though he had learned a great deal about gunnery and ballistics, his education and experience did not fit him to cope with formal sieges in the Spanish–Dutch manner, and his temper was probably too impatient to be prepared to accept the slow pace of war conducted on these lines. If he was a master of the use of the spade (as contemporaries admiringly testified), it was not because he was a scientific sapper, tunnelling to plant mines under weak points in a city's wall, but because his rapid construction of large field-fortifications – at Werben, Nuremberg, Naumburg – gave him temporary security, and obviously daunted his adversaries.

In other respects, the grand strategy which Gustavus had in mind depended for its success upon the validity of certain assumptions. In the first place, it assumed that he would be able to raise all the new troops he required. In the event this proved not to be so: instead of the 210,000 on which he had counted, he started on his Bavarian campaign with no more than 120,000 under his own command. Secondly, it assumed that the situation in north Germany was under control. But in fact it was no such thing. The failure after Breitenfeld to finish off the resistance in the Lower Saxon Circle now proved to have been disastrous. At the end of 1631 the Imperialists in this area had been reduced to a handful of strong places and an insignificant number of scattered troops. But just before Christmas Pappenheim arrived in Hameln with a general commission to organize resistance and prevent the Swedes from reducing the Circle to subjection. The resources at his disposal were modest: at no time does his army seem to have amounted to more than 8,000 men. Against him he had no less than four Swedish armies, numbering in all something like 30,000. The disparity of force was so great that Gustavus was perhaps justified in regarding the fighting in the Lower Saxon Circle as no more than mopping-up operations of peripheral importance, and in refusing to be distracted by them from his real objectives. But it soon became evident that Pappenheim had no intention of being mopped-up. The Swedish commanders with whom he had to deal were tardy, over-cautious, blind to opportunities, and disposed to quarrel among themselves. Gustavus sought to remedy the deficiencies of his subordinates by giving them more explicit orders, which were often irrelevant by the time they arrived. He tried to impose some degree of co-operation upon them by sending civilians as his legates – a measure which the generals hotly resented. If he had sent Oxenstierna, as in the end he intended to do, the chancellor's authority might have mended matters. If he had gone himself, the situation would probably have been brought under control within a matter of weeks. As it was, the Lower Saxon Circle continued to be a kind of 'Spanish ulcer'.

The heart of the Swedish position in Germany lay in Thuringia. Through the difficult defiles of the Thuringian forest passed the life-line which connected the Swedish armies on the Rhine and the Main with the coastal base in Pomerania. Upon the keeping open of this route depended Gustavus's communications with Stockholm. The great bastion of Erfurt was strongly held in order to protect it; one of the seven armies was specially detailed to safeguard it. But it formed a narrow bottleneck between Saxony and the Lower Saxon Circle. If Pappenheim should succeed in securing for himself a virtually unimpeded freedom of action in the Circle he might strike south-eastward and sever this artery. If, on the other hand, Saxony should be overwhelmed by the Imperialist forces, it lay open to attack from the opposite flank. Worst of all would be an Imperialist pincer-movement in the shape of simultaneous thrusts from east and west.

Gustavus may have underestimated the danger in the Lower Saxon Circle, but he could not be accused of lack of concern for the position in Saxony. This provided a third reason why his strategic plans for the campaign of 1632 were never suffered to develop unimpeded. John George might for the moment be loyal to the Swedish alliance, and Gustavus was usually careful to handle him tactfully, but the king had little confidence in the Elector's steadfastness, and not much more in the capabilities of his Saxon army. Moreover, the Swedish alliance by no means commended itself to all of John George's advisers: there were both pro-Swedish and anti-Swedish factions in Dresden, in constant struggle for the control of John George's troubled mind. There were still those who pinned their hopes on the emergence of a 'third party' which should persuade the Emperor to a compromise peace, and look forward to bundling the foreigner out of Germany.

It was disquieting that among them was the Elector's commander-in-chief, Hans George von Arnim. Arnim was a Brandenburger who had served under Wallenstein and had recently transferred from the Imperial to the Saxon service; he was the only one of John George's generals of any real capacity, and when he resigned his command (as he did from time to time) John George had to cajole him into thinking better of it. The terms of Sweden's alliance with Saxony left Gustavus with no control over Saxon operations, and Arnim conducted his campaigns without much consideration for Swedish grand strategy. He showed little sign of resigning himself to the passive role which Gustavus had designed for the Saxon army: instead of standing fast and serving as a kind of anchor for the Swedish position in Germany, he had in October embarked on a rash invasion of Bohemia, which (though it captured Prague) left the Saxon forces in a deep salient, in obvious danger of disaster as soon as the Imperialists could rally for a counter-offensive. Later he conducted successful but (from Gustavus's point of view) risky and irrelevant operations in Silesia. Throughout the whole of the Bavarian campaign, therefore, Gustavus was haunted by the possibility of a disaster to the Saxon armies, and a political collapse in the Saxon capital.

The situation in Saxony appeared all the more precarious,

since already on 22 November 1631 Arnim had begun personal negotiations with Wallenstein. Here entered the fourth, and in the end the most important, of those elements which combined to put Gustavus's calculations out of reckoning: the resurrection of Wallenstein. Since his enforced dismissal in 1630 Wallenstein had been lying low, awaiting a turn of the wheel which should once more give an opening to his measureless ambition. He had bitterly resented his desertion by the Emperor; he cherished a lively hatred of Maximilian; and in the summer of 1631 he may perhaps have sabotaged Tilly's activities on the Elbe, and forced him to his disastrous invasion of Saxon territory, by refusing to allow the armies of the League to draw supplies from his estates. It suited his purpose to pose as a Czech patriot, and certainly he was in touch with some of the Bohemian exiles. Through one of them, Count von Thurn, he had made contact with Gustavus at the end of May 1631, and in July had offered him support if the Swedes would provide him with an army. At that stage Gustavus had been prepared at least to listen to him; but after Breitenfeld there seemed no need to pursue the negotiation.

Yet if Breitenfeld thus meant that Wallenstein lost the chance of striking a bargain with Sweden, it opened the way to his restoration to his Imperial command. The crisis confronting Ferdinand II was now so grave that he must find a new general, and a new army, without delay. Of those who had taken the lead in forcing Wallenstein's dismissal, Maximilian was in no condition to renew his objections, and John George was already an open enemy. The Saxon invasion of Bohemia (which menaced Wallenstein's duchy of Friedland) removed the last hesitations on either side. On 5 December Wallenstein was reinstated in his command, with wider powers than ever before; and he at once began the formation of an army on Bohemian soil. It was a development which seriously compromised Gustavus's programme. For it meant that once Wallenstein had completed the process of mustering and training his troops, Silesia, Saxony and Thuringia would all be within striking distance of a force which might well be more formidable than those that could be collected to oppose it and would certainly be led by a general who would be more than a match for Arnim or William of Weimar. The very area where stability was essential was now put in jeopardy. Since this was so, the best hope must lie in inflicting upon Bavaria blows so serious that Wallenstein would be forced to come to Maximilian's aid before his preparations were complete.

In these circumstances Gustavus could not wait to bring his own army up to the strength he had considered necessary. When he started for the Danube in March 1632, he started 90,000 men short. His hope was to catch Tilly north of the river, and beat him; but Tilly was too quick for him. Gustavus therefore took the opportunity to make a detour to Nuremberg, where he was well received. Fortified by a contingent of 2,000 men and a monthly contribution of 20,000 *rdr*, he made his way by rapid marches southwards. He reached the Danube at Donauwörth. The Imperialist garrison decamped at the last moment; but this did not prevent the Swedish army from cutting down all found in arms, and many who had no arms at all: as at Frankfurt-on-Oder, Protestantism proved no protection against a mercenary soldiery. By making Donauwörth his crossing-place over the Danube, Gustavus put himself into a position to overrun that triangle of Swabian territory which was bounded by the Danube, the Lech and the Alps: in a position, therefore, to establish himself in the final base which he needed for the assault on Vienna.

On the other hand, he was now separated from his objective by the obstacle of the River Lech; behind which Maximilian and Tilly stood with their army to bar the way into Bavaria. Deep, swift, swollen with the Alpine snows, the Lech was a barrier which it was impossible to turn, and which no other commander of that age would have deemed it possible to force. But necessity left him no alternative but to try to force it, in the face of a powerful army established in a carefully chosen position. On 5 April 1632, in a classic operation, the crossing was effected: diversionary assaults to mislead the defenders, dense smoke-screens to blind them, an artillery barrage of massive proportions at the crossing-place, the technical innovation of a floating bridge almost flush with the water, and hence less vulnerable to enemy fire, and the trick was done: he was over the river. Maximilian's army retreated in confusion to the great modern fortress of Ingolstadt, carrying the mortally wounded Tilly with them, and Gustavus proceeded to occupy Augsburg, imposing on the city a stringent oath of loyalty to the Swedish crown, and a monthly contribution of 20,000 *rdr*. Bavaria, it seemed, was at his mercy; and little mercy he showed it. For this was Maximilian's base and supply area, and its resources must be denied him: the Swedish forces devastated it with unusual and systematic thoroughness.

Gustavus now hoped to keep Maximilian pinned down in Ingolstadt, which lay on the north bank of the Danube, and, while thus engaging his attention, to push eastward, complete the conquest of the Bavarian lands south of the river, and take Regensburg. But things did not work out like that. Maximilian slipped away from Ingolstadt, leaving behind him a garrison strong enough to withstand a protracted siege, and reached Regensburg with his army before Gustavus was aware what was afoot. Reconnaissance suggested that it might be almost as difficult to take Regensburg as it obviously was to take Ingolstadt. He might conquer Bavaria, he might savour the satisfaction of occupying Maximilian's capital; but there was no denying that the campaign was no longer going according to plan. Maximilian had been defeated, but he had not been knocked out. The road to Vienna was still barred. Above all, Wallenstein was still menacing Saxony and Thuringia. Gustavus had calculated that any serious threat to Bavaria and Upper Austria must necessarily have the consequence of bringing Wallenstein hurrying to the rescue. The pressure on Saxony would thus be relieved, and Wallenstein himself would be brought to battle before his preparations had been completed. But the news of the Lech appeared to make no impression in Bohemia. The threat to Ingolstadt, which Gustavus had imagined would be a powerful persuader, apparently left Wallenstein unmoved. He saw no reason to quit his excellent quarters in Bohemia, and interrupt the methodical organization of his troops, in order to lend a hand to a prince who had shown himself his enemy; nor was he particularly concerned to safeguard the Habsburg hereditary lands. He had his own game to play, and had no intention of allowing Gustavus to divert him from it.

Just what that game was, and how dangerous to the Swedish position it might be, was something that Gustavus would have given much to know. But now that he was in south Germany his sources of information were not what they had been when his armies stood on the Elbe or the Main. In particular, it was extraordinarily difficult to discover exactly what the situation was in Saxony. He knew that Arnim was

169

quarrelling with John George, that both were seriously alarmed at the prospect of an attack by Wallenstein's armies, and that Arnim was still in touch with Wallenstein. But whether the danger to Saxony was as serious as they thought, whether Arnim was any longer to be trusted, or whether his talks with Wallenstein were no more than devices to buy time – this he found impossible to decide. His representatives in Dresden continued to send him reassuring reports on the military situation; and in the light of these, and in the absence of any immediate prospect of the great battle for which he was hoping, it seemed reasonable to fall back on the other half of his strategic programme and perfect the 'linking of the Rhine and the Danube' by the complete subjugation of Swabia.

It was with this idea that, after the occupation of Munich, he turned once more westwards towards Lake Constance. But at Memmingen, on 25 May 1632, came news which forced him to a drastic change of programme. The position in the north, it appeared, was crumbling. Arnim was in full retreat from Bohemia; Saxony was threatened with imminent invasion, with little prospect of successful resistance; the Thuringian bottleneck was in danger. So critical did the position appear to him that on 2 June he wrote to Oxenstierna suggesting an immediate levy of conscripts in Sweden, in order to strengthen the army at home in the event of disaster in Germany. There was no escaping the conclusion: Gustavus had lost the initiative. So far from having succeeded in diverting Wallenstein from Saxony by his attack on Bavaria, he now found himself diverted from Bavaria by Wallenstein's attack on Saxony. The tables were turned with a vengeance.

There was only one thing to be done. Saxony must be rescued, at whatever hazard. On 4 June Gustavus broke up from Donauwörth and headed north, taking 18,500 men and seventy guns with him, and leaving the remainder of his army to guard his Bavarian conquests and his Swabian base. The prospect of victory had made Wallenstein ready to collaborate with Maximilian: on 21 June their armies effected their junction. Their united forces now numbered 48,000 men, and they were eager for battle. For Gustavus, on the other hand, the problem was how to avoid it and yet prevent the Imperialists from crushing Saxony. His answer was the Nuremberg leaguer.

Nuremberg was by this time a Swedish ally. The city was rich, untouched by the war, well fortified, and well stocked with provisions and military supplies. Outside its walls, but linking up with its defences, Gustavus now constructed a vast fortified camp, within which his army could rest secure. Wallenstein could not ignore it. His attack on Saxony had therefore to be interrupted; his plans were thrown out of gear: Gustavus had effected his object. Wallenstein was too prudent a commander to risk a defeat by a headlong assault upon the Swedish positions: as always he preferred an indirect riposte. His answer was simple but masterly. He took a leaf out of his opponent's book, and at Zirndorf constructed a leaguer of his own. Thence he could keep watch on his adversary, pounce upon him if he were so rash as to afford an opportunity for battle, and, if all went well, cut off his supplies so completely that he must be driven to a desperate sortie and probable disaster. In this calculation, however, there was more than one flaw. In the first place, Gustavus was well supplied in Nuremberg, and under no necessity to give Wallenstein the chance he was looking for. In the second, he had no intention of leaving the situation as it was. There were plenty of Swedish troops available in central Germany to come to the aid of the army in Nuremberg: all that was needed was to organize their concentration. This was not designed simply to be a relief operation to extricate a beleaguered army. It was clearly offensive in intention.

It was now Gustavus's turn to borrow the tactics of his adversary. The armies which he summoned to Nuremberg were to blockade the blockader, to sever Wallenstein's supply lines and cut him off from reinforcements precisely as he had hoped to do to Gustavus, and at last to meet him in battle with the advantage of numbers. The only questions were how far the other Swedish armies within reach could disengage themselves from their local commitments, and whether their movements could be synchronized: if not, they were in danger of being overwhelmed in detail before they could concentrate. The difficulties of communications and supply, the difficulty of obtaining speedy intelligence, made the co-ordination of these forces a matter of great intricacy. It was a sure instinct that led the king to entrust what was essentially a question of logistics to someone who was not a soldier at all – Oxenstierna.

Even Oxenstierna could not do all he would have wished. The army of the Rhine could get away without trouble, for here Gustav Horn had been conducting highly successful operations. But in the Lower Saxon Circle Pappenheim was still in command of the situation, and of the generals who were supposed to deal with him only William V had the nerve to obey Oxenstierna's summons. Further east, William of Weimar, in a sudden panic at the prospect that Saxony might make a separate peace, had actually started on an unauthorized invasion of the electorate, and was only stopped at the last minute from prosecuting this lunatic enterprise by a direct order from Gustavus. Fortunately, John George was magnanimous enough to overlook this scandalous affair, and despite the imminent danger to his country generously sent five regiments to Oxenstierna's assistance. Against all the odds, the complex operation was carried through without a hitch: on 17 August the relieving forces made their junction; and soon afterwards they arrived at Nuremberg. It was a masterpiece of precise planning.

The arrival of the relieving army did not in itself solve Gustavus's problems. It was true that he was now free to march where he would, leaving a strong garrison in Nuremberg behind him. But it was not for this that he had concentrated his forces. In central and northern Germany there was no military objective worth his while except Wallenstein's army. But if Wallenstein were to refuse to come out and fight? Gustavus had calculated, as Wallenstein had calculated, that difficulties of supply would eventually compel him to risk a battle: 'This kind of devil', he had remarked, 'cometh not out save by prayer and fasting'. But there was little sign that Wallenstein was much inconvenienced by the Swedish counter-blockade. Thus the logic of the situation was driving the king to the conclusion that even if his adversary remained within his entrenchments the risk of an attack must be taken: anything else was strategically irrelevant. And so, by merely sitting still, Wallenstein forced upon him the most difficult military enterprise of the war.

The prospects were anything but encouraging. Wallenstein had now been in his camp for nearly two months; his position was carefully prepared, and it was in itself formidable. It lay to the west of Nuremberg and to the south of Fürth, along a ridge running parallel to the River Rednitz. Attack from that eastern side was very difficult, both by the nature of the ground and because the most likely crossing-places were commanded by Wallenstein's guns. To the south and west the country was more open, but here assault was made almost impossible by lack of roads practicable for artillery. To the north the position rose gradually to a bluff hill – the Alte Feste – which lay just beyond the perimeter of the camp, where the ground fell away in rocky slopes of tangled woodland. On the night of 22–3 August 1632, after vain probings across the Rednitz, Gustavus moved his troops out to Fürth and established them in a new camp there. Wallenstein now expected that the king would move round the northern end of his position and attack him from the north-west or west, and he accordingly drew up his army in battle array on this front.

His actions were misinterpreted by the Swedish intelligence, which reported, with disastrous plausibility, that the enemy was in process of abandoning his works and in the act of decamping, leaving only a small rearguard around the Alte Feste to cover his retreat. This information seems to have reached Gustavus before dawn on the 24th. If he were to catch Wallenstein and beat him, he must act quickly. He proceeded, therefore, with the minimum of delay, to improvise an assault. He sent his cavalry far to the westward to cut off Wallenstein's presumed retreat, and hurled the rest of his army at the Alte Feste, in the expectation of an easy victory over weakened resistance. It was not long before he discovered his mistake. Throughout the whole day his troops fought their way up the difficult approaches. But the nature of the terrain was uniquely unfavourable to the new Swedish tactics: slippery ground prevented the bringing up of the guns; the combination of arms was scarcely practicable; the regiment-pieces had little chance of making their effect. The Swedish army never took the Alte Feste, and never came near to reaching Wallenstein's perimeter. When on the following morning it was decided to break off the attack, they had suffered 2,400 casualties, including over 1,000 dead, against Wallenstein's 600.

It was a serious setback, the first check in what since Neu-Brandeburg had been an uninterrupted career of victory: the legend of Swedish invincibility was shattered overnight. But it was not in itself decisive: indeed, it seems likely that Gustavus contemplated renewing the attempt under more favourable auspices. What was decisive was the events of the following week. In the crowded camp at Fürth supplies began to run out, and especially supplies of fodder: the horses died in their thousands. The men began to sicken too. Discipline was difficult to maintain; desertions began, in a trickle at first, and then by thousands: within a fortnight of the failure at the Alte Feste Gustavus had lost a third of his army. By 8 September there was no help for it; he could stay there no longer. On that day he marched the remnants of his army away, leaving Oxenstierna and a strong garrison to hold Nuremberg. Wallenstein watched his departure with composure. He could afford to do so, for he had won the game. But he had not yet won the match.

It was not easy to know what to do now, or where to go. Gustavus had lost the initiative, and it was far from obvious how he could recapture it. He might unite his forces with the army of John George. But to this there was a variety of objections: it might cause political friction; it seemed to be unnecessary, since while Wallenstein had been tied up at Nuremberg the Saxon armies had been doing well; and it would impose a heavy burden of supply upon the territories of his ally. In any case, he persuaded himself (on very inadequate grounds) that Saxony was in no great peril, since Wallenstein might shortly be expected to go into winter quarters. Or Gustavus might go at last to the Lower Saxon Circle, and finally reduce it to order. It would have meant confining his efforts to a subordinate theatre, but it would have been a practical and feasible measure, which assuredly would have paid long-term military dividends. After all, it was now clear that the original programme of finishing the war this year could no longer be carried out; if the question were (as it seemed to be) how most usefully to employ his time for the remainder of the campaigning season, this at least was a sensible answer. But he could not bring himself so easily to abandon the grand strategic design with which he had started off in Mainz. He still hankered after a campaign in Bavaria. He still told himself that if he went south Wallenstein would follow him, despite his previous experience to the contrary. He still argued that a Swedish army on the Danube would relieve the pressure on John George – and this although he was simultaneously arguing that John George was not in any real danger. The truth was that in the month or so after Nuremberg both sides were moving in a fog, blundering about in the dark for lack of early information of each other's movements, reacting nervously to inaccurate reports, and moving to counter threats which in the end turned out to be imaginary.

Within that fog, secret agents and accredited diplomats were engaged upon still foggier negotiations. The disaster at Nuremberg had made Gustavus revise his views about the expediency of treating with Wallenstein. He might not be an ally to be trusted, but plainly he was an enemy whom it was worth while to buy off. The price offered was handsome: Wallenstein should have the diocese of Würzburg, with the title of Duke of Franconia, in exchange for his lost duchy of Mecklenburg, and perhaps, if all went well, the crown of Bohemia too. But the appeal was not only to his ambition, but also to his principles, in so far as he had any. The Edict of Restitution was to be withdrawn, the ambiguities of the religious peace cleared up, Lutherans to be tolerated in Catholic countries. There was to be a large distribution of former ecclesiastical lands to satisfy the major German Protestant states; but the Elector of Mainz was to recover his electorate, and Maximilian was to be consoled for the loss of the Palatinate by being given Upper Austria. Sweden would take Pomerania in perpetual possession, but as an Imperial fief. On the religious side, these were proposals not very different from some which Wallenstein himself had recently outlined to Arnim. But in no way are they to be taken as representing Gustavus's considered plans for a peace settlement. They were terms which had to appear reasonably plausible if they were to serve their purpose of landing this big fish. Wallenstein declined the offer, and transmitted the intelligence to Vienna, But he did not break off all contacts: it was his practice always to keep his options open; and negotiation would still be a possibility in the future. Equally hollow, and equally fruitless, were renewed attempts by a couple of optimistic French agents to arrange a three months' truce with Bavaria. Oxenstierna had no doubt that these were mere 'popish practices'; Gustavus, still remembering the truce negotiations of January, put no faith in them: Maximilian, he considered, was 'as slippery as an eel'. Neither of them had the least intention of tempering their real terms for peace:

expediency might for the moment dictate a more pliant language, but the thaw would disappear once the wind blew strongly again from the north.

Meanwhile Gustavus had turned south again. On 26 September 1632 he once more crossed the Danube, and proceeded to mopping-up operations in Swabia – hardly the kind of enterprise, one would have thought, to bring Wallenstein rushing to the rescue. Before long Gustavus realized this. He accordingly turned about, and tried the effect of a threat to Ingolstadt. The result was as negative as before. Wallenstein was getting ready to deal with Saxony, and was not disposed to allow his attention to wander. Maximilian, to be sure, was worried about Ingolstadt, and on 4 October began to move his army back to Bavaria: to this extent, at least, Gustavus's diversion had been effective. But what Maximilian did was of minor importance: what mattered was that Wallenstein was on the point of effecting a junction with Pappenheim. And this was ominous. With their united armies they would be in a position to overwhelm John George; they would be able to bar the Thuringian passes; they could at will crush the Swedish armies in the Lower Saxon Circle. The news of their imminent juncture reached Gustavus at Neustadt on 5 October, and he was not slow to grasp its significance. If Saxony were to be saved, he must go north, with all speed. The operations in Bavaria were abruptly suspended; for the last time he turned his face towards home.

He reached Nördlingen on 10 October, to be met by more encouraging tidings: news that Maximilian was no longer with Wallenstein, news that the corps of Holck and Gallas had also been detached, news (above all) that Pappenheim had not yet arrived. If the king were quick, he might still be able to bring his enemy to battle on equal terms before the year was out. At Nuremberg, a week later, he learned that Wallenstein's invasion of Saxony had already begun. He now pressed on by forced marches, taking Oxenstierna with him: in seventeen days his troops covered 630 kilometres. His object was to secure the Thuringian passes before Pappenheim could reach them. For all his haste, he would have been too late had it not been for the enterprise of Bernard of Weimar, who on his own initiative moved his army into the area in the nick of time, and stood his ground until the king came up with him at Arnstadt. In a final dash Gustavus just succeeded in beating Wallenstein to the important passage of the Saale at Naumburg. Here, in a crook of the river reminiscent of the position at Werben, he constructed the last of his fortified camps and gathered his troops inside it. Wallenstein seems to have drawn the conclusion that it was his intention to go into winter quarters here, and it seemed to him that the strategy which had been so successful at Nuremberg might well be applicable now. He would cut Gustavus's supply lines, ravage his supply areas, pen him into his encampment; whether there were a battle or not, he would by next spring have established himself firmly athwart the whole width of north Germany from the Oder to the Weser, and would be in a position to bar Gustavus's escape-route to the ports of Pomerania. In these bold calculations there was but one error, and it was fatal: he mistook the intentions of his adversary.

Unlike Wallenstein, Gustavus by no means considered his encampment at Naumburg as marking the end of the campaign. He was still hoping for an opportunity for battle. And on 4 November he received the astounding news that Wallenstein, almost in the presence of his enemy, was dispersing his forces and going into winter quarters. 'Now in very truth I believe', he is said to have exclaimed, 'that God has delivered him into my hands.'

At the moment when these tidings reached Gustavus Adolphus, Wallenstein had dispersed as many as fifteen regiments to quarters at various distances from the main body. The most important of these detachments was the nine regiments under Pappenheim's command: on 5 November they were at Halle, no less than thirty-five miles away. Gustavus had at his disposal an army which had a slight overall superiority in numbers, though compared with Wallenstein's it was weak in cavalry (6,200, as against more than 8,000), and less strong in pikemen than its commander would have wished. But he had – at least, potentially – the enormous advantage of surprise: Wallenstein had no idea that he was about to be attacked. Given ordinary good fortune, and no unexpected delays, Gustavus was confident that he could beat him; and early on 5 November he set out to catch him.

But the whole history of the next two days, from the Swedish point of view, was a history of malign accidents and cruel strokes of fortune. By pure chance, an Imperialist detachment blundered into the Swedish army as it was about to cross the river Rippach. By obstinate fighting it held up their advance for several precious hours, and it alerted Wallenstein to the danger that was impending over him. Instead of being able to fall upon an unsuspecting foe on the 5th, Gustavus was forced to defer his action to the following day. Wallenstein was given not less than sixteen hours to call in his scattered detachments; which meant, in practice, to call in Pappenheim from Halle. Pappenheim did not receive the order to rally till after midnight, and the foot did not start to move till six hours after that; but the cavalry set off almost immediately. If Gustavus was to finish with Wallenstein before they arrived, it was essential that he lose no time.

His army was already within four gun-shot lengths of Wallenstein's position. That position was carefully prepared: its right resting on the village of Lützen, whose windmills formed the anchor of the whole line; its front protected by a ditch and the embanked highroad that ran parallel with it. Only his left was insecure, exposed to enveloping movements by Swedish cavalry: this was the gap which Pappenheim's arrival was designed to fill, and until he should fill it Wallenstein was in danger of seeing his whole army rolled up from its left flank. If he were to escape that danger he needed time, and he needed luck. Both were vouchsafed to him.

On 6 November 1632 the Swedish reveille sounded at 5 a.m.; the army was drawn up ready for assault by soon after 7 a.m. Even making the utmost speed, Pappenheim's cavalry could hardly be expected before noon: there was ample time for a victory. Time; but not visibility. In the early morning of 6 November the whole Lützen position was shrouded in impenetrable mist. It did not begin to clear until after 10 a.m.; operations did not become practicable before 11 a.m.: Gustavus had been cheated of four vital hours. Even so, it seemed for a little while that he might snatch a quick decision. His centre battled across the ditch and the road; his right wing began to envelop the Imperialists' left. At this moment, about noon, Pappenheim appeared with his cavalry, and it looked as though he might just be in time to avert disaster. But he had hardly begun the attack which was to restore the situation before he was mortally wounded by a cannon-ball; an Imperialist regiment refused to fight; and a panic flight developed which threatened the whole Imperialist left with disintegration. At the same moment the Swedish centre, pressing forward, captured seven of Wallenstein's guns, and turned them on his own men. The battle seemed as good as over.

At this supreme moment the mist came down again, thicker than ever; hiding the mass-desertion on the Imperialist left, concealing from the Swedes the extent of their advantage, blotting out the prospect of speedy victory. Almost simultaneously the check was followed by disaster. The Swedish left had run into tough resistance, and in an effort to lighten the pressure upon it Gustavus took the Småland regiment of cavalry to that part of the front and launched it in a charge upon the enemy. Almost immediately, he was hit; his horse carried him away from his escort; he was caught up helplessly in the mêlée. An Imperialist horseman fired a pistol into his back; he fell heavily from the saddle; and as he lay face downward in the mud a final shot through the head ended his life. The body lay where it fell. Enemy plunderers took the king's ring, his watch, the chain which he habitually wore around his neck, and one of his spurs; until at last, stripped to the shirt, the corpse lay half-naked and unregarded, while his riderless horse careered about the battlefield.

The command devolved on Bernard of Weimar, and it was Bernard who by his resolution saved the situation and turned near-defeat into clear victory. All hope of success on the right was now at an end, for Piccolomini and his cuirassiers had taken Pappenheim's place, and the Swedes could only with the utmost difficulty hold fast against his furious charges. But after exceptionally bloody fighting the Swedish centre made good its ground on the far side of the road, the Swedish left captured the Lützen windmills one after another, and every piece of Imperialist artillery fell into Swedish hands. When about 5 p.m. the light began to fail, the issue had in fact been decided. The key to Wallenstein's position was in Bernard's hands, and only the tenacity of the Imperialist foot prevented a complete breakthrough. Near nightfall, Pappenheim's weary infantry at last arrived after their long march from Halle; but Wallenstein had had enough. Ammunition was exhausted; both sides were fought to a standstill; and so ferocious had been the fighting that the Swedes lost a third of their army, the Imperialists an even larger proportion.

And so the long and fascinating duel with Wallenstein

179

reached its end: not with that victory of annihilation which Gustavus had always looked for, and which only two days ago he had believed to be within his grasp; but at least with a success which shattered Wallenstein's strategy for the winter, re-established the reputation of the Swedish arms, and made possible the prosecution of those plans for a Protestant League which were already on the agenda for the forthcoming congress at Ulm. It would not be easy, now that Gustavus was dead, to carry out his programme for Germany in its full extent; but Lützen had at least ensured that it should not be impossible.

Chapter 12

PROSPECT AND RETROSPECT

Though the mists had parted at Lützen for long enough to permit the king's death to be avenged in victory, they were visibly thickening over Germany. In the south, indeed, princes and cities who feared the resurrection of Habsburg power and the implementation of the Edict of Restitution might still place their reliance on Swedish succour, and be willing to enter into a permanent confederation under Swedish leadership. But in the north, in those regions with which, after all, Sweden's interests were most directly concerned, how would it be with them? What hope was there of inducing the great Protestant electorates to sink their interests in a Swedish-dominated security system? What prospect of enlisting George William of Brandenburg, embittered by Swedish insistence on the retention of Pomerania; or John George, for whom the king's death had removed his most formidable rival for the leadership of German Protestantism; or Frederick V, thrust aside and humiliated in the name of military necessity? And the other allies – Adolf Frederick of Mecklenburg, William of Weimar, Frederick Ulric of Wolfenbüttel, and the rest – most of whom had at one time or another been made to smart under Gustavus's impatience or contempt – how long would they continue to fight, now that he was gone, if a tolerable settlement should appear to be within sight? They had, indeed, been near to drowning; but it had been necessary to stun some of them in order to effect their rescue, and even those who had escaped this drastic treatment were beginning to feel the lifebelts which Gustavus had thrown them as being unpleasantly restrictive of their freedom of movement.

If Lützen had been a defeat instead of a victory, it would

not have been long before these discontents became obvious. Two more years of Swedish military ascendancy enabled the political organization set up at Ulm to expand into the League of Heilbronn; but it was a league from which Saxony and Brandenburg held aloof, and it depended for its existence on the continued successes of Swedish arms: the disaster of Nördlingen (August 1634) would expose its fragility. By 1635 the German Protestant princes, weary of the endless struggle, moved for once by a feeling which was akin to German patriotism and which was certainly a revulsion against the foreigner, were ready to accept the Peace of Prague, though its terms left the Emperor in a stronger position than any Habsburg had enjoyed since the battle of Mühlberg. With that, the eviction of the Swedish armies from Germany appeared a possibility. By 1638 it was clear that Sweden could hope to fight her way to acceptable peace terms only with the aid of France. Despite the Peace of Prague, the constitutional struggle within the Empire which had lain at the root of the war was by no means over, and, from the princes' point of view, Swedish or French pressure upon the Habsburgs was still a useful instrument in conducting it: without such pressure the victory of particularism in 1648 would hardly have been possible. For their part, they wished nothing better than to withdraw into neutrality and allow the foreigners to fight this battle for them. As to the religious issue, by the 1640s it had become of secondary importance.

Thus within three years of Gustavus's death the situation in Germany had been transformed. The plans which he had matured in the months after Breitenfeld had lost most of their relevance, and the whole question of Swedish involvement had to be reconsidered with these altered circumstances in mind. In the eighteen months before Oxenstierna returned home in 1636, a vocal section of the Council in Stockholm was for getting out of Germany on almost any terms. After Nördlingen it was obvious that the whole idea of erecting a Protestant alliance under Swedish leadership must be abandoned: Gustavus's solution to the problem of security had become a vanished· dream. Was there, then, any intelligible war aim that remained? Oxenstierna was convinced that there was. Though institutional security might now be unattainable, territorial security, as it had first been conceived in 1630, was still a necessity: Pomerania and Wismar were still worth fighting for. And indemnity – that was simply essential. Even in the darkest moments, when all seemed lost, the regents in Stockholm believed that they must stand out for a cash indemnity; for without such an indemnity what hope was there of paying off the arrears due to the Swedish armies?

As the areas under Swedish control contracted, it became less possible to live on the country: hence the increasing importance, in the later stages of the war, of the French subsidies. Not that the ideal element in Swedish policy had wholly vanished: Oxenstierna still felt himself (and was by Europe regarded) as the leading champion of the Protestant cause. It was Swedish and Hessian insistence that eventually obtained the inclusion of the Calvinist states within the scope of that principle of *cujus regio ejus religio*[1] which finally prevailed at Westphalia in 1648. But essentially what Sweden now wanted was territorial and monetary compensation: Pomerania and Wismar (and later Bremen and Verden) for security's sake, as outposts from which to keep a watchful eye on Germany, and as a reward for sacrifices; together with a large lump sum – originally Sweden asked for 20,000,000 *rdr* – for 'the contentment of the soldiery'.

In the end, barring a large abatement of the cash indemnity, Oxenstierna got what he wanted. The Peace of Westphalia did seem to give Sweden the security which Gustavus had sought in 1630. And it did register a final check to the danger to Protestantism from the Counter-Reformation. Despite all that happened after 1634 it is still probably true that Gustavus Adolphus, by his intervention, saved his country from a danger that was real; and also that he saved German Protestanism in its hour of greatest peril. The terms of the Peace of Westphalia ratified that achievement. Whether in the process he did Germany a service is another question: a question with which it is hardly reasonable to expect him to have been concerned. As to Sweden's security – which was undoubtedly the central element of his policy – he could hardly be expected to foresee that in the post-Westphalian world Sweden would conceivably be *less* secure than in 1630. For a century Swedish statesmen had been moved by the fear of war on two fronts. The acquisition of the empire, the standing commitment in Germany, presented them with the danger of war not on two fronts but on three, as Charles X would find out; and it was a consciousness of that implication which led to defensive measures in Pomerania which Sweden after 1660 could ill afford: Charles X estimated that the safety of Pomerania demanded an army of 8,000 in peace time and 17,000 in time of war.

From the point of view of the permanent political interests of Sweden, the German venture, after all, had been a distraction: a commitment forced upon Gustavus by circumstance, a complication not of his seeking. The struggle for maritime supremacy against the old enemy, Denmark, the defence of his throne against a Catholicizing dynastic rival – these still remained, unaffected by Breitenfeld and Lützen. They would continue to be the main preoccupations of Swedish policy for years to come. It had been the war in Poland that had provoked Swedish intervention in Russia and had led to the Peace of Stolbova, with all its far-reaching consequences for eastern and northern Europe. It had brought the conquest of Riga, and by the acquisition of Livonia had given Sweden something that might be called a Baltic empire. The years after Westphalia would see a reorientation of Swedish policy in many respects: friendship with Spain, a courting of Vienna which was a consequence of Sweden's new position as holder of an Imperial fief. But the quarrel with Poland remained alive, and one reason why it flared into open war again in 1655 was the refusal of the elder Vasa line to abandon its claim to the Swedish throne. One reason; but not the only one. For the progressive debility of the Polish republic was the opportunity of her neighbours, and particularly of Russia. Poland was becoming a power-vacuum into which states more dangerous than herself might irrupt.

It was to forestall such an irruption by Russia that Charles X launched his pre-emptive attack in 1655; it was concern to prevent Russian expansion that lay behind Sweden's amicable relations with a weakened Poland in the years after 1660. In the last half of the century the Baltic provinces would become not a bridle upon the Poles, but a bulwark against Moscow: the danger that Gustavus and Oxenstierna foresaw when they imposed the Peace of Stolbova would have become a reality. The spirit of Ivan IV was abroad again; the Russians once more sniffed the sea. In the beginning the occupation of the Baltic provinces made political sense, and was even a necessity. In the long run it turned out to be a commitment which could scarcely be sustained against the weight of Russian numbers. But it was an inheritance which no Swedish statesman could bring himself to abandon; not only from considerations of national safety, but also for economic reasons. Riga was one of the great ports of Europe, and was in wealth and population the greatest city in the Swedish dominions. Livonia was Sweden's granary: in the 1680s Stockholm on occasion depended on imports of Livonian corn to save her from famine. Even Charles XI, that most prudent and least expansionist of monarchs, was more concerned to strengthen than to relax Sweden's grip on the Baltic provinces, though he was more immediately anxious about Denmark. There the German venture had merely postponed a solution. But it had seemed to make a solution easier, for it had tipped the military balance in Sweden's favour. The veteran armies of Torstensson extorted the Peace of Brömsebro in 1645; Charles X, schooled in the German wars, imposed the Peace of Roskilde in 1658. By 1660 one great question had been settled: Sweden had attained her geographical limits within the Scandinavian peninsula, and the Sound had ceased to be a Danish stream. No longer was Sweden liable to be penned by Denmark within the Baltic. And this, certainly, was a legitimate political objective. What was not legitimate was the design, which Charles X entertained after Roskilde, of incorporating the whole of Denmark into the Swedish realm, and degrading it to the status of a Swedish province.

The empire had entailed upon Sweden the status of a great power, with corresponding obligations. With France, she was one of the guarantors of the Westphalian settlement, inescapably involved in the great questions of continental politics. In 1648 her army was the best in Europe. But she found herself after the peace with extensive overseas dominions, scattered in isolated pockets from the Weser to the Neva, facing a number of powers who might (and on two occasions did) combine to dispossess her of her gains. The defence of this realm required the maintenance of armed forces on a scale which neither the provinces nor the motherland could afford; and the peacetime army, until Charles XI reformed it, was always inadequate to the tasks it might have to perform. If an international crisis threatened, it had to be supplemented in a hurry by large recruitments of mercenary troops which the Swedish treasury was unable to pay. They had to be raised on credit. As soon as possible after mustering, they had to be transferred to foreign soil, so that they might be maintained as Gustavus's armies had been maintained: by contributions levied upon foreign territory, supplemented if possible by foreign subsidies. A war which was in appearance aggressive was almost inevitably the consequence of any mobilization, even though it might have been necessitated by purely prudential considerations. Gustavus in Germany had solved the difficult equation: he had contrived to balance the need for security against the means for paying for it. But Gustavus was uniquely fortunate: he had had all Germany to live on.

His successors were never in a comparable position. Alternative methods of providing themselves with the means of maintaining an adequate standing army in peacetime were not easy to devise. The hope that they could do it by monopolizing the Eastland trade through the control of its end-ports proved to be illusory. But one radical solution was at any rate conceivable: the conquest of the Sound. If Sweden could straddle the Sound, as Denmark still did, she might hope by the Sound Tolls to solve her financial, and hence also her military, difficulties. This lay behind Charles X's attempt to conquer Denmark in 1658–60. It failed. The trading nations of the West could not afford to allow it to succeed. The regents after 1660 fell back on an intricate diplomatic balancing-act, fortified by subsidies, which imperfectly concealed their country's weakness. Only Charles XI really solved the problem of maintaining a credible military deterrent without foreign subsidies. But since Sweden's neighbours would not permit her to sit still, in the end there was nothing for it but a return to the search for a 'radical solution', in conditions which made success at best dubious. The system which had been perfected after Breitenfeld reached its end at Pultava. For Gustavus, for Charles X, for Charles XII, the search for a radical solution revealed it to be an unrealisable dream – though not one of them would have been prepared to admit it.

It is tempting, in the light of what was to follow, to see Sweden's short-lived greatness as a misfortune and a mistake, and to condemn those of her kings and statesmen who were responsible for it or who tried to shore it up. Certainly it imposed upon the mass of the Swedish population grievous sacrifices of human life, and very heavy economic and social burdens. For the fortunate few – the successful soldiers, the entrepreneurs, the aristocracy who grew rich on the booty garnered in war or the crown's grants of land, and the topmost civil servants – it offered (until Charles XI stripped many of them of their gains) very handsome rewards. For the peasantry, who formed nine-tenths of the population, it could mean misery. Not, indeed, misery on a scale comparable with that of the French peasantry, still less the hopeless servitude of eastern Europe; for the Swedish peasant remained a free man. Still it was an existence overshadowed by conscription, and loaded with fiscal burdens which could be borne only if the harvest did not fail. Yet the presence of the Estate of Peasants in the Diet, and the support on which they could usually count from the Estate of Clergy (many of whom were of peasant origin, and almost all of whom had a lively appreciation of the hardships of their parishioners), acted as a salutary check upon the state's demands, and ensured that the country's rulers should not strain loyalty to breaking-point. There were frequent disturbances of a minor character; the king's bailiffs might on occasion be massacred; but the burden of empire was never such as to induce anything like a peasant revolt. It was, and even under the Caroline absolutism after 1680 it remained, a parliamentary state, with a Diet in which the Estate of Peasants could (and did) find a vent for explosive humours; a nation, moreover, inured even in peacetime to a hard life in a harsh climate – though certainly the wars made it harder.

Yet the imperial adventure did bring important compensations. In the Baltic provinces Swedish rule on the whole meant higher standards of government, better administration, educational advance, ecclesiastical reform, the rule of law, an amelioration of social conditions: in short, the replacement of near-barbarism by civilization. The general resistance of all classes (not least the peasants) to Russian conquest in Charles XII's time sufficiently testifies to the fact that they did not feel themselves to be victims of foreign exploitation, still less nations rightly struggling to be free. In Pomerania, Swedish rule brought with it the preservation of parliamentary institutions, in an age when over most of the rest of Germany they were being emasculated or suppressed.

As for Sweden herself, her brief career as a great power had effects which set a deep mark upon her history. In the sixteenth century she had been a third-class state, pent in the remotest recesses of the Baltic, rude, poor, backward; a power which only with difficulty had maintained its political independence, and which economically had only recently emancipated itself from the position of being a Hanseatic colonial land. By 1660 all this was changed. Economically, politically, culturally, she had found her way into the mainstream of European life. The rustic provincial nobility returned from the great wars with booty, but also with wider perspectives, changed ideas about what became a nobleman, heightened demands on life. The economic developments which Gustavus fostered laid the basis for Sweden's industrial advances, supplied the nation with a stronger middle class. His educational reforms – and especially the creation of the *gymnasia* – were as important for Swedish society as the foundation of Public Schools in Victorian England, and imposed ideals and standards which are only now beginning to be challenged. His munificence to the University of Uppsala paved the way for that cultural efflorescence which marked the eighteenth century, and was to produce a Linnaeus and a Berzelius. His administrative innovations set in motion a process of social mobility destined to be of decisive importance, and gave birth to a civil service which Colbert might have envied. The military glories of the seventeenth century might in the end prove barren of enduring consequences, the inexorable facts of the geopolitical situation might doom the empire to perish, but the great reforming measures of the reign had been intimately bound up with the demands which Sweden's international position imposed upon her. The 'Age of Greatness' may today seem no more than an aberration, a piece of the past of interest only to historians; but it gave a powerful impetus to 'the Civilizing Process'; and without it the birth of modern Sweden would have been even more difficult than it has proved to be.

It seems therefore to be a mistake to look at the reign of Gustavus Adolphus as an episode of no permanent significance. Nor will it to do think of him as a kind of tragic figure, driven by ambition or religious fervour to engage his country in an enterprise doomed to ultimate failure; or even as a man caught helplessly in the grip of circumstances the instrument of an inevitable but malign destiny. No doubt he was deeply convinced of the righteousness of his cause, of the necessity for doing what he did if Sweden were to be safe; and he consciously dedicated his life to the pursuit of those policies which he believed to be right. He could not foresee the end of the road he had taken; and in the closing months of his life we can sense a growing feeling of frustration, disquiet, perhaps even of disillusionment, at the complexity of the labyrinth in which he had involved himself. But for good or ill he made deliberate choices, and always he was conscious that he had been free to do other than he did. His reign, which meant so much more to Sweden than the acquisition of an empire, was in a real sense his personal achievement: as Robert Monro put it, 'He was both head and heart of the kingdom.'

Few sovereigns have devoted themselves more wholeheartedly to their duties; few have had a more comprehensive mastery of the business of kingship. Though his reign was filled with wars, it would be wrong to think of him primarily as great soldier: if he had never fought a battle or conquered a province, his domestic achievements would have secured him a great place in Swedish history. The years after 1617 are a period of extraordinary creative activity. He was always conscious of his responsibility to God for the welfare of his people; and if he demanded great sacrifices, and was rigorous in exacting them, he could feel compassion for those who had to bear the burden.

In many ways he was a typical Vasa. He had the family pride and touchiness: opposition to his will, a lack of proper respect, impertinent pressure by a foreign ambassador, could produce a formidable explosion. Though the pathological suspiciousness which marked the sovereigns of the two previous generations was in him much diluted, he had a morbid streak which was hereditary in his family. But he inherited also that effortless gift of words which was common to all the Vasas. In Charles IX it had taken the form of demagogic oratory. In his son it was refined and perfected. He had the faculty of concentrating on the essential, and he had the businesslike habits which had been so conspicuous in his father and his grandfather. He had, besides, qualities which they had lacked: scholarly tastes, a love of music, and, best of all, the power to charm. To contemporaries he seemed (as

189

indeed he was) a man of sanguine temper, gay, sociable, garrulous and impulsive. His affability was famous, and the Germans remarked that he was always laughing. Many a man came from his first interview feeling (as a Hessian envoy put it) that it was impossible not to love him. He was a sincerely religious man, but without the obsessive preoccupation with theology which had marked Charles IX and John III. His Lutheranism was from the beginning broader than some of his clergy would have approved, and by the close of his life his tolerance had come to extend not only to Calvinists but to the Roman Catholics of conquered Germany.

When on campaign he habitually shared the hardships of his soldiers; partly from a sense of obligation, partly from an appreciation of the basis of good discipline, but most perhaps because of his desire to do and experience everything himself: when field fortifications were to be constructed he did not think it beneath his dignity to do his share of the digging. His audacity in reconnoitring, his eagerness to be in the thick of the fight, were condemned by his contemporaries – he was twice seriously wounded, and several times in great danger of his life – but these traits were typical of the man; for he loved fighting and adventure, just as he loved hunting, dancing and fencing, and other vigorous exercise. He did not share the contemporary habit of heavy eating and drinking, though he could hold his liquor when the obligations of hospitality required it. Despite this habitual abstemiousness, and a life of constant violent exertion, he became in his later years decidedly corpulent; but to the end of his life his golden hair and beard, the bright blue of his protruding myopic eyes, the characteristic backward poise of the head, made him an unforgettable figure.

The mercenary soldiers in his armies certainly did not forget him. In his lifetime he had seemed a comrade as well as a leader; devotion to his person was a link that bound them together; and after his death he became a legend. His own subjects were in no doubt as to his stature: within a decade of Lützen they were habitually referring to him as 'Gustavus Adolphus the Great'. No Swedish monarch has been more beloved in his lifetime; none has enjoyed a more lasting popularity with posterity – and even with historians. By any standards this was a wonderful reign; and if strength of character, devotion to duty, and success in enterprise, are

190

acceptable criteria of greatness, then he was assuredly a great ruler, as he was certainly a great man.

. . .

NOTES

1. The principle that the religion of a territory should follow that of its ruler.

BIBLIOGRAPHICAL ESSAY

The most important printed primary sources are Gustavus's own writings: *Konung Gustaf II Adolfs skrifter*, ed. C. G. Styffe (Stockholm, 1861); Gustav II Adolf, *Tal och skrifter*, ed. C. Hallendorff (Stockholm, 1915); *Schriftstücke von Gustaf Adolf, zumeist an evangelische Fürsten Deutschlands*, ed. G. Droysen (Stockholm, 1877), and above all his letters to Axel Oxenstierna, of which a fair number are in German: they form the first volume of Second Series of *Rikskansleren Axel Oxenstiernas skrifter och brefvexling* (Stockholm, 1888) and cover nearly 900 pages. The treaties and agreements concluded during the reign are printed in *Sverges Traktater med främmande Magter*, vol. v, part 1 (Stockholm, 1903): many of them in are German or Latin. A sidelight on the king is provided in *Letters relating to the mission of Sir Thomas Roe to Gustavus Adolphus 1629–1630*, ed. S. R. Gardiner (Camden Society, 1875).

The best short study is Nils Ahnlund, *Gustav Adolf den Store*, fortunately available in English translation as *Gustav Adolf the Great* (Princeton, 1940), which is not so much a narrative history as the reflections of a great authority on various aspects of the reign. It is complemented by Ahnlund's masterpiece, *Axel Oxenstierna intill Gustav Adolfs död* (Stockholm, 1940), the first volume of a biography which was never completed. There have been many studies in German: the best is still Johannes Paul, *Gustaf Adolf*, i–iii, (Leipzig, 1927–32): the emphasis here is mainly on the German war. In English, the pioneer works were *Monro His Expedition with the Worthy Scots Regiment (called Mac-Keyes)* (1637), which conveys the feel of the German war better than any other book, and the blow-by-blow account of the fighting in *The Swedish*

Intelligencer (1632). A remarkable work for its time is Walter Harte, *The History of the Life of Gustavus Adolphus*, I–II (1759). The most recent work in English is Michael Roberts, *Gustavus Adolphus: A History of Sweden 1611–1632*, I–II (1953, 1958), which attempts to combine a general narrative with analytical studies of (for example) the constitutional situation, the economy, the Church, education, and so forth: both volumes have very full bibliographies. Insights into the king's mind are provided by E. Kohlmeyer, *Gustav Adolf und die Staatsanschauung des Altlutherthums* (Halle, 1933); by J. Nordström, 'Historieromantik och politik under Gustav Adolfs tid' (*Lychnos*, 1937) and by his book *De yverbornes ö* (Stockholm, 1934). The competing influences of Grotius and Gothicism are dealt with in Lars Gustafsson, '*Virtus Politica*'. *Politisk etik och nationellt svärmeri i den tidigare stormaktstidens litteratur* (Uppsala, 1956).

Foreign policy is dealt with satisfactorily in the concise study of Wilhelm Tham, which forms vol. I, part 2, of *Den svenska utrikespolitikens historia* (Stockholm, 1960). Swedish attitudes to Russia are analysed in Kari Tarkiainen, '*Vår Gamle Arffienden Ryssen.*' *Synen på Ryssland i Sverige 1595–1621* (Uppsala, 1980: English summary). Relations with Poland are the subject of the excellent dissertation of Axel Norberg, *Polen i svensk politik 1617–1626* (Stockholm, 1974: German summary). Sverker Arnoldsson, in *Krigspropagandan i Sverige före trettioåriga kriget* (Göteborg, 1941) discusses official attempts to condition public opinion at home. The theory that Gustavus intervened in Germany in order to provide a vent for Swedish copper is propounded in Friedrich Bothe, *Gustav Adolfs und seine Kanzlers wirtschaftslichen Absichte auf Deutschland* (Frankfurt, a.M., 1910). Three important contributions to the debate on Gustavus's intervention in the German war are Nils Ahnlund, *Gustaf Adolf inför tyska kriget* (Stockholm, 1918); Johannes Kretzschmar, *Gustav Adolfs Pläne und Ziele in Deutschland und die Herzöge zu Braunschweig und Lüneburg* (Hannover und Leipzig, 1904); and Bertil Boëthius, *Svenskarne i de nedersachsiska och westfaliska kustländerna* (Uppsala, 1912). G. Irmer, *Die Verhandlungen Schwedens und seiner Verbündeten mit Wallenstein und dem Kaiser von 1631 bis 1634*, I–II (Leipzig, 1888) sheds light on one aspect of the perennial problem of Wallenstein's motives. Michael Roberts, in 'The Political Objectives of Gustav Adolf in Germany, 1630–2', in *Essays in Swedish History* (London, 1967), discusses some of the theories which have been put forward. A new approach to the question was provided by Artur Attman, in *Den ryska marknaden i 1500-talets baltiska politik* (Lund, 1944), which argued that the real motive behind Swedish foreign policy from the mid-sixteenth century onwards was an attempt to obtain control of the trade between Muscovy and the West: recently this view has tended to become almost a historiographical orthodoxy. It is conveniently accessible in English in the same author's *The Russian and Polish Markets in International Trade 1560–1650* (Göteborg, 1973) and his *The Struggle for Baltic Markets. Powers in Conflict 1558–1618* (Lund, 1979): it found an early ally in Per Nyström, 'Mercatura Ruthenica' (*Scandia*, 1937). For a sceptical view of this theory, see Michael Roberts, *The Swedish Imperial Experience* (Cambridge, 1979), pp. 26 ff. Documents on Swedish–Russian economic contacts in this period are printed in *Ekonomiska förbindelser mellan Sverige och Ryssland under 1600-talet. Dokument ur svenska arkiv*, ed. A. Attman, A. D. Narotjnitskij et al. (Stockholm, 1978).

On constitutional questions and administrative reforms, standard works are Nils Ahnlund, *Ståndsriksdagens utdaning 1592–1672* (Stockholm, 1933); Nils Edén, *Den svenska centralregeringens utveckling till kollegial organization i början av sjuttonde århundratalet (1602–1634)* (Uppsala, 1902); J. A. Almquist, *Den civila lokalförvaltningen i Sverige 1523–1630*, i–iii (Stockholm, 1917–22). English translations of the Charter of 1611 and of the Form of Government of 1634 are available in Michael Roberts, *Sweden as a Great Power 1611–1697* (Documents of Modern History) (1968) On the general constitutional debate, Fredrik Lagerroth, *Frihetstidens författning* (Stockholm, 1915) and Erland Hjärne, *Från Vasatiden till Frihetstiden* (Stockholm, 1929) are two classic works which approach the subject from different angles: they have to some extent been superseded by Nils Runeby, *Monarchia mixta. Maktfördelningsdebatt i Sverige under den tidigare stormaktstiden* (Uppsala, 1962): see also Michael Roberts, 'On Aristocratic Constitutionalism in Swedish History', in *Essays in Swedish History* (1967). For the Swedish Church, and its relations with the state, there is a lengthy essay by Michael Roberts, in *Sweden's Age of Greatness 1632–1718* (Problems in focus, London, 1973). On economic developments Eli F. Heckscher, *Econonomic History of Sweden* (Harvard, 1954) is the translation of the abbreviated (and partly revised) version of his famous book *Sveriges ekonomiska historia från Gustav Vasa*, I–II (Stockholm, 1939–49). Two important specialized works are Georg Wittrock, *Svenska Handelskompaniet och kopparhandeln under Gustaf II Adolf* (Uppsala, 1919), and Einar Wendt, *Det svenska licentväsendet i Preussen 1627–1635* (Uppsala, 1933).

For military and naval reforms see G.B. C:son Barkman 'Gustav II Adolfs regementsorganisation vid det inhemska infanteriet' (*Meddelanden från Generalstabens krigshistoriska avdelning*, I), (Stockholm, 1931), and for Gustavus as a tactician and strategist, Michael Roberts, 'Gustav Adolf and the Art of War', in *Essays in Swedish History*. For the navy, *Svenska Flottans Historia*, I (Stockholm, 1942). For the sinews of war, see Sven Lundkvist, 'Svensk krigsfinansiering, 1630–1636' (*Historisk tidskrift* 1966), and the collective work of Hans Landberg, Lars Ekholm, Roland Nordlund and Sven A. Nilsson, *Det kontinentala krigets ekonomi. Studier i krigsfinansiering under svensk stormaktstid* (Kristianstad, 1974: summary in German). A very important book, which gathers together several of its author's works in this field, is Sven A. Nilsson, *De stora krigens tid. Om Sverige som militärstat och bondesamhället* (Uppsala, 1990). It examines the impact of war upon a predominently peasant population, and makes a convincing case for considering Sweden to be an example of 'the military state': the long final chapter, summarizing the whole, is in English. The antecedents of the military state as it was shaped under Gustavus Adolphus are examined, though less convincingly, in Gunnar Artéus, *Till militärstatens förhistoria. Krig, professionalisering och social förändring under Vasasönernas regering* (Stockholm, 1986), with particular reference to the emergence of 'the Army Command'. There is a considerable literature dealing with the military state: for example, André Corvisier, *Armies and Societies in Europe 1494–1789* (Bloomington, 1979); Alfred Vagts, *A History of Militarism* (Westport, Connecticut, 1959), which makes clear the important distinction between military states and militaristic societies; *The Military Revolution and the State, 1500–1800*, ed. Michael Duffy (Exeter, 1980); Stanisław Andrzejewski, *Military Organization and Society* (London, 1954). The military and social implications of changes in the art of war in this period are examined, from different points of view, in Geoffrey Parker, *The Military Revolution* (Cambridge, 1988) and Michael Roberts, 'The Military Revolution, 1560–1660' in *Essays in Swedish History* (1967).

The view that Sweden's wars were inspired by a greedy, 'feudal', nobility is aggressively put forward in Axel Strindberg, *Bondenöd och stormaktsdröm*, (Stockholm, 1937). The effect of conscription on one village community is examined in detail by Jan Lindegren, *Utskrivning och utsugning. Produktion och reproduktion i Bygdeå 1620–1640* (Uppsala, 1980: English summary). The suggestion that the policy of the state was 'control for control's sake' appears in David Gaunt, *Utbildning till statens tjänst* (Uppsala 1975: English summary) in regard to the expansion of the civil service; and in regard to education, in Bengt Sandin, *Hemmet, gatan, fabriken, eller skolan. Folkundervisning och barnuppfostran i svenska städer 1600–1850* (Lund, 1986). The relative social and political importance of the Army Command and the bureaucracy, and the superiority of the latter (even in a military state), is demonstrated in Ulf Sjödell, *Riksråd och kungliga råd. Rådskarriären 1602–1718* (Lund, 1975); but see also Björn Asker, *Officerarna och det svenska samhället 1650–1700* (Uppsala, 1983: English summary). On the Swedish administration of Livonia, Ragnar Liljedahl, *Svensk förvaltning i Livland 1617–1634* (Uppsala, 1934) remains the standard work.

196

LIST OF DATES

1560   Reval calls for aid from Sweden; becomes a Swedish town
1581   Swedish forces capture Narva.
1594   9 December: birth of Gustavus Adolphus.
1595   Peace of Teusina between Sweden and Russia.
1600   Deposition of Sigismund III; usurpation of Charles IX.
1601   Charles IX invades Livonia.
1605   Catastrophic defeat of Swedes at Kirkholm.
1610   Charles IX intervenes in Time of Troubles in Russia.
1611   Christian IV of Denmark declares war on Sweden (the 'War of Kalmar').
1611   Death of Charles IX; accession of Gustavus Adolphus.
1612   1 January: Accession Charter imposed on Gustavus Adolphus.
1612   6 January: Axel Oxenstierna appointed chancellor.
1612   26 November: Gustavus's Proclamation revoking alienations of crown lands and revenues.
1613   21 January. Peace of Knäred between Denmark and Sweden.
1613   Election of Michael Romanov as Tsar.
1614–15   Judicature Ordinances reforming judicial system.
1617   Peace of Stolbova between Sweden and Russia.
1617   Statute of Örebro against Roman Catholic and Polish intrigues.
1617   *Riksdag* Ordinance regularizes procedure at Diets.
1618   The Treasury organized as the first *collegium*.
1618   Chancery Ordinance creates central organ of government.

1618 Truce of Tolsburg, for two years, with Poland.
1618 Defenestration of Prague.
1618 Oxenstierna's Statute for towns.
1619 January: Truce of Deulinie, for fourteen years, between Russia and Poland.
1619 Swedish Trading Company founded.
1620 Reform of local government, completed 1624.
1620 Gustavus marries Maria Eleonora of Brandenburg.
1620 Gustavus draws up 'Ordinance for Military Personnel'.
1621 Gustavus draws up 'Articles of War'.
1621 War with Poland resumed: Gustavus takes Riga.
1624 Gustavus's Poor Law.
1624 Gustavus's endowment of Uppsala University.
1624 Crisis with Denmark: agreement at Sjöaryd registers Danish defeat.
1624 Anglo-Brandenburg proposals for a Protestant League.
1626 Swedish victory at Wallhof enables Gustavus to transfer seat of war to Prussia.
1626 Wallenstein appointed Imperial Commander.
1626 Decisive defeat of Denmark at Lutter-am-Baremberge.
1627 Imperialists overrun mainland Denmark and much of Baltic coast.
1628 January: Swedish–Danish defensive alliance.
1628 January: Secret Committee authorises intervention in Germany, at king's discretion.
1628 Swedes begin collection of toll at Baltic harbours.
1627 July: Stralsund saved by Danish intervention.
1629 7 June: Christian IV concludes Peace of Lübeck with Emperor
1629 September: Gustavus concludes Truce of Altmark with Poland, for six years.
1630 26 June: Gustavus lands in Pomerania.
1630 August: Diet of Regensburg. Wallenstein dismissed from command.
1630 1 August: Magdeburg allies with Sweden.
1630 November: 'Contingent Convention' with Hesse-Cassel.
1631 February: Leipzig Convention of German Protestant states.
1631 January: Treaty of Bärwalde with France.
1631 3 April: Gustavus storms Frankfurt-on-Oder.
1631 10 May: Tilly storms Magdeburg.

1631 August: Tilly invades Saxony.
1631 2 September: Swedish–Saxon alliance.
1631 7 September: Battle of Breitenfeld.
1631 12 December: Mainz capitulates to Gustavus.
1632 5 April: passage of the Lech: Tilly mortally wounded.
1632 23 August: unsuccessful attack on Alte Feste.
1632 6 November: Battle of Lützen: death of Gustavus.
1632 December: Congress of four southern Circles at Ulm lays basis for League of Heilbronn.
1634 Form of Government accepted by Diet.
1634 August: Swedish disaster at Nördlingen.
1635 Peace of Prague.
1636 July: Oxenstierna returns to Sweden.

MAPS

1. The Baltic region, 1610–30

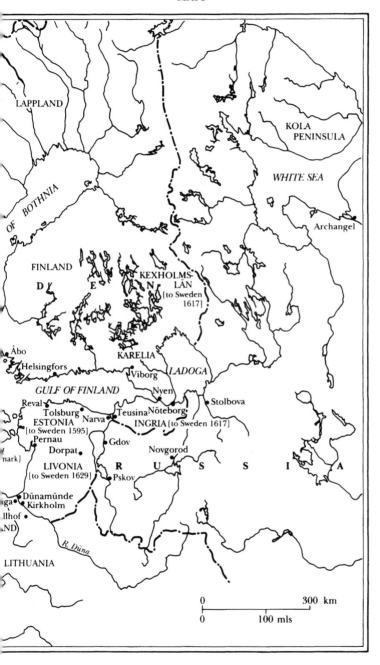

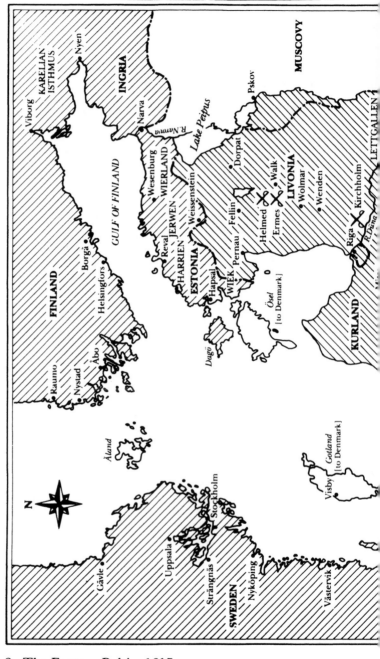

2. The Eastern Baltic, 1617

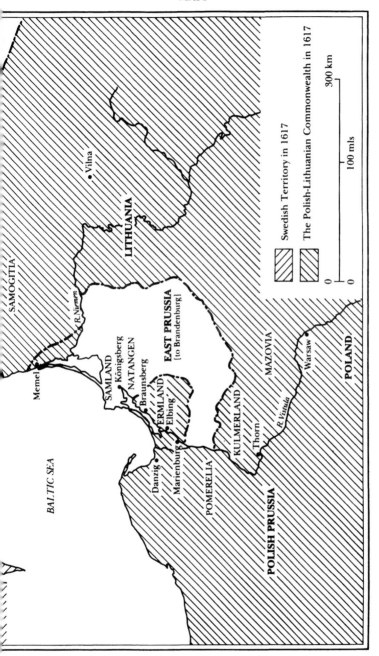

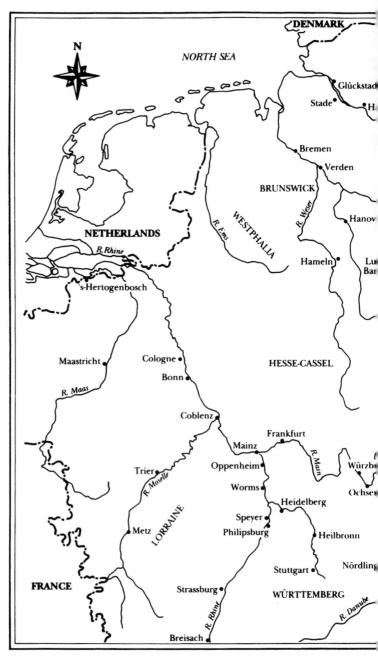

3. Germany in 1630

INDEX

208

Protestant Union, 47; seeks peace with Poland (1621), 48; takes Riga, 48; a preventive war with Denmark (1623)?, 50; a campaign in Prussia (1623)?, 51; terms for joining Protestant league (1624), 52; renews war in Livonia (1625), 53; motives for invading Prussia, 54; tries to bully Danzig (1626), 55; intransigent towards Poland (1627), 56; on danger to Sweden, 59–60; allies with Denmark (1628), 58; aids Stralsund, 61; virtually annexes it, 62; intervention in Germany?, 60, 63; campaign in Prussia (1628–29), 65; in danger, 65; hesitations of, 67–8; fear of Denmark, 68; and a 'just war', 68–9; diplomatic offensive by, 69; the Lion of the North, 70; not France's lackey, 71; farewell speech of, 70–1; lands at Peenemünde, 72

Speech at Örebro *riksdag* (1617), 73; and the Diet, 29–30; and the Council, 81–2; increasingly authoritarian, 29; educational reforms of, 85–6; munificence to Uppsala University, 86; and the navy, 91–3; military reforms of, 103 ff.; his Articles of War (1621), 103; his 'Ordinance for Military Personnel' (1620), 96; and artillery 106; his new taxes, 112; alienates crown lands and revenues, 113–14; fosters industrial development, 114; founds towns, 115; and trading companies and monopolies, 117–18

Offers to John George (1630), 128; politico-military dilemma of, 129; and Magdeburg, 130 ff.; forces alliance on Pomerania, 131; fails to coerce George William, 135; fails to persuade John George, 136; encamps at Werben, 138; allies with John George, 139–40; wins Breitenfeld, 140; strategic dilemma of, after Breitenfeld, 141; enters Mainz, 143; diplomacy of, (1631–32), 144 ff.; aids Tsar to recruit, 146; intrigues in Poland, 147; allies with Holstein-Gottorp, 147; Richelieu's rival for Rhine, 150; mistrusts Maximilian, 150; rebuffs Richelieu, 150; deaf to English diplomacy, 150; harsh terms for Frederick V, 151; organizes conquered Germany, 151–2; dictum of, 153; dictatorial attitude

Viborg, Treaty of, 10;
conference at, 36
Visingsö, 57
Vittsjö, skirmish at, 33

Wallenstein, Albrecht von,
raises army for Ferdinand
II (1626), 55; occupies
Mecklenburg, 57; made
Duke of Mecklenburg, 57;
General of Oceanic and
Baltic Seas, 57; tries to
take Stralsund, 61; wants
peace with Denmark, 63;
makes peace with
Denmark, 64; sends aid to
Sigismund, 65; dismissed,
127; resurrection of, 167;
negotiates with Arnim,
167, 176; at Alte Feste,
173; plans junction with
Pappenheim, 178; strategy
of, 177–8; beaten at
Lützen, 178 ff.

Wallhof, battle of, 54
'Walloon-smithing', 114
Werben, 138
Westphalia, Peace of, 183
White Mountain, battle of,
43
William, Duke of Courland,
40
William V, Landgrave of
Hesse-Cassel, 129; and
Contingent Convention,
131–2; undaunted, 138;
and Swedish plans for
Germany, 156; a
constitutional iconoclast,
158
William, Duke of Saxe-
Weimer, 129, 137, 172
Wimpffen, battle of, 51
Wismar, 57, 153, 182
Würzburg, 142

Zirndorf, 171